88
SONGWRITING WRONGS & HOW TO RIGHT THEM

ABOUT THE AUTHORS

Pat and Pete Luboff are songwriters, music publishers, music business photojournalists, teachers and arts administrators. Their songs have been recorded by Patti LaBelle (gold album) and Bobby Womack (Number Two Black Single), among others. They publish their own songs through Pea Pod Music.

They are currently editors of the *L.A. Record* for the Los Angeles Chapter of the Recording Academy and the *California Copyright Conference* newsletter and have contributed articles to many music business publications. They are past editors of *Grammy Pulse* and *Songwriter* magazines.

Pat and Pete have been teaching songwriting since they founded a song evaluation workshop for the National Academy of Songwriters (NAS) in 1979. Pete continues to run the workshop at NAS's Hollywood offices every Monday night and teaches an advanced songwriting course at UCLA Extension. They have traveled throughout California and to Arizona, New Mexico and Minnesota to conduct songwriting workshops.

Pat is a past president of NAS (formerly Songwriters Resources and Services). Pete was vice-chairman of the NAS board for seven years and was First Vice President and a National Trustee for the L.A. Chapter of the Recording Academy. He is currently serving on the boards of both organizations. The Luboffs homeschool their two children, Paladin and Pepper.

Pat and Pete Luboff are available for workshops in your area. For more information, call Pea Pod Productions at 310-674-9222.

88

SONGWRITING WRONGS & HOW TO RIGHT THEM

Concrete Ways to Improve Your
Songwriting and Make Your Songs
More Marketable

PAT & PETE LUBOFF

Writer's
Digest
Books

Cincinnati, Ohio

88 Songwriting Wrongs & How to Right Them. Copyright © 1992 by Pat and Pete Luboff. Printed and bound in the United States of America. All rights reserved. No part of this book may be reproduced in any form or by any electronic or mechanical means including information storage and retrieval systems without permission in writing from the publisher, except by a reviewer, who may quote brief passages in a review. Published by Writer's Digest Books, an imprint of F&W Publications, Inc., 1507 Dana Avenue, Cincinnati, Ohio 45207 (1-800-289-0963). First edition.

Other fine Writer's Digest Books are available from your local bookstore or direct from the publisher.

96 95   5   4   3

Library of Congress Cataloging in Publication Data

Luboff, Pat
    88 songwriting wrongs & how to right them : concrete ways to improve your songwriting and make your songs more marketable, including : developing a professional attitude, building song foundations, writing and constructing melodies, rewriting, collaborating, recording and pitching demos, and much more / Pat & Pete Luboff. — 1st ed.
        p.   cm.
    Includes index.
    ISBN 0-89879-508-7 (paperback)
    1. Popular music — Writing and publishing. 2. Music trade.
I. Luboff, Pete. II. Title. III. Title: Eighty-eight songwriting wrongs & how to right them. IV. Title: 88 songwriting wrongs and how to right them.
MT67.L8   1992
782.4216413 — dc20
                                      92-4026
                                           CIP
                                         MN

Edited by Mark Garvey

ACKNOWLEDGMENTS

The information contained in this book comes literally from a cast of thousands. Our gratitude pours out to:

Helen King, who founded Songwriters Resources and Services (now the National Academy of Songwriters), for being the first to open a door for us. That door has led to all the others. To our friends at NAS who make the world a better place for songwriters, especially to past executive director Kevin Odegard and the current champions of songwriters, Dan Kirkpatrick and Steve Schalchlin.

To our two favorite legal eagles, Kent Klavens and Al Schlesinger, for being there for us with good advice. Much of what we have written was gathered over seventeen years from countless interviews with songwriters, music publishers, producers, and record company executives and with recording artists, from ABBA to "Weird Al" Yankovic. We thank them all for giving so generously of their time and information.

To the good people at the National Academy of Recording Arts and Sciences, especially L.A. Chapter executive director Marla Hein for her constant support. The Clive Davis quote in Chapter 75 is reprinted from a NARAS publication, *Grammy in the Schools® Career Handbook*. To the California Copyright Conference for keeping us on the cutting edge of developments affecting copyrights.

To all our A.R.T.S. buddies for surrounding us with love and approval. And to our wonderful, talented collaborators, particularly Harold Payne, Bob Martinez, Jarrett Michaels and Jim Eubanks for believing in the dream.

To our parents for teaching us by their mistakes, and to our children, who teach us ours. To Gunilla for being far more than a mother to us. To Bert Pollens for being better than a father. To our dear friends Rich and Ginny Wiseman for inspiring us to live the creative life.

To Writer's Digest Books for hiring people of remarkable integrity, with extra thanks to Julie Whaley for taking on this project and to Mark Garvey for seeing it through to the sweet end.

To all the songwriters for bringing tears to our eyes and smiles to our lips.

To our Higher Power, without whom nothing is possible and with whom everything is.

---

*This book is dedicated to all songwriters for their
courage to create the mirrors of our lives.*
•

CONTENTS
......

From the Authors

PART ONE
_____ IN THE BEGINNING _____
Wobbly Song Foundations

PART THREE

MAKING THE MUSIC

Melodic Mistakes

PART FOUR

ONCE WRITTEN, LOOK TWICE
Rewriting Wrongs

PART FIVE

TWO HEADS, OR MORE, ARE BETTER
Collaboration Misconceptions

PART SIX

GETTING IT ON TAPE

Demo No-No's

PART SEVEN
ALLOW ME TO PRESENT MY SONG
Pitching Package Pratfalls

PART EIGHT
MAKING DISCONNECTIONS
How Not to Get Your Songs Heard

PART NINE

The Final Vinyl

Post-Record Release Problems

FROM THE AUTHORS

*The mistakes are all there
waiting to be made.*

*Chessmaster Savielly Grigorievitch Tartakower (1887-1956)
on the game's opening position*

This is a book about common mistakes that song-writers make, written by two people who believe there are no such things as mistakes. Songwriting is like flying a plane. Pilots don't just stick the plane in the air, point it in the right direction, and sit back while it flies in a straight line to its destination. Their instruments constantly feed back information, and the pilots constantly correct the course. In one sense, they are constantly "making mistakes" that have to be corrected.

The creative process in songwriting is the same: You take off in one direction with a song, and the song feeds back information about whether you are on the right course. Each song is a learning experience that leads to the next song. We agree with Vilfredo Pareto, who said, "Give me a fruitful error anytime, full of seeds, bursting with its own corrections. You can keep your sterile truth for yourself."

Dean Pitchford, world-class groundbreaking writer of such hits as "Let's Hear It for the Boy," recorded by Deniece Williams, "All the Man I Need," recorded by Whitney Houston, and the script and songs for the movie *Footloose*, told us something that gives us great hope as we work— all anybody has in this business is his opinion. Your opinion becomes more valuable with experience, but it's never more than an opinion. Your opinion only becomes stronger with each chance you take. There are no failures, only new avenues to explore.

One day we were doing a science experiment with our children. The assignment called for us to make a hypothesis about the outcome. We did so and conducted our experiment. Our hypothesis was incorrect, but we realized in a blinding flash that we had learned just as much from making an incorrect hypothesis as we would have from making the so-called correct one.

We once saw a video of Pablo Picasso giving a tour of his studio. Among hundreds of paintings stacked in every nook and cranny and sculptures scattered on every surface, there was only one little hand-lettered sign. He kept it always where he could see it. The sign said: "Unless your picture goes wrong, it will be no good."

We have personally made *every mistake in the book*, and we always get better at what we're doing. We have learned to love every step of the process, from writing, producing, pitching our songs and marketing ourselves to accepting economic success as a means to write another great song.

We've learned ways to attain economic success with our music. We've also seen others do it in as many ways as there are people doing it. The main thing is to be standing in line prepared for action when someone else has dropped out. Any way you get in line is the right way; any way you prepare yourself is the right way. Somebody will make up the rules about how to do it after they've seen how you did it.

Our sincere thanks to all the songwriters who have permitted us to use their songs in this book, for their generosity, courage and inspiration.

Yours in song,
Pat and Pete Luboff

PART ONE

IN THE BEGINNING

Wobbly Song Foundations

1

THE ONES THAT GOT AWAY

*Be prepared to capture musical and
lyric ideas when they come*

You're having dinner at a crowded restaurant, and the couple at the next table are experiencing a challenge in their relationship. You can tell by the way they're discreetly yelling at each other, not loud enough to get thrown out but with sufficient volume for you to hear every word.

As a songwriter, you know it's in your job description to eavesdrop on conversations. The basic, real-life emotions that people express in their everyday relations with each other are the building blocks of songs that tap into the lives of your listeners. So, you listen, and sure enough, one of the combatant lovers comes up with a great title in the middle of a heated sentence. You smile as you slice your next bite of food. Great title, you think, I'm going to remember that.

But by the time you're ordering the dessert course, you're asking yourself, What was that she said? It's too late to ask that question. The phrase has escaped your mind completely. You feel empty in spite of your meal; maybe you let a great song get away.

The solution to this problem is simple. Never let the possibility of a great idea get past you. Scribble it on a napkin if you must, but put it in writing or on tape when it first sparks your enthusiasm. Later, you may look at it and wonder what you saw in it. Then you can deliver your paper napkin to the local recycling station with a clear conscience, knowing you gave the idea a chance to be seriously considered.

Song titles and ideas are in the air. You'll hear them in phone conversations, see them in the newspaper, find them popping out of the depths of your mind as you're driving down the highway. As a songwriter, it's your job to be ready to catch

these fleeting thoughts as they fly by. Ideally, you should be prepared in an organized way (see the next chapter). But if boy or girl scouting is not in your history, it's up to you to improvise when a song title appears at a restaurant and finds you without a pencil or scrap of paper. Many great songs have been written on paper napkins with borrowed pens.

Particularly in Los Angeles, where the automobile is a second home, plenty of songwriting goes on in moving vehicles. Since it's not easy to find someone to borrow a pencil or paper from at fifty-five or even twenty-five miles per hour, you should equip your car with these two pieces of equipment at least. Some writers pull over to the side of the road when inspiration hits; others speed on and scribble. Billy Steinberg, the lyricist in the Tom Kelly/Billy Steinberg collaborations of "Like a Virgin," "True Colors," and co-writers on "Eternal Flame" and "I Touch Myself," admitted to us that he's been known to swerve a bit when a hit has hit him on the road.

As in every songwriting "rule," the exception has validity. Case in point: Willie Nelson, who told us that he never writes anything down in his writing process. He feels that if it can be forgotten, it wasn't strong enough. He wrote "Crazy" in his car, retreating from Nashville, where he wasn't being accepted and where his house had just burned down, to return to his home state, Texas.

Most songwriters, however, must catch the first inspiration, the seed of the song idea, to have the chance to see what it could grow into with some cultivation. A commitment to getting the idea into some tangible form for later consideration is a basic commitment to yourself as a songwriter.

2

IT'S HERE SOMEWHERE

Have an organized place to keep your song notes

Step number one is to catch the inspiration, the line, the melody, and record it somehow no matter where or when it hits you. Caught with no pen or paper in the restaurant, you borrow the waiter's pen and scribble your inspiration on the paper napkin. You slip the napkin into your pocket and launch into your linguini, satisfied that you have not let that one get away.

After dinner, you're off to the movies, and by the time you get home, you have just enough energy to throw your clothes into the hamper and crawl between the sheets. One thing leads to another; your great idea goes through the wash and is gone with the rinse.

Getting it down in writing is not enough. Putting it some place special, somewhere it can be retrieved from and reconsidered, is essential. If you are already prepared with a system for gathering your song seeds, you won't be left hunting for long-lost napkins in your lint filter.

A song-catching system can be as simple as a box or a drawer that you throw all your scribbled-on scraps into. Then you can pull out song ideas like raffle tickets and work on them at random for the fun of it. A more sophisticated system, but still easily within the reach of most of us, consists of a small bound notebook. Keep a pen clipped to the notebook and carry it with you at all times.

If categorizing appeals to you, a notebook with index tabs separating sections is a good organizing tool. Label the sections "Titles," "Songs in Progress," "Connections" (potential collaborators, people to pitch songs to), and "Tax-deductible Expenditures" (mileage, recording tape, and so forth), or whatever suits your style of organizing. A list of titles is a wonderful starting point for a writing session, especially with a collaborator.

If you're serious about being a songwriter, you will eventually have to set up a filing system for your copyrights and royalty statements. Why not start now? A section of a desk drawer or filing cabinet should be dedicated to your songwriting. Each completed song will need its own file folder, labeled with the title. The contents of the folder might be: the copyright registration form for the song, a collaboration agreement among the writers of the song, an original final lyric sheet and some copies for pitching the song, and/or a publishing contract for the song. Other files can be set up to hold lists of titles and receipts for expenditures. As you develop a number of music business connections, you will need a filing card system to keep track of names, addresses, phone numbers, and which songs were pitched to whom. If all this is Greek to you, read on. We will explain later.

If you are electronically inclined, set up a computer disk dedicated to your songwriting (with a backup, of course). The disk can contain all the data on the creative and business aspects of your songwriting. You will still need a filing system as described above to deal with hard copies of lyrics, receipts, copyrights, and so on.

Many songwriters prefer to record their inspirations on cassette or minicassette tape recorders. This system is the favorite of Steve Allen who, with thousands of songs to his credit, has been cited in the *Guinness Book of World Records* as the world's most prolific songwriter. He is never without one or two minicassette recorders, and he fills up tapes rapidly because he's constantly open and receptive to the nonstop flow of ideas.

Use of a tape recorder, however, requires another step—you have to transcribe the tapes to have access to the ideas you've captured. Mr. Allen has that one licked, since his creativity has paid off in the form of a pool of secretaries to do that job for him. He is living proof of the value of catching ideas as they come to you.

Mr. Allen wrote the tune most closely associated with him, "This Could Be the Start of Something," in a dream. He woke up with the song still playing in his mind and quickly got it down on tape. The moral of that story is: When you open up the channel, be ready to receive. Keep your notebook or your tape machine next to your bed. And may you dream a hit tonight!

3

THE TOO-EARLY EDITOR

Don't stop the creative flow by judging too early in the process

You've managed to catch the inspiration on the fly and wrestle it down onto paper or tape; now you sit or lie down and try to write the song. You write one lyric line, look at it, wrinkle your nose as if there were a skunk in the vicinity and cross the line out. You try another line. "That's bad, and I don't mean Michael Jackson bad," you grumble at yourself as you scratch out line number two. After about five or ten minutes of this, depending on your personal tolerance for pain, you become convinced that the original idea wasn't worth the paper napkin you scribbled it on. Maybe it's just that you're a lousy writer. Maybe you never should have been born. You've edited your song and yourself out of existence before either of you had a chance.

If you're a writer who edits your ideas before they've had a chance to flow, take yourself to the nearest mirror and tell yourself firmly to *stop that*. The crystal clear ideas that flow in a song come from a deep well of human emotions. In order to tap into that source of ideas and let them flow through you, you have to prime the pump. Have you ever used an old-fashioned sink pump? Remember pumping the handle up and down, up and down? How many times did you pump before any water came? At first it was just a trickle. But after a while, a steady stream came easily with each push on the handle.

How do you prime your songwriting pump? One good way is to free associate. Psychiatrists use free association as a way of revealing their patients' unconscious. Dr. Freud would say "mother" and the patient, instructed to reply with the first word that popped into her head, would usually say "father." If the patient screamed "butcher knife," Dr. Freud knew he had a guaranteed steady income.

Suppose the phrase that caught your ear in the restaurant was, "What happened to the passion?" No wonder you liked that—*happened* and *passion* resonate with each other in a near rhyme (as opposed to a perfect rhyme, like *slow* and *go*). There's also a strong emotional tone to the line and a ring of universality. Every good relationship develops from an initial heated attraction to the more subtle rosy glow of commitment—if the couple can hang in there.

Now, it's time to free associate. Let your mind spew out every word that comes into it without editing *at all*. Here's a sample of a free association on *happened*: lost, found, missing, missing in action, gone, faded, pale, cool, cold, frozen, ice, hard, easy, easy does it, don't do it, do you, will we, why not, why bother, hopeless, sad, sorry, it was an accident, slipped away, fell down, crashed, burned explosion, and so on. Now, let's try *passion*: heat, hot, fire, burning, yearning, desire, love, attraction, magnetism, electricity, lightning, thunder, rain, excitement, hunger, need, craving, thirst. Keep going until you feel you're done. You could also try looking up the words in a thesaurus, but only after you've free associated on them. Your connections will probably be more creative than the ones you will find listed there.

What you've done is similar to what an artist who is about to create an oil painting does: You've put your colors on the palette. Now you can see what you have to work with. A couple of these words may jump out at you from the page and say, "Use me, I'm unique. I call up a great image." You may be inspired to write lines around those words. Follow the urge but maintain the frame of mind you developed in the free association exercise. Write everything that comes to your mind and do not judge one bit of it. Remember where judging got you before, staring at a line of dark scribbles and contemplating nonexistence. Tomorrow will be soon enough to ask yourself if you like what you wrote today. Right now, you're just getting out the raw materials. Don't try to rhyme. Don't try to write the finished lyric at all. Just pump, pump, pump out those ideas. Some writers find a thesaurus is a handy tool for priming the word pump.

Musical free association can also be done with or without a tool in hand. A drum machine is fun to use to get your musical juices flowing. Start by creating a pattern on your machine. Drum feels in themselves suggest an attitude. If you just start singing over a feel that turns you on, unexpected inspiration can strike. Don't forget to have your tape machine rolling to catch what comes to you.

If your tool is a guitar or piano, try practicing scales, chord inversions, difficult rhythmic combinations, anything that pushes the limits of your skills. You might find your fingers wandering in the middle of your F-sharp melodic minor scale because they want to "play hooky" from their studies. If they happen to hit upon a hot lick that could turn into the beginning of a song, follow that creative gust.

When creativity flows, it often digs channels. You find yourself always going to the same rhythms, the same chord changes. One way to break out of your rhythmic rut is to play both drum machine and guitar/piano at the same time. With the drum machine going, play chords with no real concern whether one follows the other. When and if they do come together, you will often find yourself in a musical place you wouldn't have gone on your own.

Another way to break away from the musical places your hands tend to go to by themselves is to create your music without that tool in your hand. Take your title or lyric ideas and sing them a cappella (without instrumental accompaniment).

Make up lyrics as you go along. These can be silly or nonsense lyrics. You might even blurt out a really striking lyric line, especially if you keep your list of brainstormed phrases in front of you. The resulting gibberish is called a "dummy lyric." Maybe the dummy words you mumble will create an interesting metric pattern or a catchy melodic phrase. Later you can put the dummy lyric in a musical setting with a drum pattern and guitar or piano arrangement. Then you can fine-tune the words on the melody.

The point of these techniques is to free yourself to create something new and fresh. You need to keep interested in your creation. Free exploration of unknown territories, taking creative risks, having fun with your writing—none of these are possible if you have a judge screaming in your head that you're wrong before you even begin.

For some people who want to write, the inner critic is so negative that the entire process gets frozen. If you have read this chapter and find you cannot stop the judge from pounding the gavel as soon as pencil approaches paper or fingers touch musical instrument, there is help. A self-help group called A.R.T.S. (Artists in Recovery through the Twelve Steps) uses a slightly amended version of the twelve steps of Alcoholics Anonymous to get beyond paralyzing self-criticism, writer's block, and invalidating attitudes. There are no dues or fees for membership. There may be a meeting in your area. If not, you can start one with help and literature from the A.R.T.S. World Service Literature Distribution Coordinator, P.O. Box 175, Ansonia Station, New York NY 10023-0175; phone 212-873-7075.

4

········

DON'T MESS WITH MY MUSE

Don't think that discipline will hamper your creativity

Living on the other side of the looking glass from the songwriters who suffer from the too-early editor are the songwriters who refuse on moral principle to question anything they do. We've seen many of them in our workshops.

Their basic philosophy is that their creative process is a delicate flower that will wither if disturbed in any way. Discipline is a dirty word to them, as is any word having to do with the commonly accepted tools of the songwriting trade, including rhyming, structure, title, chorus and clarity. They become angry in the workshop when we talk about these things and tell us in no uncertain terms that they want nothing to do with them. They see no value in learning about what goes into a song, only a threat to their ability to connect with their mystical muse.

We wonder why they come to the workshop at all if they feel this way. If they are convinced before they enter the room that they don't want to change their ways—that is, to learn something new about songwriting—why are they there? Thomas Edison said, "We don't know a millionth of one percent about anything." The more you know, the more you realize how little you know. Don't make the mistake of limiting your opportunities by pretending you know everything there is to know. Learning is fun and fuels the creative process. Knowing how songs are put together will not prevent you from putting yours together, or force you to do it in a way you don't like, or dry up your creative well.

A song is a particular kind of art form. It has a definite shape, just as an artist's canvas has measurable dimensions. The canvas can be tiny or huge. The tiny painting can fit in anyone's home. Only a mansion or a museum has a wall large enough for the huge painting. If your aim is to get your song recorded and played on the radio, there is a limit to the length of time you have to get your message across. There are many other variables that come into play if your song is to be chosen from the thousands upon thousands of others that are vying for the same three-minute slot on the radio.

Maybe the idea of taking these things into consideration while you are writing makes you nuts. It could be that you don't really want to write songs as we know them today, that you seriously want to go where no songwriter has gone before and create an entirely new song art form.

We went to a concert of works written by contemporary composers several years ago. One young man sat down at the piano and proceeded to play something that sounded like he was just banging anywhere on the keyboard with his flat hand or his elbows—no regular rhythm, no melody, no chords we recognized. We thought, this guy could be making a million mistakes and no one would ever know. Five seconds later, he stopped dead, apologized to the audience, and said that he had made a mistake and wanted to start from the beginning. When you're creating out there where the buses don't run, you can make your own rules, and who's to know if you break them?

The reality is, however, that most songwriters really do want to write songs as we know them. It's just that some songwriters have swallowed the myth that the creative person can only function as some untamed force of nature, operating above the rules that govern everyday life. The rules of the songwriting craft are not there to stifle your creativity. Rather, they are there to give you a framework, to challenge you to fill that framework with such skill that those who hear your message will dance, cry, make love, sing.

Songs express the full range of human experience: prayer, pride in country, the call to war, the joy of personal love or misery at its loss, rage at social injustice, the teaching of our children, story-telling, both serious and hilarious, dancing, and just plain having fun.

About 150 years ago, Stephen Foster crystallized the form of the American popular song. A study of the structures in his songs will reveal the roots of the verse/chorus and verse/bridge forms we explain in chapter eleven, "No Bones About It." You probably can sing these songs without referring to sheet music: "Beautiful Dreamer," "Camptown Races," "Swanee River," "Oh! Susanna," "Jeanie With the Light Brown Hair," and "My Old Kentucky Home." Those are the cream of the crop of over two hundred songs published before his death at the age of thirty-seven.

The fact that these forms are still in use today is a testimony to their value. There is something about the way our thoughts line up, the way music and words come together to express a reality more focused and pure than real life, the way rhymes satisfy our ears and repetition enchants us, that wants to fit itself into these song structures.

You wouldn't be a songwriter if you didn't love songs. But if you want to be a serious songwriter, there comes a time when the honeymoon is over. You get past thinking it all happens by magic. Get on your work clothes, grab your monkey wrench, and take apart any song you love until you understand why it is great. You'll see that great songs are a highly disciplined art form. They are both 100 percent creativity and 100 percent structured, proof that structure and creativity are not mutually exclusive.

Fear not for your creativity. It is safe and can only be enhanced by learning what makes a great song great. You wouldn't try to read without knowing the alphabet first. Why try to write songs without a basic knowledge of the tools and structures of songwriting?

5
NOWHERESVILLE
Know what you're trying to say

Have you seen the great old Ernest Borgnine movie, *Marty*? Marty asks his friend, "What do you want to do?" His friend replies, "I don't know, Marty. What do you want to do?" Marty answers, "I don't know. What do you want to do?" They do this quite a lot in the movie. Finally, Marty breaks away from his friends who can't decide what they want to do and takes the big risk of offering himself to a nice girl. He is rewarded with the happy ending of a promising relationship, while his friends are still hanging around the corner asking each other what they want to do. If you want a happy ending to your songwriting process, you, too, will have to take the plunge. You have to ask yourself, What do I want to do with this song? You need an idea of where you're going, or you won't get there.

At a songwriting workshop we taught at Santa Fe Community College in New Mexico, Andy Lovato played a song for us that he had co-written with Tollis Pompeo. The demo was excellent. From the first note of the introduction, you got the feeling that the song was about something heavy. The atmosphere of the song was ominous. Ironically, it turned out that he had used the same demo service that we use for some of our songs.

The song was called "Trouble Boy" and the lyrics follow:

Standing on a corner hanging out, passing the time
Not too hard to tell what's on his mind
He don't wanna play any games, follow no rules
He ain't gonna change and let down his cool
If you ask where he's going, he'll just laugh and look away
And say it don't matter, he just lives day to day

CHORUS:
He's a trouble boy, trouble boy, trouble boy
Take your trust and break it like it was a
*   toy*

Cruising down the street late at night, he's
never done
Waiting for the chance to have his fun
Hiding out in back of his shades, what does he
care
He ain't losing sleep, he's getting his share
Keeping wild, crazy hours with his crazy bunch
of friends
Living in a dream where the party never ends

CHORUS: *repeat*

You don't know what trouble is
Till you mess around with a trouble kid

CHORUS: *repeat*

© 1989 Andrew Lovato/Tollis Pompeo

After we listened to the song and complimented Andy on his demo and the way the mood was communicated in the song, we asked him some questions: "What were you trying to make us feel? Are we supposed to feel sorry for the person in the song? Are we supposed to be moved to advocate for better social services for children so people won't grow up into this desperate state? What message did you want to get across?"

He answered, "Gee, I never thought about that." His answer floored us. Here's a smart guy who has spent hours and hours crafting this song and hundreds of dollars getting it on tape, and he didn't stop to think what he was trying to say in the first place!

In chapter three, we left you with your palette filled with lyrical and musical possibilities. You are like an artist who has put every color in the rainbow on the palette in preparation for a painting. Now you turn to the canvas and say, "I'm going to paint a still life of a bowl of fruit." Or, "I'm going to do a bold abstract painting that will express the joy I am feeling now." You have an intention, an idea that you want to communicate.

The same is true for writing a song. Song is a powerful, emotional method of communication. What do you want to express, to communicate?

Turn to your song canvas and tell it what you have in mind. You might say:

● This song will make people cry.

● People will jump up and dance when they hear this song.

● I'm writing a number one hit song.

● I'm writing this song to pitch to Patti LaBelle.

● I will use this song to promote myself as an artist.

● I would like a country artist to record this song.

● I want to change the world with this song.

● This song is personal, to tell my husband I love him.

Let's go back to the song we were writing in chapter three, "What Happened to the Passion?" Suppose you decide to make people cry with this song. Then you would take the title in the direction of the end of a love affair. The singer could be extremely sad because he wants to continue in the relationship, but his lover isn't interested anymore. The tempo might be slow to medium, the range of the melody could be wide, rising and falling to emphasize the depth of emotion felt by the singer.

How about making people dance with the song? This time, the singer might be angry, ready to walk but getting in one last dig at the lover, something like, "You came on so strong, like you wanted me so much, but now that you have me where you wanted me, you don't want me anymore." The beat would be hard and fast. The melody might not have a very wide range, and the notes could fire rapidly.

Now, consider the proposition that you want to write a number one hit song. A study of the charts in *Billboard* magazine (the main trade magazine of the record business) will show you that very few artists record "outside" songs, that is, songs that were written by someone other than themselves, their producers, or their band members. It's up to you to identify the few artists who do record outside songs so you can aim the song you're about to write in their direction. All artists have an image, a look and sound that make them special. This image also includes the kinds of messages they will sing. Which ones might sing the message, "What Happened to the Passion?"

Patti LaBelle is an artist who records outside songs—a gold record on our living-room wall attests to that. She recorded "Body Language," a song we wrote with Harold Payne, on her *I'm in Love Again* album. She is very popular now, capable of having a number one hit. Her image as a strong, independent woman could accommodate the demand "What Happened to the Passion?" So, you decide that Patti LaBelle is the artist you want to write for. Visualizing her singing the song you are writing will help. (Don't forget to leave some room for her trademark vocal trips into the ionosphere.)

If your goal is to perform and record your song as well as write it, other factors have to be considered. Is this message important to you? If it became a hit, could you sing it over and over again for years and still mean it? Does it communicate the image that you want to have as an artist?

How about trying to change the world with the song? "What Happened to the Passion?" could be a song that asks why there is so much apathy and self-doubt in America. Why are we suffering from one political scandal after the other? Why doesn't everyone stand up and stop all the craziness? What happened to the energy, the coming together, that we had in the sixties? Could it be a country song? Asking yourself these questions in the be-

ginning will help you focus on what you want to communicate and how you want to express it.

The decision to write a very personal song is a liberating one. You know who you're writing to intimately and you know, no matter what, the song will be a hit with that person. The details of your relationship will give you all the inspiration you need. In the end, this song may even be a number one hit. That's what happened for Randy Goodrum when he wrote "You Needed Me" as a love song to his wife. Only 100+ turn-downs later, Anne Murray recorded it. It's also likely, though, that your personal song will remain just that, strictly personal. "What Happened to the Passion?" can become "I Love What Happened to the Passion" for your personal love song to your spouse. The lyrics could speak to your experience of a broader and deeper feeling than the first rush of attraction, and how great it is to experience that growth in your relationship.

Now, can you sense how each of these intentions affects the direction that the song takes? Having an idea of where you're going with the song will help you to make choices all along the way. Starting to write without your intention in mind is like taking a cross-country trip to an unknown destination. How will you know which way to turn when you come to a fork in the road? Without a clear intention, you wind up in Nowheresville.

6
....

HEARD BUT NOT SCENE
*Have a clear idea of all the details
of the setting of the song*

Songwriters come from far and wide to the workshop we started in 1979 at the National Academy of Songwriters in Hollywood. John Oriettas from Quebec, Canada, brought this song in:

SOMEHOW

*Girl little did we know
How fast that love could grow*

*The time was short the time was sweet
Ooh girl I never will forget you*

*There's a place in my heart
It will never part
But now I have to leave
Ooh girl I will never forget you*

CHORUS:
Somehow the moment that I met you
Somehow I knew I never would forget you
*   girl*
You made a change in my life
And somehow we've got to make it last
*   forever*

That look upon your face
I never will replace
You made me laugh you made me smile
Ooh girl I never will forget you

BRIDGE:
Me and you
Make our dreams come true
We're gonna make them last forever

© 1990 John Oriettas

This song left us wondering about many things. Who are the people involved? Where and when did this encounter happen? Is the relationship over or not? If it is, why? Somehow, this song did not get across any hard information.

Have you ever noticed how the first few shots in a motion picture, the ones behind the title and the credits, tell you so much about where and when the story is taking place? That process in a motion picture takes about as long as you have to complete your whole song: three minutes. You don't have time to get into long shots of landscape. The listener has to have a pretty good idea within the first few seconds about the where, when, who, what, and why of your song.

But how do you get all that into those few seconds? You may not literally put descriptive words into your opening lyrics, but you have to have a clear picture in your head of who is singing, why he wants to sing, what the message is, and where and when the singing is taking place.

When we write a song, answering these questions is one of the first activities in the process. We talk about who the people are. We call them the "singer" and the "singee." For instance, the singer in one song is a woman who can't stop thinking about her husband, who has divorced her to marry another woman. She still lives in the home they shared together. It was a total shock to her, she had no idea there was anything wrong in their relationship. She is in pain and really wants to forget this guy. She has started a new relationship with another man and she and the new man are on the brink of becoming intimate with each other. She's not in love with the new man.

It's after dinner, and they are in her house. They are both middle- to upper-middle-class working people. She is in her thirties and he is about forty. She has no children. She's a bank teller, and she met this guy when he came to make a deposit. She drives an old beat-up VW. . . and we could go on to hair and eye color, height, weight, and so on. The point is, we have a real person in mind, a person with a lifestyle. She's more important in this song than he is, so we didn't go into so much detail in his description. For some songs, we do a full characterization for both the singer and the singee.

Having all this background fleshed out builds a firm foundation for your song's unity. Picturing a specific person as the singer helps you choose the language the singer will use. The little details may never find their way into the song, but they will be there in your mind, keeping the story of the song building in a realistic way. The reason we all love great stories is because we come to care about the people in the stories. We know about them. They become our friends. We identify with their feelings. The feelings don't exist without the people who feel them. That's why our songs have to be sung by characters who are real to us, because we have given them fully fleshed-out lives.

Without those details, "Somehow" has nothing that reaches out and grabs us. We find it hard to care about the people in the song because they have not been made real to us. We recommended that John go back to the drawing board with this one and work up a picture with lots more details than he actually needs in the song.

How about this for a story line? The singer is a male. He is on a business trip to a distant city, and he meets a beautiful woman who happens to be attending the same convention. She has long, thick red hair that she keeps up in a bun at the business meeting. But when they go out for dinner that night, she lets her hair down, symbolizing that they are both very relaxed with each other and share openly. They really have a great time together, and he wants to continue the relationship, but they live very far apart, and they both have to return to their hometowns in two days.

On the last night they can be together they make love and it's wonderful. Now, he's singing to her in the hotel room on that last night, desperately trying to think of a way to keep the relationship going, somehow. Phone calls, letters, trips, none of that would be enough because he wants her so much. Both of them have good jobs that would be difficult to give up. Both want the relationship and, at the same time, are fearful that they are moving too fast toward a big commitment that would uproot at least one of their lives.

Notice that the exact time and place of the singing of the song is mentioned. This is an extremely important bit of information. The writing technique of keeping the song *in the moment* of the emotion forces the lyrics to be immediate, highly charged with feeling, concrete and direct. What kinds of things would this man actually say in this situation at this very moment? Answering that question you'll be inspired "somehow" to write a strong melody and powerful lyrics.

If you don't make the supreme effort to have your lyrics communicate your message with precise images, you can say along with William Safire, "Is sloppiness in speech caused by ignorance or apathy? I don't know and I don't care."

7

WHY BOTHER?

Make sure each song will motivate an artist to sing its message

One of our favorite possessions is an R. Crumb adult comic book entitled *Despair*. On the cover, the husband stares out the window and says to the wife, who sits rigidly in a chair staring off in the opposite direction, "See if there's anything good on . . ." In the balloon over her head is her reply, "Why bother?"

This scene never fails to amuse us. We've been there, in the doldrums of existence where even television offers no hope. This is real-life pain, the stuff that makes for the best laughs. So, even though the punch line is, "Why bother?" there's a very sharp point being made by this image.

Why bother to write songs? It's difficult and frustrating most of the time. Ultimately, we do it because we have something to say and we want others to hear it. We've covered the necessity of knowing what you want to write about in chapter five, and who and where you are writing about in chapter six. Why? is another important question you need to answer in your songs. Consider this song:

LETTER TO A FRIEND

Dear old friend
It's been a long time
How have you been?
I'm doing fine

I'm alone now
Mary is gone
Isn't it strange
How people move on?

CHORUS:
Just wanted to keep in touch
To let you know I think of you
Especially when times are tough
But nothing much is new

I'm out of work
But that's okay
I watch the TV
Night and day

So say hello
To the old crowd
And drop on by
When you're in town

© 1990 James McCarthy

James wrote a lovely melody for this lyric and the song was a pleasure to hear. But after it was over, we asked ourselves and the workshop participants, "What's the point of this song?" Everyone was most interested in the lines about being out of work and still being okay. We all wanted to know how he accomplished that feat! But besides that, very little information was actually transmitted. Most important, there was no feeling of a burning reason that motivated the message.

Why did he write this letter to this person in particular? He tells us he's out of work and his wife is gone, and that is the sum of the information. We get letters like this from our cousin, and after we have read them, we are left feeling confused. Why did he write if he wasn't going to tell us anything?

The message and the motivation for the message are like a two-headed snake. These animals are quite common in nature. The reason we don't see more of them is that they can't agree on which way to go, and while they're deliberating, they get eaten. In your song, the motivation and the message have to be headed in the same direction, too. And you are the one who has to make the decision about the direction they will take together.

You've heard actors talking about acting. When they prepare for a scene, they think long and hard about the character they are portraying. They make decisions about how that character would react to the situation presented by the drama. Before they act or speak, they ask themselves as the character, What's my motivation? To play the part convincingly, they need to know why they are saying this or doing that.

When you create a song, you're creating a movie in which the singer is the character, the actor, the star—in fact the only person in the whole film (unless you're writing a duet). If you get that person clearly focused in your mind and really work from the point of view of that charac-

ter's intense need to express the chosen emotion at that particular moment to that particular listener, your song will automatically come from an authentic emotional stance.

Note that we said *intense* need. There have been eighty zillion songs that say, "I love you." If you want to write a song about that time-honored message, what will make your version of it special? What makes this love so intense that the singer feels the need to burst into song? In other words, why is your character singing this message? The better the reason is, the better the song will be.

If James wants to tackle a rewrite of this song, we suggest he keep the pretty melody and go back to the drawing board with the lyrics. He might try choosing a situation that wouldn't be so emotionally removed. Perhaps the singer could actually run into this old friend and be face to face with him, filling the listener in on some telling details of the changes that have occurred in his life.

Maybe the singer could actually cry and then get embarrassed. The desire to look good for very old friends that we haven't seen in a long time is universal. Perhaps this singer had the bad luck of running into an old friend when he was especially low and unable to put up a good front. How about if it wasn't just an old friend, but an old lover, or even an ex-wife? You can see that these situations would be much more emotionally charged than James's current choice, which suffers from lack of focus and tension.

If you are writing a song for your sweetheart and you don't intend it to go any further, you are free to sound like any greeting card on the shelf. But if your intention is to write a song that can be pitched to and recorded by a recording artist, you're up against a challenge.

Your song will be competing with thousands of other songs. You want to write a song that will move someone to tears, make their heart stop or suddenly beat faster. Only a strong emotional motivation will inspire lyrics that cut to the bone and a melody that soars. That's what you will need to make your song stand out from the crowd. That's why you need to know why your singer is singing.

8

MUSIC FROM THE HEAD

*Avoid writing songs that are too philosophical,
emotionally removed and cerebral*

Songwriters will be songwriters. We love to play with words. We seek the universal truths. We sit up late at night and travel the uncharted seas of thought in our minds. Let's face it, we're bonkers.

An excellent lyricist who comes to the NAS workshops wrote a lyric that shows what happens when we indulge in philosophizing:

VISIONS OF THE FUTURE

*I'm seeing shadows
Outlines in my mind
They're soft and hazy
Obscure and undefined*

*They're like a memory
Of something yet to be
They're getting closer
Now my eyes can see*

> CHORUS:
> *Visions of the future
> Pictures in my head
> Visions of the future
> In shades of gold and red*

*The colors haunt me
Daring me to ask
"Is this the future
Or something from my past?"*

*I stand unmoving
Watching them draw near
My fascination
Struggles with my fear*

> CHORUS: *repeat*

*Lives I haven't lived yet
Sights I've yet to see
Mirrors of my soul
Of what I know will be*

> CHORUS: *repeat*

© 1991 Tama Winograd

Tama wrote another lyric, entitled "Mother Earth," that inspired Bob Martinez and Pete to write a beautiful melody. Every time Pat hears that song, she cries because it is so moving. But "Visions of the Future" is another song entirely. It doesn't move us because it takes place entirely above our ears. You have to touch the heart or wrench the guts to move your listeners.

Tama brought "Visions of the Future" to the workshop and the consensus was that the subject matter was too philosophical to be entertaining. Tama knew when she wrote it that she wasn't trying to write a recordable song. She was just feeling "spacey," so she wrote a "spacey" song. This is fine, if you realize what you're doing and you do it to get it out of your system. Nobody can tell you not to write what you feel a need to write.

The trouble is that many newer songwriters are not as self-aware as Tama. They write songs that could be footnotes in *Being and Time*; then they make a big investment of time and money to demo them and pitch them. There's a big difference between writing anything you feel like writing and pitching anything you write. The first is something you do for yourself. The second requires an investment of money, presumably because you think the money will be recouped and additional income will be generated. If you're thinking you can get your philosophical treatise on the pop charts, you've got the wrong idea. The pop charts concern themselves with areas between the shoulders and the knees.

There is a market for songs of a philosophical nature, the growing New Age market. Anything goes in this field, from pure vocal sounds without words to poetic spiritual lyrics. Generally, New Age artists write and record their own material, and many have their own labels. There are also New Age record labels that sign artists and distribution companies that specialize in distributing New Age labels. Many of these artists start out by selling their own tapes through mail order or by placing them in local stores. This is an alternative market that is worth looking into if you are of a spiritual or philosophical bent.

If you are drawn to New Age music and would like to gather with more than a thousand similarly bent souls, you may want to attend an International New Age Music Conference. Conferences are sponsored in Los Angeles each spring by the International New Age Music Network (INAMN), a nonprofit organization dedicated to education, research, and international networking in the New Age music field. For more information on INAMN, call 213-935-7774. *Billboard* magazine has a New Age music chart of the top artists that includes publisher and label information.

To research possible outlets for your self-produced New Age project, consult the directory of *New Age Marketing Opportunities* compiled by Sophia Tarila. It's available from First Editions, P.O. Box 2578, Sedona AZ 86336; phone 602-282-9574.

It's up to you to distinguish the origin of the music you are writing. If they are strictly songs from the head, they may have a chance in the New Age field, but only if you perform them yourself. They probably won't be suitable for the pop, country or R&B fields. If those are the fields you'd like to cultivate, you need to connect with your own emotions so your songs will connect with the listeners' emotions.

There's a fine point to be made here because many songwriters write songs in which the singer is talking about being in love, but the emotions are once removed. The singer is talking about it instead of expressing it. For example,

From the head . . .
You say that you don't love me
You say you've had enough
I don't know what to say
I feel so out of touch

From the heart . . .
You don't have to tell me
I can see it in your eyes
Your heart has left already
Your touch has turned to ice

Can you feel the difference in emotional intensity? The words that come from the heart are direct. They're not talking about what someone else is saying, they're saying what they want to say and using pictures to convey ideas. Writing from the heart means just that, *from* the heart, not about the heart. Next time your head tries to take over while you're writing a song, let your heart tell it who is boss. Songs that are visceral have more impact than songs that are cerebral.

REALITY ISN'T EVERYTHING

*Don't force a song to fit your reality;
let it have its own integrity*

Writers are told all the time to write from experience, to write about the things they know, the things they've seen, the things they feel, the places they've been. This is all true. But when it comes to writing songs, sometimes reality gets in the way. Here's a strong song that Gail Jennings brought to our Santa Fe workshop:

QUEEN OF THE GYPSIES

*You treated me like the Queen of the Gypsies
Something I could never be alone
You cast me as the star of the movie
I played the role of the bird that's flown*

> *Would you believe I was lost in a forest
> I can't find my path through the trees
> If I said diamonds don't turn to rust
> Would you be there for me?*

*You let me be the Queen of the Gypsies
But everything was better before
You made me feel like the star of the movie
Oh, oh, oh . . . I still wanted more*

> *Should I say I was lost in the downpour
> Drowning in my silent screams
> You delivered me from the raingods
> Once more will you rescue me?*

*You loved me like the Queen of the Gypsies
Like a perfect jewel you'd found
You worshipped me like the star of the movie
I don't know, I don't know, why I let you down*

*You let me be the Queen of the Gypsies
But gypsies usually don't hang around*

© 1990 Gail Jennings

This song is filled with terrific images. Let's summarize what the song is saying. The first verse says that his love made her feel very special, like the queen of the gypsies or a movie star. However, the last line says she left him. The second part,

which is like a bridge, says she's lost and confused and makes a reference to a Joan Baez song that the listener may not understand and then asks the lover to be there for her. The second verse says he made her feel great, but she wasn't satisfied. The second bridge-type part says she was in big trouble and he saved her, and she wants him to save her again. The third verse says he was great, but she felt compelled to let him down. The tag says she has left him.

How can she ask him to save her and leave him at the same time? When we asked Gail about these conflicting messages, she explained that the song was about a real relationship of hers. Then we understood that this song is a very good example of how real life and art are like oil and water, you can shake them up, but they don't really mix.

Real life doesn't make a lot of sense a good deal of the time. Art is a world that makes perfect sense within its own limits. We go to art for an escape from the chaos of reality. Maybe the whole impulse to create art comes from this urge to have some islands of perfection amid the imperfections of real life. Real life confronts us with diametrically opposed ideas that have to be held in our minds simultaneously, like reflections in a shattered mirror. Art is purified ideas, focused as in a single point of light.

When you draw from your own life for a song, there's a tendency to lose objectivity about whether the song makes any sense. Gail is such a good writer that we don't wonder what she's saying, but we do wonder how she can say so many conflicting things at once. Conflict and drama are great in a song, especially when expressed in rich images, as Gail has done in this song. The combination of the messages, "You were great, you made me feel great, you saved me and I want you to save me again, and I left you," is entirely believable in real life but confusing in a song. Perhaps the song would be stronger if Gail chose just two of these, for example: "You were great, you made me feel wild and free, so I left you." Life is not that simple, but we're talking about a work of art here, not life.

When you draw on your own experiences to write a song, remember that you are the creator here. You don't have to write down your experiences verbatim. In fact, you are much better off picking and choosing among them. Then you can put together a song that has a life of its own, a more orderly life than real life can ever have.

10

I DID IT THEIR WAY

Don't write to impress or please others; write from your own passion

We've all heard about writing songs from the heart, but whose heart? Billy Steinberg made Tom Kelly realize that he had "meandered in a musical direction which didn't reflect his real passion for music." Tom tells the tale: "I had slipped into this clique. I was singing background sessions and hanging out with a lot of really slick musicians. I lost my grounding, where I came from as far as where my real school of music is and what I love. Because I was a good singer and I got into this background scene, all of a sudden I was associating with a different type of people musically and my writing was being affected by that.

"When I met Billy, we discovered we shared a great common love of Buddy Holly, the Everly Brothers, Roy Orbison; it was truly uncanny how all of our favorite artists were the same. I really have to thank Billy because he encouraged me to use less chords and to unsophisticate myself. He said, 'Let's write a really simple rock 'n roll song.' I had been going in the opposite direction.

"I was writing for the wrong people, writing to impress somebody of a certain musical genre. Because they were the people I was around all the time, I wanted to write something that would turn their heads. In reality, it was not where my background was and not what eventually made a success for me."

Billy adds, "I think a lesson people can learn from that is that some up-and-coming writers don't allow themselves to write freely from what they love about music. They look at the charts and they say, 'Oh, dance music is making it now,' or 'Rap music is in now.' Then they try to make themselves do those things. A good piece of advice would be to follow your instincts and write the best songs you can."

The question of whether a songwriter should try to write commercial sounding songs to impress or write strictly from the heart without regard for commerciality ranks right up there with "To be or not to be." On one hand, if your songs are out of touch with what's happening in the current music scene, it may be impossible to find a commercial outlet for them. On the other hand, if you write just to sound like a hit song and you don't believe in what you're doing, the song will be an empty shell. On the other hand, it is necessary for your creative life to be true to your self as a songwriter, and there are more markets than the mainstream in which to get your songs heard. On yet *another* hand, there are lots of people out there making lots of money writing songs with no substance, a.k.a. "records."

We could go on until we had described a millipede's worth of hands. The considerations are endless. In the end, it comes down to you. You will have to decide what you intend to do with your songwriting and then go for it. Whether you choose to make music from the heart or music for the charts, you will have to live with the consequences. If you don't like the way the path you choose feels, you can always change course.

We think that the heart/charts dichotomy is a false one. We've met many of the great writers of the hits we were weaned on and the ones on the charts today. It's obvious they're doing something they love. It's also obvious that they're writing songs with a keen awareness of past and present great songs and what makes them work. As with all other aspects of songwriting, here too we're called upon to achieve a delicate balance between concepts that appear to be in opposition.

The trick is to keep your heart connected while you plug into the current of what's selling. If you do that right, you write a song that lasts forever and is recorded by everyone. These songs are called standards. Songs such as "The Wind Beneath My Wings," "I Love You Just the Way You Are," "Unchained Melody," "I Heard It Through the Grapevine" and "Yesterday" express universal emotions. Everyone wants to be valued, loved unconditionally, loved eternally. Everyone fears the loss of love and knows the pain of losing it. People never tire of hearing these songs and singers love to sing them. That's quite a standard to live up to.

11

NO BONES ABOUT IT
Give your songs structure

Can you picture how your body would look without any bones? What if the bones in one arm were a lot longer than the ones in the other? We take for granted the support and symmetry that our bones give our bodies because bones are inside where they can't be seen. Songs need skeletons, too.

This idea seems to anger some young songwriters when we present it to them in a workshop. We'll never forget the young man in Minnesota who came up at the end of the day to argue with us that his favorite bands did not have structure in their songs. Since this was a two-week workshop, we had some time to work this out, and we asked him to bring in some of his favorite albums the next day. He showed up with a stack of heavy metal albums under his arm the next morning and was shocked as we pointed to verses, bridges, hooks and choruses. Every song had some kind of structure. Even rebels need a structure on which to hang their battle cries!

We can tell right away in our workshops if a song that is presented has structure because we ask the writers to hand out copies of their lyric sheets to everyone. Some lyrics wander all over the page, with one very long section labeled "Verse" and another quite short section also labeled "Verse." Sometimes the "Chorus" section doesn't have the title in it. Or the lyrics may be just strung along in one long poem shape, with each of the lines varying in length. When the structure is clean and clear, that's also obvious on the lyric sheet.

What is song structure? We wrote the copy on pages 18 and 19 as an information sheet for the National Academy of Songwriters.

There are two basic structures. Once you get a strong feeling for these, other combinations can be made. The best way to learn about what song structures are being used today is to listen to the radio and identify the parts of the song structure as you hear them. Then, try writing songs in the various structures you hear. An extended explanation of this technique is included in chapter thirty-two, "The Long and Winding Melody."

You may notice that certain ideas tend toward a verse/chorus construction and others cry out to be in verse/bridge construction. When you play

COMMON SONG STRUCTURES

The structure of a song is the skeleton that gives it shape. A clear structure is a must in a song, particularly if you intend to be commercial, i.e., you want to make money with your song.

There are two main types of song structures: the verse-chorus and the verse-bridge.

VERSE-CHORUS STRUCTURE

The verse-chorus structure is the one most prevalent on the radio. The verse-chorus structure usually starts with a verse. The verse states the problem, gives details of the situation, or in some way sets the stage for the coming title, which will solve the problem or sum up the situation. In order for the structure to stand, each lyric line must be strong enough to stand on its own. If you say the line out of the context of the song, it should express an understandable, complete thought or give the listener a complete visual picture. Each lyric line rests on the one before it, like a stack of child's blocks. If one is not placed solidly, the whole meaning can collapse. Melodically, the verses tend to be background in feel, leading on and up to the impending climax of the chorus.

In the verse-chorus structure, the title tends to be at the beginning of the chorus, in the first line. It may also be on every other line of the chorus, every line, or just the first and last lines. It is always in a prominent place and you should know what the title is after one hearing of the song.

The title is almost always called the hook, because it grabs you and pulls you into the song. (Other kinds of hooks may be found in the lyrics, melody or arrangement.) It is good to visualize the title as the hub of a wheel, with all the lines of the song pointing to and converging on the title like spokes. The title is what the song is about, the main message of the song.

The chorus lyrics explore the ramifications of the title, maybe saying the same thing in several different ways. The melody of the chorus lifts and stands out from the verse as a separate, and probably stronger, more dramatic section. It is usually best to make your verse and chorus sufficiently different from each other that they are easily distinguished as separate sections. An easy way to guarantee the separation is to make sure your verse lines are much longer (more beats on the line) or much shorter (fewer beats on the line) than those in your chorus. Varying the number of lines in each section helps, too. For example, a four-line verse could be followed by a six- or eight-line chorus.

After one verse and one chorus, a song in verse-chorus structure usually returns to a verse section, which gives more details to support the main point of the title. Ideally, the second verse should match the first identically, as far as beats on the line, placement of accented beats, and number of lines in the section. The lyrics should be different from those in the first verse, adding more information and, hopefully, introducing a new twist to the meaning of the chorus the second time around.

For the most part, choruses are repeated identically—both lyrics and melody. So far, we have had Verse One, Chorus, Verse Two, Chorus repeat—and we might express that basic form as A,B,A,B. Here is a diagram of verse-chorus structure dynamics:

Our favorite example of a verse-chorus song is *You Light Up My Life*. The verses lead up to the chorus unerringly and the chorus takes off like it had wings. The only wandering from the pure verse-chorus form is the little bridge inserted in the last repeat of the chorus: "It can't be wrong when it feels so right."

Bridge is the term used loosely to refer to a small section of the song that is a departure from the rest, in lyrical point of view and/or melodic feel. In the verse-chorus structure, the bridge tends to be short, as in the example above. The basic form of a verse-chorus song with a small bridge (usually placed between the last two repeats of the chorus), would be A,B,A,B,C,B. A=Verse, B=Chorus, C=Bridge. In the verse-chorus structure, we don't write a bridge unless it really adds something wonderful. It is not always necessary between the last two repeats of the chorus, and extra excitement can be created by simply repeating the chorus a tone or a half tone higher (called modulation). The basic form would then be: A,B,A,B,B. On the positive side, a bridge may be just what your song needs to perk up interest at the end, to break up the monotony, or to add a new twist to the last go-round of the chorus.

VERSE-BRIDGE STRUCTURE

In the verse-bridge construction, the bridge is much more important. Some ideas tend to write themselves into this form, and it's gaining more acceptance or, we should say, coming back into style. Many of the songs of the forties were verse-bridge forms, then called "pop" songs. In the verse-bridge structure, the title is in the verse. It may begin or end the verse but it always appears in the same place in every verse once the place is established in the first verse. Almost everyone knows the song *Don't It Make My Brown Eyes Blue*, which is a straight verse-bridge structure, with the title at the end of each verse. The verses tend to have a completed feel, as opposed to the suspended feel of a verse that is leading up to a chorus. The thought contained in the verse is the main idea of the song and the melody seems to land in a resting place at the end of the verse, especially if the title is at the end. After verse one, there's usually another verse with exactly the same construction, but with different lyrics—except for the title.

Now we come to the bridge, which usually does not contain the title, but does build up to the emotional high point of the song. Usually the strongest emotional appeal in the lyrics comes at the end of the bridge in a verse-bridge song. It's "say anything, but don't say goodbye" in

Brown Eyes Blue. The melody builds to a high point there. And if you look at the bridge, you'll see that it's no secondary or offhand construction. It's actually a major structural part of the song.

After the bridge, there is usually a third verse, which is again different lyrically except for the title. And that's the whole form: A,A,B,A. A=Verse, B=Bridge. The form is extended by repeating the bridge verbatim, and the verse of your choice (usually the first or the last). And a diagram of the dynamics looks like this:

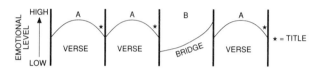

To further your understanding of song structure, you need only turn on the radio and listen. Write down the lyrics and pick out the structure behind the songs.

Here's a list of titles of well-known songs. See if you know their structures:

1. *Just the Way You Are* by Billy Joel
2. *The Way We Were* by A&M Bergman and M Hamlisch
3. *I Never Promised You a Rose Garden* by Joe South
4. *Killing Me Softly With His Song* by C Fox & N Gimble
5. *Yesterday* by McCartney & Lennon
6. *Margaritaville* by Jimmy Buffett
7. *I Write the Songs* by Bruce Johnson

1. verse-bridge
2. verse-bridge
3. verse-chorus
4. verse-chorus
5. verse-bridge
6. verse-chorus
7. verse-chorus

your song without singing the lyrics, or if you write melody first, the structure should be obvious from one hearing of the song. It should also be obvious where the title will sit in the melody. The title must be in the most outstanding repeating notes of the melody. If you play your melody and no one spot really stands out, you have a problem we will cover in chapter thirty-six, "Don't Play It Again, Please."

Why do we need structure in songs? Songs are aural art, heard over a period of time. The listener wants to be interested in and excited by the song. If the listener feels lost and confused while listening to the song, they will tune out and turn the radio knob to another station. Radio stations know this, so they play songs that they feel pretty sure their listeners will love.

What makes you love a song? Don't you love it when the chorus comes around, and the melody jumps out and grabs you and makes you want to sing along? Right at that same spot, the main idea of the song, the lyric you wish you wrote because it's so true for you (and millions of others), fits right on that melody like a glove. It's so satisfying when that all comes together, you want it to happen more than once. So, as the emotional intensity in the song drops back during the verse, you can't wait for it to hit that high spot again. Never fear; the verse builds, perhaps a two-line lift takes you even further up and then, bang, the chorus returns like emotional fireworks.

It's the regularity of the rise and fall in the structure that makes a listener feel satisfied. The verses are the setup, both in the information they contain and melodically, and the chorus (or the title in the verse/bridge form) is the payoff. In a song, the structure gives listeners several opportunities to experience this setup and payoff experience. It also gives you, the writer, the chance to come at your point with several new twists.

So, don't let your songs lie there in a blob. Give them some bones to dance with.

12

....

WRITING YESTERDAY

Don't try to write a song like today's hit;
don't write dated material

Play a song from your past, any song, and you will remember who you were with when the song was a hit, what you were doing, and even which street you were walking or driving down when it came on the radio. Pat remembers the first time she heard Elvis Presley singing. She was nine years old and drifting off to sleep wondering what could be the meaning of a song playing on the radio called, "A Malt Shook Up."

You can mark the times of your life by songs because songs are so much a part of their time. Songs set, as well as express, the mood of the time. When a song is a huge hit, you can bet that it has tapped into something going on right at that time in the world. Cole Porter's smooth sophistication,

Dylan's anthems, the Beatles' psychedelic visions, the outraged and outrageous rappers, all express the values of the era from which they sprang. Should we conclude from this that it would be a good idea to consciously imitate songs that are like the ones on the charts right now?

The answer to this is a definite *no*. The songs that are on the charts right now were written a year ago, or more. When you are writing, you need to think about tomorrow, not yesterday. Certainly, there is a lot to be learned from the songs that are currently enjoying success. We can study and imitate their structures and production values to a point. But if we really want to make an impact as songwriters, we have to go beyond today's songs and try to take the next step. It's our job as songwriters to express what's on everybody's mind before they are even aware of it.

Songwriters need to be students of society. You don't have to look too far for information about what is happening now. It's coming at you from all directions: television, radio, newspapers, magazines, movies, and advertising billboards, commercials, jingles ad nauseam. It's a media jungle out there! It's hard to see the future through the media overload. Step back and make a point of thinking about where all the present madness is leading. You also might try reading some of the magazines that specialize in scientific and philosophical forecasting, such as *Omni* and *New Age Journal*.

Some writers bring songs to our workshops that have gone beyond the today-is-too-late line and slipped right into the past. Musically, melodies can be updated in the arrangement. But lyrically, if the concept is old-fashioned, there's not much you can do about it except change the words. Here's a ditty we wrote back in the days when women's liberation was a new idea:

HURTIN' YOU IS HURTIN' ME

I told you you don't need no job
To satisfy your goals
A wife should keep the kitchen clean
And sew up socks with holes
But when I went and broke my leg
You stood up for us all
I'm sorry that I ever made you feel so small

   CHORUS:
   Every time I put you in your place
   Reality has hit me in the face
   It's finally penetrating into me
   Hurtin' you is hurtin' me

I would come on big and strong
Superior to you
No way you could equal me
Physically it's true
So then I tried to prove my point
By pushing you around
You knocked me cold with a frying pan
This king got crowned

CHORUS: *repeat*

© 1973 Pea Pod Music

We still like this song, but it's obviously from another era. With the way the economy is today, men can no longer afford the luxury of being the sole bread-winner. Women are still being battered, and now that we look at this second verse, we realize that the image of the woman fighting back was ahead of its time.

The battle of the sexes rages on forever, but the style of fighting changes with the times. We need to consider how men and women relate to each other today and where that might lead tomorrow. Consider the changes that have taken place in the last twenty years. People used to marry right out of high school or college and have babies right away. The wife stayed home and the husband worked.

Now, people wait to get married and wait some more before they have children. Many first-time mothers are between thirty and forty. That means today's young adults live as single dating persons for a longer time. Older singles get more set in their ways before marrying. Women develop careers before having children. Women and men choose to be single parents. The baby boomers, the big bulge in the population, are in their mid-forties now and will all be senior citizens at the same time, around the turn of the century. Your songs reflect this world. What do you think are the implications of these situations?

The fact that songwriting provides a constant stimulus to learn is one of its most attractive features as an occupation. Songwriters need to tune in to what's happening in the world on as many levels as possible. The information you gather reading newspapers or books, talking with friends, and examining your own experiences and feelings is the stuff that your songs are made of. The more input you have, the more intelligent your output can be.

You are the poets and the philosophers of tomorrow. Keep your eyes open and tell the world what you see coming down the road.

PART TWO

WHAT IN THE WORD?

Watching What You Say
in Your Lyrics

13
....
THE CASE OF THE MYSTERIOUS MESSAGE

Don't be intentionally obscure in your lyrics

Some songwriters think it's a good idea to leave their listeners guessing. They write songs that are like riddles. Try as the listener might to decipher it, the meaning of the song remains a mystery. For example, try to figure out this one, written by two songwriters we know pretty well:

YOU'RE NOT THE ONE

by Pete and Pat Luboff

> CHORUS:
> *You're not the one*
> *You're the next best thing*
> *You're not the one*
> *My heart is taken*
> *I need you*
> *More than I want to*
> *But you're not the one I love*

The woman I love, she looks like you do
With auburn hair and smiling eyes
She sings to me just like you do but
She wouldn't leave and make me cry, saying

> CHORUS: *repeat*

The man you love, he's not like I am
He's just the opposite of me
He tells you lies and he's unfaithful
He throws away what I most need, saying

> CHORUS: *repeat*

© 1975 Pea Pod Music

It would take Sherlock Holmes to decipher that the singer loves the woman he is singing to, but she's not the one, because he loves the illusion of who he thought she was and not the reality of who she actually is. In the second verse, we can't even remember how to explain it, but the end result is that there are only two people referred to in the song, not four. It sounds like four because the lyr-ics refer to both the surface person and the secret or fantasy person within each character in the song. Have we tried your patience enough with this?

Patience is one thing a listener does not have, whether it's a publisher, producer, some other music business professional, or a kid listening to the radio. If you're asking your listeners to stop and think about what you're trying to say, you're asking too much. The beauty of a great song is that it says what it says so clearly. The listener doesn't have to think about it. The message hits home and all the listener has to do is say, "Yeah, that's exactly how it is."

We love a good mystery—book, that is. It's fun to read through the chapters and guess "who done it." But songwriting has a very different set of rules. The only mysteries allowed in songs are the multiple meanings evoked by very rich images. Even if phrases like "marshmallow skies," "moon river," or "the sound of silence" don't have an immediate concrete meaning, they do have an unmistakable emotional significance.

People don't want their newspapers to keep them guessing about what's happening. They want information clearly communicated. Can you imagine a newspaper writer trying to be more interesting by making the reader wonder what the story means? Perhaps because of the old troubadour connection, in which songs are a form of transmitting news, we want the message in a song to be clear and direct. Whatever the origin of their expectations, your listeners want to know right away who's doing it, what they're doing, and why they're doing it.

Truth clearly delivered in words that communicate action and emotion through images is fascinating. Don't try to be interesting by being obscure. It will frustrate and alienate your listeners.

14
·········

NOWHERE PERSON

*Don't give the singer a negative persona
to identify with in your lyrics*

Some days you feel so low, worms could use your head for a doormat. This is a great time to write a song to express these feelings and relieve the pressure. Pain has its purpose; it forces you to grow. This fits right in with writing songs, so go on and do it. There's nothing wrong with that.

The problem comes in when you take that song too seriously just because it came from a serious place in yourself. Here's an example of a song that we wrote on a particularly bad day:

WHO AM I?

*You're easy to talk to, you're easy to like
You make it seem easy to share
You're someone to look at and someone to
    want
I love you, but then, who am I?*

*I'm no one to speak of and I've no one who
    cares
I'm home and alone most the time
I wait for the evenings when I find you here
I love you, but then, who am I?*

*Who am I to tell you I love you?
I can hardly say it to myself
Who am I to ask you to listen?
I love you, but then, who am I?*

*I'm so lonely, can't you see?
Everyone else is so special
Why not me?*

© 1974 Pea Pod Music

There's even more to this sad tale, but we can't bear to subject you to it. Who will want to sing this song? Remember that when an artist sings a song, that artist takes on the image of the character expressed in the song. Who wants to be such a pathetic loser?

Country music has room for losers, but they're losers on a grand scale. Our loser is too real, too ordinary. The country loser is bigger than life, as in "Always on a Mountain When I Fall." When a lover is lost in a country song, he's really lost, as in "He Stopped Loving Her Today" (because he died). In those country songs, they lose so much, you have to admire them. Country is special that way. Then there are the blues, which by definition is the musical home for losers.

For the most part, however, a pop artist doesn't want to look like a loser. We don't want our artists to look like losers. We want to see them as beautiful, successful, glitteringly perfect and imagine that such a thing exists in real life. They are the mythological creatures of our culture. We want to look up to them and identify with them. They take us with them to a place of beauty and power. We spend most of our time muddling about, trying to make sense of a crazy world. We want our artists to lift us up out of it, not drag us down into it.

That's why your real-life songs about your real-life down days need to be carefully considered before you invest time and money in pitching them to recording artists. Perhaps their usefulness stops with having helped you get through a rough day. Perhaps there are some parts that are real gems that can be used as seeds to start a finely crafted song on a day when you're in top form.

There are some wonderful songs that carry painful messages. "Crazy," by Willie Nelson and "Love Hurts" by Boudleaux Bryant are two of our favorites. They are distinguished by a high level of craft and an air of wisdom in the point of view of the singer. But your ordinary "I'm bummed out and life stinks" song is best tucked away in the back of your file where you can find it years later and say, "Yecch, who wrote this?"

15

WHO'S YOU?

Don't mix up pronouns in a lyric

If you haven't seen the classic Abbott and Costello "Who's on First?" routine, check it out of your local video store and keep your tissue box nearby while you watch it. You're going to laugh until you cry watching Lou Costello sputter and fume as he gets more and more confused.

Confusion in a song, however, is no laughing matter. One area to watch is in your use of pronouns. Case in point: a beautiful song brought to the Santa Fe workshop by Candace Magner.

NO WAY OUT

On a cold December afternoon
with a cold rain fallin' down
she packs the last box to leave in her folks'
* storage room*
'cuz she plans to leave this town
She sets her suitcase on the seat of the bus.
She tells him, "this town isn't big enough for
* people like us,*
*   but I'll be back, I'll be back, 'cuz there's*

*   No way out*
*   No way out*
*   of a love that goes on and on*
*   on and on and on."*

On a warm May morning
with a warm wind blowin' through
she throws down her books and leaves her last
* class at school*
as she wonders what she'll do.
She writes, "I'm lookin' for a job in L.A.
I hope you're coming soon but if you can't get
* away,*
*   then I'll be back, I'll be back, 'cuz there's*

*   No way out*
*   No way out*
*   of a love that goes on and on*
*   on and on and on."*

He mails her a letter, sayin'
"This town feels too big
when you're far away, far away, but there's

No way out
No way out

On a steamy August evening
with the storm clouds rollin' in
she dials him at home, and cries "L.A.'s too
* big,*
and I feel I don't fit in
too many people, there's too much to fear,
I haven't got friends, I don't know anyone
* here,*
*   so I'll be back, I'll be back, 'cuz there's*

*   No way out*
*   No way out*
*   of a love that goes on and on*
*   on and on and on*

© 1991 Candace A. Magner

This song has a lovely melody. We wish we could have included a tape with this book so you could hear it. We love the unity that Candace builds in this song with the similarity of the opening lines in each verse. The information about the season and the weather produces immediate emotional pictures.

For us, though, the song hit a major pronoun "bump" in the first verse: "She sets her suitcase on the seat of the bus./She tells him, 'This town isn't big enough for people like us.'" That bump sidetracked us. Was the heroine talking to the bus driver? Or, might she have been talking to her father, since her folks were mentioned? Who is this "him," and where did he come from?

Until that point, there's no mention of a love interest. All we know is that she's leaving home because she doesn't like small-town life. Even in our confusion, we can't believe that she's really in love with the bus driver. But if she's talking to a lover and saying, "This town isn't big enough for people like us," why is he staying and she leaving? As we ponder these mysteries, half of the song flies by unheard.

It's hard to take, but it's true. A little two- or three-letter word like "he" or "she," "him" or "her" can throw the whole sense of your song off track. This is especially true if you start out using "she" to refer to someone in the song and then switch to "you." We don't know the origin of the old saying, "Don't switch horses in midstream," but we've seen enough songs go wrong to know why it's essential not to switch pronouns in mid-song.

Pronouns are also confusing when there's more than one "he" or "she" being tracked in one song. So, mind your he's and she's and don't let him or her enter without an introduction. When we're listening to your songs, we always want to know who's on first.

16

NOT NAMING THE GAME

Make sure the title is not buried or nonexistent

David Ziems brought this moving lyric, written to a very pretty melody, to our workshop in Santa Fe:

I could never let you down
I will always be around
We will be the best of friends
'Til this life is through

I will always come to you
Any time you want me to
If you ever need my love
I will soon be there

There are times when the world is hard
Maybe times when your heart is tired
But you know you can always count on me

I'll forever trust in you
I'll forever love you too
'Til the rivers all run dry
You'll never be alone

© 1991 David Ziems

Now, there's a friend all of us would like to have. Let's say we heard this song on the radio and wanted to run out and buy it. What would we ask for? Ah ha! Stumped you, haven't we? That's a big problem. How can we buy it? How can everyone who tracks income for it identify it? This is a song with no name. David told us when he pre-sented it that he couldn't think of what to call it, so he just called it "Song for Kate."

There are a few exceptions to the rule that a title must be prominent, repeated, and obvious from just one hearing of the song. George Michael saved his title for the very last line in "Kissing a Fool" and "One More Try" on his *Faith* album, but he is an artist who does not need to pitch his songs elsewhere. Also, the titles of the first songs to sell the album were unmistakable. How many times do you think the title "Faith" was repeated in that song? 8 + 8 + 3 + 8 = 27 times.

Do your own survey of the songs you hear on the radio or watch on MTV. Just a bit of this should convince you that titles really are important. The title is almost always our starting point for writing a song. The title is the hub of the wheel of the song. All the lyric lines should point to the title, enhance it, support it, and lead up to it. The title is your main idea, the essence of what you're communicating. Knowing this will help keep you focused on what your message is. Stick to your title and you won't wind up wandering all over the universe in your song.

The title needs to sit on the most exciting part of your melody. The emotional high point of the melody can be created very literally by having the highest notes in the melody at the title, but there are other ways of setting the title apart melodically. An interesting syncopated rhythm, such as the one Diane Warren created for the title in "Rhythm of the Night," can do the trick. Notes of long duration in a very melodic phrase will stand out in the midst of narrow range, quick notes that resemble speech. When you sing your song without lyrics, the place where the title should go should be obvious to your ears, unless your melody has no single phrase that stands out from the rest of the song. In that case, you need to work on the melody until it does. (See chapter thirty-six, "Don't Play It Again, Please," for more on how to build some peaks and valleys into your songs.) The whole song vibrates when you sing your melody without words, but the part that jumps out and declares, "Here's the title," should vibrate the most.

In the verse/chorus structure, the title is usually in the first line of the chorus. It may also be in the second, third and fourth lines. When the title is great, the melody is catchy, and the message pays off in a satisfying way, we love to hear the song over and over.

In the verse/bridge construction, the title repeats in the verses. It may be in the first line or the last line of each verse. Chapter eleven, "No Bones About It," gives examples of each type.

What makes a title great? Great titles are often drawn from everyday phrases in their usual form or in a slightly twisted form. A glance at the list of Song of the Year Grammy winners and Grammy award-winning best songs in the R&B and country categories will give you plenty of examples: "That's What Friends Are For," "What's Love Got to Do with It," "Every Breath You Take," "Just the Way You Are," "If You Don't Know Me by Now," "Giving You the Best That I Got," "Lean on Me," "After All This Time," "Hold Me," "9 to 5." All of these were commonly used phrases before they became song titles.

We like to look through a dictionary of American idioms for inspiration. For instance, the phrase "two heads are better than one" became our song title "Two Hearts Are Better Than One." Other song titles you can find as entries in this dictionary include "Behind Closed Doors," "Knock on Wood," "The Time of My Life," "That'll Be the Day," "I.O.U." and many more.

Our song on Patti LaBelle's *I'm in Love Again* album, "Body Language," was a book title and a common phrase in the jargon of popular psychology. While we were waiting for the album to be released, two other songs came out with the same title. Titles are not copyrightable, except in very rare circumstances, such as when the title word is a creation of the songwriters. "Supercalifragilisticexpialidocious" fits this description.

There must be a million songs entitled "I Love You." If you are moved to write a song with that title, the song better be dynamite to make up for the triteness of the title. Better yet, add something special to those three little words to distinguish your song from the 999,999 others. Four examples: "I Honestly Love You," "I Just Called to Say I Love You," "I Can't Help It If I'm Still in Love With You," and "I Love You for Sentimental Reasons."

Great titles have drama and conflict. They almost write the whole song by themselves because they call up so many images. A great title arouses your curiosity about the song. Add poetic devices to your conflict (see chapter twenty-four, "No Reason to Rhyme") and your title is stronger and more memorable. Country songs are often all that and humorous, too. "Heaven's Just a Sin Away," "A Boy Named Sue," "(Hey Won't You Play) Another Somebody Done Somebody Wrong Song" and "80's Ladies" are a few examples of titles that do it all.

Let's get back to David's song with no name. Since the song has a verse/bridge structure and the melody calls for the title to be on the last line of the verse, we suggested that David pick one of his ending lines and settle on it as the title. For instance, he could choose "You'll never be alone" from the last verse and substitute it as the last line in verses one and two. The line carries the basic intent of the message of the song and the repetition would establish it as the title.

Or he could choose to replace his current last line in each verse with a new line, such as "I'll be there for you." The problem with either of these choices is that they're not outstanding dramatic lines in themselves. With a really dynamite title, this song could move up a dozen notches in impact. David will have to decide whether he's willing to spend some time coming up with about three hundred titles until he finds one that is really strong and unique.

Then he'll have another problem to solve. The

current rhyme scheme does not lead in well to the title. (For an extended definition of rhyme schemes, see chapter twenty-four.) It would be much more satisfying to the ear if the line just before the title set us up by rhyming with the title. The current rhyme scheme is A, A, B, C. That is, the first two lines rhyme with each other and the second two don't. A better rhyme scheme would be A, A, B, B, or two sets of two lines that rhyme with each other. If David chooses to rewrite this song, it would be a good idea to show the devotion he's expressing in pictures of hands touching, shoulders to lean on, or lives intertwined like vines in the lines that he rewrites. His language is beautifully direct, but a few sharp images will make this good song even stronger.

Remember the concept of the title as the hub of your song wheel. Your title shouldn't be an afterthought. A great title makes for a great song. Keep your ears out for the great titles that are constantly floating in the air around you and collect them. They make good starting points for writing sessions, either solo or with collaborators.

Once you have your great title, honor it. Stick with the message it wants to get across. Without a strong connection to your title throughout your song, the spokes collapse, and your song can't move on down the road.

17

I'M BIDING MY LINES

Don't take too long to get to the point

In one workshop in Santa Fe, a songwriter presented the following song to the group:

RHYMING LINES

Where you been so long?
So good to see ya here;
C'mon and join our song.
Lend us all your ear.

The first time I saw you, you really
  turned me on;
I never thought I'd stand a chance,
You showed me I was wrong.

Life hands us people
We may never want to see again;
Reach out to someone,
Someone you could call a friend.

You know it's true,
Love is all around.
Feel it in your heart,
Remember where it's found.

It isn't always easy to be where you
  want to be.
To make your life do one thing right;
Imagine what comes naturally

Make something happen;
Recognize the signs.
For the verses of destiny,
We write the Rhyming Lines.

© 1980 Denny Cicak

What's wrong with this song? Denny took the whole song to get around to his point, which is in the last two lines. The first two lines could have been an okay start to a song about meeting a long-lost lover again. The second two lines come from some other point of view, and it's not clear whose. The second three-line section goes back to the lover, but doesn't relate to the idea of how or why they've been apart. The next three sections are a philosophical discussion of love and friendship. The title idea, which is the foundation on which the entire song must rest, is not even hinted at until it shows up in the last two lines.

A song is a three-minute motion picture. In those three minutes, the songwriter has to give the who, what, where, when, and why of the situation. Most, if not all, of this information has to be stated or implied in the first two lines. If listeners can't relate to the people and the situation by then, they'll turn off their ears. Check out the first two lines in your favorite songs on the radio and see how much information they convey.

If a song is going to get through the gauntlet of publishers, producers, artists, record company executives, promoters, and radio programmers and get out where it can be heard by the general public, it has to grab the listeners by the ears in the first line and never let them go. The message has to be emotionally intense, and we have to know who is singing and care about the person delivering the message right at the top of the song.

A song could be thought of as a commercial that sells the central idea you've chosen to express. Just like in the ad game, you have to tell them what you're going to say, say it, and then tell them what you said. In a song you start telling them what you're going to say in word number one.

We told Denny that the last two lines of the song were a good starting point for his rewrite. One way to go would be to make those two lines the first two lines in his chorus. Because it's best to keep the language in a song conversational, it might be better to switch the order of the lines to say, "We write the rhyming lines for the verses of destiny."

It's not unusual to come away from hundreds of lines of work with only one or two lines worth keeping. We have written as many as three hundred titles for one song before hitting the one that satisfied. Songwriting is like mining for diamonds: You have to move a lot of dirt to get to one little gem. Once you've sorted out the gem from the dirt, you're ready to begin writing the song.

Getting back to Denny's song, let's start with the central concept that "We write the rhyming lines for the verses of destiny." There are as many ways to go with that idea as there are songwriters to think about it. This song could be about responsibility to preserve the earth's resources, a wronged husband's reply to his wife's excuse that the affair "just happened," or the New Age theme

that we are responsible for everything we see, to name a few of hundreds of possibilities.

The essence of the message is choice. What greater choice can we make than to marry someone? This could be a wedding song one spouse sings to the other, or a duet they sing to each other. The combination of the here and now in the intense emotion surrounding of a couple getting married will bring the philosophy down to earth where we can feel it and see it.

Now load your image palette by free associating on wedding images as described in chapter three. With all your wedding words available, you're set to start. The first line could let us know that we are at a wedding by including one or two unmistakable images. Keep the song right in the moment. Don't leave the church! There's plenty going on right there; you don't have to wander down the aisle and out the door.

The only connection you need to make is the one between the choice the two lovers are making at that moment and the long-range implications of that choice: a lifetime of commitment, children, grandchildren, facing the unknown together, and so forth.

Now, you've really got a gem that sparkles. All of its facets concentrate the light on the one shining idea that you started out with in the first few lines and brought to a climax at the title. When you get done cutting and polishing this one, it could last forever.

What if the song is actually coming from a true situation in your life? The process is still the same. You need to perceive yourself and the person you want to sing to as dramatic characters. How would you describe yourself? What makes the singee the unique person he or she is? What particular emotional moment are you trying to capture in the song? We still need to know who, what, where, when and why.

You have to be especially careful when the song is about you, or from you to your lover, to include identifying details, because the tendency is to think that all these things are already understood. See chapter thirty-eight, "Stranger in a Strange Song," for techniques that will help you judge what your songs are actually saying.

18
·······

ONE SONG, MANY LANGUAGES

Don't write lyrics with an inappropriate mix of conversational tones

We are fascinated by people who study language dialects and know them so well that they can tell where you come from after listening to you talk for a few minutes. Our son, with the egocentricity of youth, said the other day, "Everyone else has an accent, but I don't." We told him that, to other people, he does have an accent. Strangely enough, since he's a native Californian, it's a New York accent that he picked up from Pat.

The language we use gives more information than just the literal meaning of the words. It identifies us in terms of education, social status, geographic origin and level of relationship to the listener. This identification was the basis for the plot of George Bernard Shaw's *Pygmalion*, which in turn became the plot for Lerner and Loewe's *My Fair Lady*. The college professor says, "How do you do?" The teenager says, "Hi." The ghetto rapper says, "S'up?" From the first word of greeting, we identify ourselves with a particular style of language.

This truth comes into play when we write lyrics. Every word we put into the singer's mouth must be authentic; it must come from the personality we created when we decided exactly who was singing this song.

Here's an example of tone gone wrong that we treasure because it is proof that top-of-the-line writers eliminate perfectly good writing from their songs. If the verse doesn't fit, don't keep it. Guess what song this verse never made it into:

You've got a long list
With so many choices
A ventriloquist with so many voices
And your friends in high places
 say where the pieces fit
You've got too many faces in your make-up kit

But I see your true colors . . .

© 1987 Tom Kelly/Billy Steinberg

This was the original first verse to the wonderful hit song "True Colors," written by Billy Steinberg and Tom Kelly. Billy, who is the lyricist of the team, liked the writing in this verse very much. But, he told us, they decided that this verse limited the song because it spoke to a particular kind of woman. They saw that this song had universal potential, and in fact, what they wanted to go for was something that anyone could say to anyone else: father to son, daughter to mother, man to woman, friend to friend. So, without ado, out went a perfectly good verse. It doesn't matter how good it is. If it doesn't serve the song, off with its lines!

We also feel that the language in this verse doesn't match the tone of the message. The song gives us something we all need, 100 percent unconditional support. This verse is slightly judgmental, a put-down. It's very clever, but clever is not what this message needs—sincerity is.

When choosing your words, consider both ends of the spectrum. Would this person use this word? And does this language suit the message? If the answer to both of these is yes, you've found the right word.

Do you remember why you loved—or hated—Winnie the Pooh? Maybe Sleeping Beauty was your favorite, or Tinker Bell. Each of these fictional characters has a distinct personality. That personality is expressed in their physical appearance, their actions, their clothing, their dramatic situation and their language. We are drawn to our favorites because we feel some kinship with the character. For us to feel that kinship, the character must be, on some level, believable. We would never believe in Tinker Bell if she talked like a truck driver. And you know what happens when you don't believe in Tinker Bell. Her little light goes out!

Every recording artist also has a distinct personality, and it's no accident. They pay people lots of money to advise them about the image they present. Just like our fairy tale heroes and heroines, they have to project believable personalities. It has to do with the way they dress, their grooming, their performing style, and the songs they choose to sing. The lyrics in the songs must fit perfectly into their jigsaw puzzle of personality or we won't believe enough to keep them alive as artists.

Try listening to three distinctly different types of radio stations: R&B, country, and rock 'n roll. Jot down some of the words that jump out at you. Here's our quick sample:

- **R&B**—Baby, baby, baby! sweet love, got to find a way, pump it, do you right (lots of words too suggestive for this publication);

- **Country**—It hurts, dreams, road, don't need nobody, freedom, lonely nights, stand up tall

(and a selection of puns and new turns on old phrases, like "setting fancy free" and "one man woman");

- **Hard rock 'n roll**—Camera eye, celestial, arrogant, discontent, fast machine, bloodstain, noose (and a lot of angry philosophy screamed at megadecibel level).

Making sure that your choice of words is precise and appropriate for the personality who is singing and the message you're expressing is the logical extension of the groundwork you laid in creating your original character, the singer and the singee (see chapter six). Putting just the right lyrics into the singer's mouth creates a sense of unity and integrity that will make your listeners believe and give real life to your song.

19

X-RATED

Be careful with sex in your songs

In workshops and collaborations, we've noticed that songwriters like to play with words, all kinds of words. When the word-play ball gets rolling, it often bounces back and forth from risky business to risqué business. This is good for some laughs, but should we put it in our songs?

The answer to that question is too complicated to boil down to a simple "yes" or "no." Let's take the "no" side first. Sex is a big deal in everyone's life. Therefore, it's a natural subject for the songwriter to tackle. But if your intention is to pitch the song to a prominent recording artist, any references to sex have to be made in the porcupine style—very carefully. You can't get more direct than John Bettis, lyricist of "Slow Hand," with the lines:

I want a lover with a slow hand
I want a lover with an easy touch

I want somebody who will spend some time
Not come and go in a heated rush . . .

© 1980 Warner/Tamerlane & Sweet Harmony Music

Notice the high level of craft in these lines. There's nothing crude about the way John put them together. The phrase "slow hand" is fresh, unique, and creative; it conveys a precise and unmistakable image. That image is reinforced by the next line with the phrase "easy touch." John's talking about some really laid-back sex here without sounding the slightest bit offensive. The third line says the same thing in another way and sets you up for the killer fourth line, where the censors are ready to hear "come and go" without so much as a twitch in the direction of their blue pencils.

On the contrary, the message conveyed by

"Slow Hand" is one of sensitivity and thoughtfulness. This is a classy love scene! This is something we'd all like to experience, and the proof of its universal appeal is that it was a hit in both country and pop/R&B, by Conway Twitty and the Pointer Sisters respectively.

By way of contrast, here's a song we wrote a million years ago:

UP IS IN

Start out from the bottom
Take it from the top
I don't care where you begin
Long as you don't stop

> CHORUS:
> *Up is in   Get up, get up and do it*
> *Up is in   Get up and get into it*
> *Up is in   Use it or you'll lose it*
> *Up is in   Down is out, up is in*

Once you have it goin'
Give it all you got
Fill your cup up to the brim
Get it while it's hot

> CHORUS: *repeat*

Come on keep it coming
Come into your own
Get off on what's happening
Feel it in your bones

> CHORUS: *repeat*

© 1974 Pea Pod Music

No matter how much we tried to say that this was a song of encouragement and enthusiasm about life in general, those who listened heard it another way. All right, we meant it both ways. But the song never got anywhere, and we believe it was because of its crude undertones.

Our "no" answer to the question of sex in songs is a highly qualified one. You might as well try to say no to arms and legs! It's interesting that we are constantly bombarded with sex and violence on television and the movies, but sex in songs causes such an uproar. What makes songs so much more powerful that people react so strongly to them?

When we say "yes" to sex in songs, we arouse the ire of well-meaning parents and vote-seeking politicians. Book burning and record burning are nothing new. You can check in your history books to see who struck the matches, and we bet you won't like them. Yet, the blatant sex and violence in rap, metal, and hard rock music might make you think that those historical bad guys didn't have such a bad idea. For your own sake, please think again.

Personally, we don't like songs with that lyrical content; we find them offensive, but we will defend the right of those creators to say what's on their minds. We don't buy it, we don't listen to it. That is the ultimate voting power, and everybody has it. Political resistance to this kind of music makes big headlines and boosts the sales of mediocre material that would otherwise have languished on the shelves.

Pardon our getting on a soapbox here, but we are in good company. The National Academy of Recording Arts and Sciences (the Grammy ® organization) and the National Academy of Songwriters are both involved in the battle to curb censorship of creators of music. If we start to say that this songwriter or that one shouldn't be allowed to have his or her song heard, where will it stop? Where would we be now if the people who wanted to ban rock 'n roll because it was "lewd" had prevailed? Before that, it was the Charleston that was too outrageous, and before that, the waltz!

Who's to say where the line between what's art and what's not is drawn? Art is in the eye of the beholder. Let's draw our own lines; we're the artists! If we are not free to choose what we express, how can we create?

So, take your own position on sex in your songs. Crude sex in a song doesn't make it less of a creation, but it does narrow the song's appeal. Most people prefer candlelight and tenderness to elevate sex from a mere release of tension between battling genders to a romantic experience between caring lovers. The words you choose will establish which of these two very different worlds of sex your song is expressing. Your listeners will respond negatively or positively according to their tastes and values. You won't be able to please them all, so make sure you please yourself by being true to your vision of the song and what it wants to say.

20

SING ME A ?

Don't depend on punctuation marks to give meaning to your song

Did you ever see Victor Borge do his punctuation marks act? He'd tell a story, and he would indicate the punctuation marks by drawing them in the air and making hilarious noises with his mouth. A period was a finger pointing at the audience and a quick rude blowing sound, like the opposite of a kiss. To make a question mark, he'd trace a curve in the air of the appropriate shape and make a ratchety sound in the back of his throat, like a New Year's Eve noisemaker, then finish it off with the period beneath.

As the story progressed, his speed accelerated and commas, periods, question marks, quotation marks came rapid-fire, until everyone in the audience had fallen out of their chairs in hysterics. This is the only known instance in the universe of punctuation marks being obvious in an aural presentation (we are not including dictation to a secretary in this unofficial survey of the aural universe).

We'd like to try an experiment with you. Don't read the lyric below with your own eyes. Ask someone to read it to you and listen without looking at it. Then you will have the real experience of the person who listens to the song, which is not the same experience as the person who reads the printed version. Have your helper start reading now:

Jane Aker brought this hard-hitting lyric to our Santa Fe workshop:

GIMME A DIME AND I'LL CALL SOMEBODY
WHO CARES

You been pokin' at some sore spots
I'd just as soon avoid—
Like, "Red on black
They're trading blood for oil."
Like, "When you gonna get a job?"
And, "Why so paranoid?"
Like, "Where you goin'?
Where you been?"

And "D'you believe in Sigmund Freud?"
The thing I'm trying to say is that
I ain't climbin' your front stairs
But gimme a dime
And I'll call somebody who cares.
It ain't much.

Can't afford to get involved
Been down this road before.
Like, "Ain't you Weasel Smith from Nam?"
And, "Ain't it a shame we didn't win that
war?"
You say times have changed since then?
And life's not really fair?
Whoa! Flip me two bits
And I'll call somebody who cares.
It ain't much.

Lookin' to put some distance
'Tween my present and my past.
Today ain't much to brag about.
Yesterday's long gone—it flashed.
Paid my debts.
You got your share.
Ya' saying one check ain't been cashed?
Honey, lend me some coin
And I'll call somebody who cares.
It ain't much.
C'mon, gimme a dime
And I'll find somebody who cares.

© 1991 Jane Aker

Are you lost? Just listening to this lyric, it's easy to go down dead end trails of what it might mean. That's because understanding this lyric depends so heavily on knowing where the quotation marks are. Victor Borge is not here to guide you, so you hear, "You've been pokin' at some sore spots I'd just as soon avoid like red on black . . ." and you draw your own conclusion from what you think that means.

Since there is no way to hear a quotation mark,

you need to broadcast the fact that you're about to quote someone. You need to come right out and say it in words. We suggested to Jane that she substitute the words "You say" on the front of each of those lines that contain a quotation, instead of "Like" or "And."

This will get her into a little trouble in the lines where she is already using the words "You say," because she has used those words to introduce indirect quotations and turn them into questions posed by the singer. Any solution she chooses will change the tone of those lines a bit.

Even with our eyes wide open and drinking in all those punctuation marks, there's confusion about what's going on here. We asked Jane, "Who is the singer in this song?" This is a question we should not have to ask; it is something we should be certain of from line number one. We thought we knew until we got to the Weasel Smith line and then we got lost. And who is the singee that the

singer keeps quoting? How can we get our bearings if we don't know who's who and what's what?

Jane answered that the singer *is* Weasel Smith. The singee is someone who knew him vaguely in Vietnam. Knowing these two facts goes a long way toward helping us understand the song. So we suggested to Jane that she have Weasel introduce himself in the first line and singee in the second line. Once we know who the singer and singee are, the whole song makes a lot more sense.

If your song has a lot of punctuation marks in it, give it the aural test. Close your eyes and say the lyrics to yourself to see if understanding their message depends on those aurally invisible punctuations. Or try writing out the lyrics without any punctuation and see if any of the meaning is lost. Rewrite to remove the message's dependence on the punctuations. If that doesn't work, maybe it's time to revive Victor Borge's technique and sing those question marks.

21
....
LYRICAL HANGOVERS
Watch out for lyric phrases that hang over to the next melody line instead of ending with their own melodic phrase

There are many ways to envision how a song is built. We've already talked about the song as a wheel, with the title at its hub and each lyric line as a spoke. Another image we like to use is a tower of building blocks. We've all tried at some time in our childhood to see how high we could stack our wooden blocks before the tower tumbled.

Being the instinctive scientists that we are, we soon figure out that the tower stands better if the biggest block is on the bottom and the blocks get smaller as the tower gets higher. We also see that the tower is more stable if the blocks are placed

directly over the ones below. The block that hangs off to one side of the block beneath it is sure to fall, and soon.

In a song, each lyric line is like a building block. It holds up the ones that come after. Consider the tower that Ron Whitmore of Santa Fe built:

LOVE IS HOLDING YOU TIGHT

*Ran around in circles, trying to find
looking for answers, locked in my mind
Didn't know if love was, more than a score
Then you walked through my door, now*

CHORUS:
Love is holding you tight
Getting up at night
to see if baby is crying for you
and as you hold her to your breast,
I can't start to express
all the love I'm feeling for you
True love takes two

Did my share of looking, had my share of fun
every time I got too close, knew I had to run
When my eyes first looked in yours
Knew my race was through
now I spend my life loving you, cause

CHORUS: *repeat*

© 1990 Ron Whitmore

Take a close look at Ron's first line. Do you notice how it doesn't complete a thought? This is what we call a lyrical hangover. The melody comes to the end of a phrase at this point, but the lyrics hang out waiting to—what? ʾ   question is partially answered in the ne͵   ͵t the real subject matter—love—isn'ʾ   ͵ntil the third line. If you look at /   ͵s by themselves, Ron could b͵   ʾhing. He also painted the sin͵   ͵rson. Where are his redeemin͵

Compare the first versͻ
pretty clear in the first two ͵
verse that we're talking about ͳ͵
singer has been around, had fun, a͵
of commitment. He knows as soon as ͵
wife that she's the one for him and no͵
happily married. That says a whole lot mo͵
puts the singer in a much better light, all witι
lyrical hangovers.

We suggested to Ron that he scrap the first verse and use his current second verse to start out with. This is the equivalent of putting the biggest block on the bottom of your tower. To get people involved in listening to your song, open up with your strongest verse. Put your best lines forward! Larry Gatlin doesn't beat around the bush. He starts many of his songs with the hook line/title. Listen to "All the Gold in California," "Take Me to Your Lovin' Place," and "Statues Without Hearts" for examples of this technique to start your song off with a bang.

There was a unanimous feeling among the workshop participants that the line "True love takes two," which was such an afterthought that Ron had written it in at the bottom of his typed lyrics, was really the high point of the song, both melodically and lyrically. The alliteration, inner rhyme, and message of the line appealed to everyone. We all suggested that Ron rethink this song or start another one with that as the title.

Here is another example of a song with lyrical hangovers, written by Cindy Bellinger and brought to our Santa Fe workshop:

THE HARDEST THING I'VE DONE

Every night I go to bed
Wishing you'd call—instead +
The silence only pulls me down
to the quiet all around . . .

If you'd only trusted more
that I could be—your +
one reason to change your life
and take me as your wife . . .

© 1991 Cindy Bellinger

These are only the first four lines of the first two verses. These verses are excellent examples of the most common kind of lyrical hangover. At the points marked with a +, the thought is begun in one line and left hanging over to be completed in the next line. The musical phrase completes at the +, but the lyrics don't. This interrupts the natural ͵w of the language. It's like taking a long pause ͵dsentence. We cannot hear those dashes be- ͵ʝg, so it doesn't help to put them on the ͵ sheet.

You may be able to point to some songs that have "made it" in spite of suffering from this flaw. Rules are made to be broken, but you must know the rules first. Some songwriters who are also artists break these rules because they can get away with it. A writer/artist doesn't have to work under the same rules as a songwriter who must pass through a gauntlet of ears between writing the song and getting an artist to record it.

Build your song carefully. Put the biggest, strongest lyric blocks down first and keep your thoughts complete within each melodic line. You may be able to build a song that reaches to the top of the charts.

22
....

TO SING THE UNSINGABLE WORD

Beware of tongue-twisting word combinations and hard consonants on long notes

Singers sing because they love to sing. Like anything that anyone does well, they get good at it by doing it over and over again until they get it right. And like trapeze artists, singers seem to sing with the greatest of ease. But take a closer look. What's really happening is that the singer has turned his or her own body into a finely tuned musical instrument by studying and practicing for years. You will also notice that great singers are always singing great songs. They know what they like, and they choose a song because it feels great to sing it. Songwriters who do not take this into account will not endear themselves or their songs to singers.

You know what it doesn't feel great to sing? Try singing a long, high note on the word "sing." Now try singing the same long high note on the word "you." You can feel the difference easily. If you did extend the word "sing" by concentrating on the vowel sound in the middle and sticking the *ng* or the *g* on quickly at the end, you were trying to make the best of a bad word choice for a long note. The trouble is, the listener will wonder why you are singing about sin. The *g* will probably get lost in the shuffle to the next word. Nasal tones and consonants are almost impossible to extend. They are more suited for shorter notes that flow into words starting with a vowel sound.

Why should a consonant flow into a vowel? Try singing or saying, "The best dog sits still." Notice how much your mouth has to work to get from the end of one word to another. Now sing or say, "I want to give you my heart." Your lips and tongue do not have to stumble over each other

to make the transitions between these words, do they? Singers love to sing words that flow into each other that way. The tongue-twisting variety of lyrics may have a place in a certain kind of song where they add to an expression of anger or agitation, but for the most part, for words to sing well they must flow gently into each other.

The best sounds for those long, high notes are open vowel sounds. Check out all your favorite ballads and see if it isn't the case that the main sounds on the extended notes are *a*, *e*, *i*, *o* or *u*. Singers just love to let loose on those sounds because it does feel good. Our vocal apparatus is physically suited to making those sounds with ease. Try opening your mouth and saying the vowels without moving your lips. It's easy.

You might think of the movements that singers make with their mouths as a dance. You have to choreograph that dance so that it can be done smoothly. There are physical limitations. You can't ask a dancer to be in a totally curled up position on one side of the stage and in a flying leap on the other side of the stage by the next beat. You can ask singers to sing the unsingable word, but chances are they will choose not to. Make your songs feel good to sing and you will increase your chances of attracting singers to it.

Do your own choreography check by paying attention to your lips as you sing the song. If they have to do too many twists and turns and flying leaps, you need to make adjustments in your choreography. Like our moms told us, "Watch your mouth!"

23

I CAN'T SEE IT

Use picture words in your lyrics;
instead of talking about the subject, express it directly

We are constantly bombarded with words. A steady stream of them washes over our ears from television and radio. Most of us have learned to tune out a great deal of it for the sake of what's left of our sanity. In this scenario, words are as meaningful as "white noise." To illustrate the state of mind of the average listener, Pat sometimes wears a special pair of earrings to songwriting workshops. One earring says, "IN," the other one says—you guessed it—"OUT."

Listening is an art that takes time and concentration to master. Wouldn't it be wonderful if the art of listening was recognized as a necessary component of everyone's education? It would be a very different world if we all really listened to each other. Unfortunately, this is not the case.

Songwriters listen to songs all the time, yet most new songwriters attending our workshops haven't noticed that the songs they're listening to have structure. There's listening, and then there's *really* listening to hear what's going on under the surface of the song that makes it great.

So, if even songwriters aren't hearing all there is to be heard in a song, what can you expect from the average listener, who doesn't have that extra interest? Not much. If you really want to get your message across to Mr. or Ms. Average Listener, you need to involve more that just their ears. You must grab the attention of their mind's eye with words that make them see what is happening in the song. This technique will quadruple the chances that your message will be received and remembered.

JoAnna O'Keefe, who writes beautiful inspirational poetry that is published on greeting cards and posters, came to our Santa Fe workshop to learn how to adapt her talents to lyric writing. She brought this lyric:

REMEMBERING

Many months have passed
since our time

of togetherness,
leaves of dark green
have turned to gold.

CHORUS:
Autumn winds are blowing
embers are glowing
and I remember,
oh, I remember.
It was springtime
and I remember.

It's been so long
since you've held me
in your arms
that I'm beginning
to lose the feel
of your touch,
and your face,
like an old photo,
fades in my memory.
Your gentle voice
grows softer:
still, I listen—

CHORUS: *repeat*

Sometimes I wonder
if you are but a dream
if we met in the mist
of my imagination,
Then I ask my heart,
and I know.
You are real,
and you touched me.

CHORUS: *repeat*

© 1991 JoAnna O'Keefe

Question: What's wrong with this picture? Answer: There aren't enough pictures to make the message of the song stick in that space between our "IN" ear and our "OUT" ear. As it stands, all we know is that she once had a lover, and now he's gone, but she remembers him. The words are lovely. They mean more every time you read them. But Average Listener is not going to be looking at the printed words. To get people to hear your song, you need to use picture words so they will see it.

Especially since the title of the song is "Remember," we asked JoAnna to fill in the blanks. What is it the singer remembers? Remember the great duet with Hermione Gingold and Maurice Chevalier in *Gigi*? They differ in their recollections about what time it was, what they wore, where they went, and so on, yet both feel they remember their past love affair very well.

JoAnna wrote to us after the workshop, saying, "I would love to shape that poem into a song—guess I'll have to read your book to find out how." Well, JoAnna, here goes. You've got a good start here because you're capturing a special feeling that probably everyone experiences, looking back on a love that was good and is now gone.

Remembering that "Remembering" is your title, put it squarely in the center of your song wheel. "Remembering" needs to be the repeated word in the chorus, not "I remember," unless you want to change your title to "I Remember."

You are taking five lines at the top of the song to say what can be said in one picture phrase. You want to set the stage that they've been apart for a while. How about:

In the cool shade of this tree
we warmed by the fire of our kisses
Now the branches are bare
in the cold winter air
But I still us see there

This establishes that they had a romance in the summer in the first two lines. The second two lines say that it's now winter. More than two seasons may have passed, but the images symbolize that the heat of the past has turned into coldness. The fifth line leads into the idea that you are remembering the love affair and, consequently, into your chorus.

Now, what is it that you remember? Close your eyes and picture it. Free associate, using as many descriptive words as you can. What color were his eyes? What were you wearing? What color was his hair? What was so special about your relationship?

Was it the long talks you had together, and the way he seemed to understand you? Was it his sensitivity to your needs? How did he show that? What kinds of things did you do together? You might want to keep the whole song in the one spot under the tree. You had a picnic there. You kissed. You talked about your future together. You fell asleep in each other's arms. You drank wine (symbolic of sharing an intoxicating experience of love). You laughed and played at tickling each other like children.

This kind of background material should be in your verses. Your chorus should give the overview. Are you glad to be remembering, or is it painful? This might depend on why you're not together anymore. Remember the song Anna sings in *The King and I*? She's remembering her husband, who is dead. She has many good memories, but they're focused on one particular night. She sings about how the earth smelled, how the sky looked, and how the mists settled on the hills. Although she's sad that her husband is dead, she's grateful and glad for the love they shared because it makes her feel a part of all lovers. So she sings, "Hello, Young Lovers." You need to choose your emotional stance and then choose words that will deliver it in pictures.

When it comes to song lyrics, everyone is from Missouri; you have to show them. Don't talk about the situation in an indirect way. It's almost as if a song were a slide show. Each line of lyric needs to project a picture on the screen of the listener's mind. The more colorful and emotional the picture, the more likely the listener will be to be moved by it. Think about the difference in impact between a phrase like "an old car" and this one, "a yellow '57 Chevy." The first is too vague. On hearing it, you might call up a picture in your mind, but not necessarily the one the writer has in mind. The second image is unmistakable.

Picture words are extremely important in a lyric, but don't stop at making your listeners see your song. Pull in as many senses as you can. If you can make them taste its strawberry sweetness, smell the smoke from a burnt-out desire, or feel the luxurious softness of velvet, you're going to have an involved, moved listener.

We'll give you more about how to turn this poem into a song, JoAnna, in the next chapter.

24

NO REASON TO RHYME

Avoid inconsistent or nonexistent rhyme schemes

Something else is missing from JoAnna's "Remembering" lyric. Did you notice that there were no rhymes? It may not have struck you just reading the words on the paper. But if they had been sung to you, you would feel something was wrong at the ends of the lines where you have come to expect rhymes in songs.

We call this inner sense that something's "off" in the song a "bump." It reminds us of driving along a smooth road and then hitting a speed bump. Something inside you jumps. When a song is crafted to perfection, it doesn't have any of these bumps.

You may be able to find one or two examples of absolutely wonderful songs that don't have the usual complement of rhyming lines. "Gentle on My Mind," written by John Hartford, is an excellent example. Many of the lyric lines don't rhyme. Only one or two lines rhyme with the title line, but somehow you just don't miss the rhymes. Maybe it's because each line is so rich with images that the song flows gently by without any bumps. Those few exceptions aside, 99.44 percent of the time, song lyrics should rhyme.

Why? There's something in us that loves a rhyme. As very young children, we love our Mother Goose. There's something immensely satisfying about the cadence of language that repeats word sounds and rhythms. Pat will never forget our son's favorite book when he was two. It was a story told in rhyme, and he asked for it several times a day for months and months. After reading it five hundred or so times, Pat had it memorized. Ten years later, with a little prompting, she could probably still recite it.

That's another reason why rhymes work in songs. Rhyming makes things easier to remember. No one likes to feel lost and confused. Rhymes are the signposts in a lyric. They say, "Here we are at the end of the line! Doesn't that make you feel just fine?"

How do we rhyme? Let us count the ways. There are perfect, near, and inner rhymes. In a perfect rhyme, the two words end in exactly the same sound: line-fine. Marilyn and Alan Bergman ("The Way We Were," "Windmills of Your Mind") are committed to perfect rhymes. They refuse to settle for less. But most modern songwriters feel that a near rhyme is close enough for rock 'n roll: line-mind. The slight difference in sound doesn't disqualify these two words from being a rhyming pair.

Inner rhymes can be perfect or near rhymes. What makes them inner rhymes is their location. Inner rhymes are similar-sounding words that are scattered throughout one line of lyric. "The Rain in Spain" from *My Fair Lady* is an extreme example of inner rhymes. When you have too many in one line, it can get comical. But a few well-placed inner rhymes can pack a line with dynamite.

Rhyme schemes, or how the rhymes fall on the line, are usually referred to with capital letters. For example, an A, B, A, B rhyme scheme is a four-line song section in which the first and third lines rhyme, and the second and fourth lines rhyme. Another common rhyme scheme is A, B, C, B; the first and third lines do not rhyme with each other, but the second and fourth lines do. A third possible rhyme scheme for four lines is A, B, C, C. Notice that in each of these rhyme schemes, it is the last word in the last line that rhymes with at least one other line in the section. That's what gives the feeling of completion to the section.

Whatever rhyme scheme you set up in the first verse, stick with it for the rest of the verses. The repeating rhyme scheme gives listeners the satisfying feeling of knowing where they are and what to expect in the song. Life is uncertain enough. People don't want to feel confused by a song that constantly switches its rhyme scheme around.

On the other ear, a problem of too much rhyming can occur when you fall into an A, A, A, A rhyme scheme, a.k.a. the "moon, June, spoon, tune" syndrome. We call that writing yourself into a corner. All too quickly you find yourself grasping at ridiculous rhymes to meet the demands of the rhyme scheme. As a result, you wind up "going for the rhyme" and losing touch with the meaning of the line. This is a sure-fire way to write a "bump" into your song.

If we find our lyrics falling into a rhyming rut like that, we steer in another direction. It's hard enough to carry off one verse like that. The second verse is worse, and the third is even verser. If you do manage to come up with something that makes sense in the A, A, A, A rhyme scheme, you run the risk of boring your listeners with too much repetition.

Every songwriter should have a rhyming dictionary to consult when stuck for a rhyme. There may just be a word in there that you won't come up with on your own.

Rhyming is the main poetic device to use to make your lyric memorable and impressive. There's nothing like a clever rhyme that really works. Another device that makes a lyric satisfying to the ear is alliteration. Alliteration means using several words with the same initial sound in a single lyric line. We've loved alliteration ever since Mary had a little lamb, little lamb, little lamb. There's no reason to stop now.

Take a minute to think of the titles of some of your favorite songs and you will see these poetic devices at work. Some of our favorites are: "Don't It Make My Brown Eyes Blue" (alliteration); "I Don't Have the Heart" (alliteration); "Blame It on the Rain" (inner near rhyme); "Sensitivity" (inner rhyme and alliteration in the same word!).

Now, do the same thing with some of the lyrics from your favorite songs. Take a close look at the rhyme scheme, the use of inner rhyme and alliteration. You'll be surprised at how much is going on in even the simplest song. It is a feat to pack all that in a song and make it sound so natural that you don't notice it. A quote from the classic movie *The Red Shoes* applies here: "A great impression of simplicity can only be achieved by a great agony of body and spirit."

Agony is not in your job description as a songwriter, but hard work is. Because the great songwriters make it look so easy, we are shocked when we get involved in the process and find out just how hard it is. Songwriter/singer Morgan Ames, one of the Inner Voices, said at a University of California at Los Angeles (UCLA) Extension seminar on women in songwriting, "There's a difference between the romance of songwriting and the doing of it. The doing of it doesn't always smell good. You sit in a room and you sweat and it's not the dream. A lot of people get stuck between the dream of what they want and the unglamorous process of doing it."

So, while you're sweating out the delicate balance between too little and too much rhyming, keep your cool. We dedicate the following poem to all of you brave and hard-working songwriters who stalk the wild word that not only rhymes but perfectly expresses your intended meaning, all the while sounding like it naturally fell off the tip of your tongue:

ODE TO A SONGWRITER IN SEARCH OF A RHYME

When you're racking your brain for just the right rhyme
And you think you can take it no longer
Remember that writing a great song takes time
And what doesn't kill you is making you stronger!

25

....

EPIC PROPORTIONS

Write songs of reasonable length

Back in ancient Greece, the great-granddaddy of all rappers, Homer, had the *Iliad* and the *Odyssey* memorized. He would rhyme on for days about a giant hollow horse, lotus eaters, Cyclops, Sirens, and battle after battle. But then, they didn't have TV and radio. Homer didn't have to pause for a station break or a commercial.

Consider this song, brought to our NAS workshop by Sharon Angell:

I WANT YOU BACK JUST SO I CAN DUMP YOU

When you left me, baby
You weren't much fun
It was cold Christmas Eve
At a quarter to one
I gave you ten presents
But you gave me none
Then you packed your things
And ignoring my gun, you said
Bye-bye, Baby
I'm dumping you
You've been an angel
But I'm just passing through
Gotta hit the road
Gotta have my space
Gotta do my own thing

And all those other stupid things
That boys always say

> CHORUS:
> *When you left me, baby*
> *You made me so blue*
> *Now I want you back*
> *Just so I can dump you!*

I'll be sweet for a while
Massaging your gums
You'll be so content
You won't know what's to come
Then you'll get 'pendicitis
Doubled over in pain
You'll beg me for help
That's when I'll explain

Bye-bye, Baby
I'm dumping you
You've been a bad boy
And you know it, too
Gotta clean up your act
Gotta make it up to me
Gotta learn a lesson

And all those other stupid things
That girls always say

> CHORUS: (variation)
> *When you left me, Baby*
> *You made me so blue*
> *Now I got you back*
> *Just so I can dump you*

I'll cut off the phones
There'll be no nine-one-one
I'll do you in
Without shooting my gun
My home fried chicken's
Germ warfare, it's true
You came back to me
And now I've poisoned you

Bye-bye, Baby
I'm dumping you
And when I dump somebody
They're really through
Only a stomach pump
Can save you now
But the one I had
Got lost somehow

> CHORUS: *repeat*

You'll never make
Another girl cry
Lovers like you
Just have to die
Here's the red dress
I'll wear to your wake
Now kiss me goodbye
You coldhearted snake

Bye-bye, Baby
You've breathed your last
Let bygones be bygones
Let's forget the past
I won't hold a grudge
Cuz I got even with you
I got you back
Just so I could dump you

CHORUS: *repeat*

Don't get mad . . . get even . . .
I saw Fatal Attraction *twenty-seven times . . .*
No bad boy's gonna ruin my Christmas Eve . . .
More fried chicken, honey? . . .

© 1990 Sharon Angell

You have to hand it to Sharon, this song packs a wallop. The message comes across loud and clear. She's focused on the emotion of the moment, and she tells the story with definite images. The only problem is that a radio station would have to play the song in three parts to insert the required number of commercials in the time it takes to sing a song this long.

In order to fit the lyrics on one sheet, Sharon typed them in two side-by-side columns. The sight of that many words squeezed onto a lyric sheet might be enough to scare away a publisher who knows that the time limit for songs played on pop radio stations is about three minutes. This could be a fun album cut for Sharon if she wants to record it herself, but the length of it will probably limit its attraction for any other singer.

The current structure of the song is: verse A, verse B, bridge, chorus; verse A, verse B, bridge, chorus (variation); verse A, verse B, chorus; verse A, verse B, chorus and tag. That's eight verses and four choruses. Usually a song has two or three verses. It's not just that we're a generation of people who insist in instant gratification. Songs have been that way for a long time.

The great ballads of the thirties and forties were written into a strictly 32-bar form. Practically all of the Beatles' fantastic songs had three or fewer verses. You can't judge the length of the song you can write by the album cuts of artists who write their own material. They work under a different set of rules than the songwriter who is pitching songs from outside the artist's inner circle. Artist's can get all the album cuts they need from within. The only songs they might consider from the outside are those that have *hit* written all over them. And hit is a very short word.

Putting aside the question of whether an artist would be willing to take on the persona of a woman who takes revenge by poisoning her boyfriend, let's look at the message of the song. If Sharon wanted to edit this song down a bit, we think that the story wouldn't suffer if she eliminated the first two sets of verses A and B with their bridges, and the first chorus. Starting the song with the chorus (variation) and then picking up with "I'll cut off the phones" and going on from there will tell the story.

There is a problem with the literal sense of the second set of verses, anyway. After hearing the threat of the first chorus—"I want you back just so I can dump you"—why would he come back? It makes more sense to pick up the story in the middle. She could emphasize that he has returned by repeating the line "Now I got you back" two or three times in the introductory chorus. That might also emphasize the humorous side of this otherwise dark song. If she did decide to cut out the first four verses, she would have to rewrite the Christmas Eve line in the tag, too.

There are some wonderful epic-length songs in the folk field and special material such as soliloquies in musicals (such as "My Boy Bill" in *Carousel*), but for the most part, your job as a songwriter is to write a three-minute miracle. That's one of the special things about a great song: so much meaning packed into such a nice, tight package. Great songs hit you quick and have a big impact. They strike you like lightning, brilliant and fast. After they hit you, you're never quite the same.

26

NOT ENOUGH IS NOT ENOUGH

Write enough to express your ideas completely

The flip side of the epic-length song is the mini-song. Some songwriters get the impression that a song has to be short. They take it to the extreme of cutting off the writing process before they get around to fully expressing the idea. Here's an example of a very short song by Joseph M. Tapia:

LOVE SHOCK

Every day is another
everything's a bother
I need to shake it
my soul just can't take it.

> CHORUS:
> *You're gonna get me over this block*
> *Give me a love shock*
> *Give me a love shock*

I can't help the urge
being with you causes such a surge
night or day night or day
you lift me away

> CHORUS: *repeat*

© 1991 Joseph M. Tapia

This is a great beginning for a song. The title is unique and calls to mind all kinds of wonderful images. The workshop participants had a ball free associating on the electricity/love theme. The air virtually crackled with current, sparks, wires, plugs, positive and negative charges, magnetism, lightning, power, energy and attraction. We encouraged the songwriters to go with the flow by exclaiming, "Socket to us!"

Although the structures of the verses do not match (the number of beats is 7, 6, 5, 6 in the first verse and 5, 9, 6, 5 in the second), the rhyme scheme shows careful thought. But the overall effect of the song in its present form is that it hasn't been taken to its limit.

Part of this might be due to many songwriters' mistaken idea that the song should just flow out easily. Some think that the original thoughts should be accepted in the form in which they first arrive, especially if they pop out rhyming. The concept of writing a hundred lines to get the one good one never occurs to them. They stop when the writing gets hard.

It does get hard rather early in the game, especially when the songwriter tries to make the first thing put on paper a "finished" line. The process of free associating on the song's images and self-talking about the who, what, where, when, and why of the song before trying to write the finished product makes writing much easier by providing a wealth of raw material to work with. It beats trying to grab the perfect word out of thin air.

Without doing that groundwork, you run the risk, as Joseph did here, of not getting your message across. We suggested to Joseph that he play more with combining the ideas of electricity and love and use the associative phrases he comes up with in his verses. Also, as it stands, the chorus is really only the title. The chorus is where you need to make your point—hard to do if you haven't decided what your point is. Joseph needs to think that out and expand his chorus to make the song's point of view clear.

What is the difference between a song fragment and a complete song? The difference is that the fragment only communicates part of the message and the complete song communicates the complete message. How do you tell the difference in your own songs? How do you see the mote in your own eye? That subject is worthy of a chapter all its own, so read on to chapter thirty-eight, "Stranger in a Strange Song," for hints on how to get an objective view of your songs.

In cooking, it's best to go easy on the salt because you can always add more later. If you put in too much salt at the outset, you've got a problem on your hands. But when you're cooking up a song, the opposite applies. Go ahead and write too much. Then you can cut down to the parts that feel the strongest to you. If you write too little, you may never get to the good parts.

27

SORTING THE MUSE

Don't mistake poetry for lyrics

When you're courting the muse, you take what she gives. You capture it on tape or paper with gratitude. Tuning in to what messages you have to give to the world is a worthy endeavor no matter what comes of it. One of the most joyful aspects of being a songwriter is opening up to whatever is coming up from your subconscious, or down from on high, or wherever you envision the flow originating.

After you've taken down the first outpouring without hindering the flow by making judgments about it, it's time to consider what raw material you have to work with and what you want to do with it. Here's a song that Dot Regelski brought to the Monday night workshop at NAS:

HAUNTED DREAMS

When dreams disturb my slumbers
In the vastness of my bed
And I sink in solitude
In sunlight I do tread
Sol warms me with his fire
But my cheeks will never dry
For you are ever with me
Your spirit stays by my side

   CHORUS:
   Haunted Dreams
   Dreams of long lost love
   Is it your face I see?
   I reach but never touch

I turn to wine to lose
Your presence in my mind
But your face still appears
Even when I'm blind

Why give me endless pain?
Why won't you give me peace?
I pray through reddened eyes
That I will find surcease

   CHORUS: *repeat*

© 1991 Dot Regelski

After you have given the muse her day in court, it's time to sort. If what you've been given sounds like "Haunted Dreams," it's a poem, not a song lyric. How will you be able to tell the difference?

Conversational tone is a good basic measuring tool. The message in most contemporary pop songs is carried by words that are commonly used "on the street" in conversations. Word order in lyrics is generally best when the words flow as in the order of normal conversation. For example, when talking about what you do in the morning, you say, "When I wake up." "When dreams disturb my slumbers" is a lovely poetic phrase that could have been written by Emily Dickinson, but it's not pop song lyrics.

Dot has a good image in her second line but again chooses a less than conversational word, "vastness." The word "big" would be more accessible and even have the advantage of alliteration with "bed." The line could be rewritten into a more conversational phrase, such as "My bed's too big for me."

The conversational tone test is easy. Just picture yourself going up to someone on the street and saying the line. Then imagine the look on his face as he either lights up with your crystal clear idea or fogs over in confusion. If someone came up to you and said, "And I sink in solitude," how would you react?

One response might be, "Take me to your poetry reading." It just doesn't sound like something said on the street; it's way too lofty in tone. Picture yourself as the singer in the song. You want the message to get across in all its urgency, with the most emotion you can muster. You could say, "I'm so lonely, lonely, lonely," thus getting the intensity across with repetition.

Or you might deal with a problem that the lyric has in its current form, which is that the "you" or the singee is not introduced until line seven. Up to that point, this could be a song about someone who is just constantly lonely because she can't form a decent relationship. Remember to get the who, where, when, what and why in as early in the song as you can. With that in mind, line three could say something like, "Your cold pillow in my arms." It keeps the bed images going and tells in a picture that she's singing to someone she wants to hold who is not there.

Among the other words and phrases Dot uses that are more at home in a poem than a song lyric are: tread, Sol, ever with me, presence, reddened eyes and surcease. These are all very good words, but they're not the way we talk to each other today.

Now why she should jump out of bed and go treading outside is a good question. Especially when the title, "Haunted Dreams," calls up images of sleeping and, therefore, bed. You've heard the Latin proverb, "carpe diem," which means "seize the day." Well, you don't have enough time in a song to seize a whole day, as a rule. The idea in a song is to seize the instant, seize the moment, seize the emotion right now. Keep the lonely person in the bed right on the sword point of the pain and loneliness. These are the feelings that we've all had and can relate to on a gut level.

Also, remember the title is the hub of your song wheel. The rest of your lyrics need to support the main image conveyed by the title. This title calls for lyrics that tell a story like this:

I woke up crying
My bed's too big for me
I hug your cold pillow
It's dark and I can't see

I heard you call my name
Just before I woke
I heard you say, "I love you"
Where did you go?

CHORUS:
Haunted dreams
Tell me you're still here
But I can't find you
Through my tears

When choosing where to go from here, you have to keep in mind where "here" is. The singer just woke up from a dream; it's probably the middle of the night. She's in bed in a dark room. What does she do next? Does she turn on the light and look around the room and talk about all the evidence of his having been there? Does she stay in the dark and pretend he's there? Does she go over in her mind what led to the break-up or death? Or maybe he is really in the next room, but the relationship is in trouble and she's fantasizing about the inevitable end. We'll leave this story for you to finish.

What separates poetry from song lyrics is the method by which the message is delivered. Poetry is meant to be read. You can hold it in your hand and look at it a long time and ponder its depths. Song lyrics, on the other hand, flow past you like a river. You can't put your toe in the same place twice. The information is received through your ears, not your eyes. Each line of lyrics has to stand on its own and deliver a complete thought. Each line needs to lead to the next and relate to the central thought, expressed in the title. That way, your brain can put the picture together. Otherwise, you're lost, confused, bored, or even angry for being made to feel the fool because you can't understand what's going on.

If the muse hands you a poem, by all means do the poem the honor of pursuing it to its creative conclusion. Maybe you will be lucky enough to be given a poem so strong and beautiful that it can be set to music and be totally valid in both worlds of poetry and song. "The Rose" is such a poem song. Amanda McBroom told us that "The Rose" came to her all in one piece, written almost as fast as she could play it through the first time.

You may object to this division between poetry and song lyrics. You can provide many examples of song lyrics that are extremely poetic, written by great songwriters such as Lennon and McCartney, Paul Simon and Bob Dylan. Then there's rap music, which is a form of poetry spoken over rhythms. This is all true, and if you can write real poetry that sings, go for it. The problem is that so many songwriters get lost in the pursuit of poetic language and wind up obscuring the emotions of the song. That's why we recommend that you be direct and conversational with your lyrics if you're aiming at writing a mainstream pop, country or R&B song.

All that rhymes is not poetry, and pure poetry does not a good song lyric make, necessarily. Now, don't you wish we'd said that straight out?

PART THREE

MAKING THE MUSIC

Melodic Mistakes

28

TO STUDY OR NOT TO STUDY MUSIC

Don't think you have to study music theory extensively or play a musical instrument expertly

Some people who aspire to songwriting think that they need to study music theory at great length to be a songwriter. Others think that what is really needed is a highly refined skill on a musical instrument. They may even go ahead and spend years and years studying theory and practicing their instrument. Then they try to write a song and they can't. This is one career where a formal education can get in the way.

We're not saying, "Don't bother to get educated." We're saying that formal training in music theory is not the education you need to be a songwriter. Some of the world's greatest songwriters cannot read or write musical notation. Many of them say that too much musical education hampers songwriting creativity. They find this out when they try to collaborate with someone who is highly trained. The trained musician often has trouble breaking out of the rules that have become a habit from many years of practicing. Trained composers tend to lose sight of song structure, doing variations on a theme when they should be repeating the chorus.

The good news here is that you don't have to be a virtuoso musician to be a great songwriter. What you need to know to write great songs is what makes a song great. You can study this on your own and in your own way. You don't have to know the names of the chords that are being played or the theory behind their progression. If you can play by ear, that's great.

Irving Berlin couldn't read music, and he played all his songs on the black keys of the piano. With today's keyboard technology, you don't have to be able to play up to speed. You can input the notes and indicate the times for the notes, then the synthesizer will play them back.

You don't even need to know a black key from a white key to be a great songwriter. If you have a keen ear for how words sit on a melody, you are a very valuable commodity. There are lots of people around who can play instruments and write melodies; very few can come up with just the right words.

We think playing a musical instrument is one of the finest occupations in the world. It's a beautiful and peaceful thing to do. Unfortunately, technology is taking over the livelihoods of musicians. Here's the situation: "There's a frog driving one way down the highway and a French horn player driving in the opposite direction. What's the difference?" The answer is: "The frog might be on his way to a gig."

Even so, some recording sessions still use real live musicians. If you were one of those musicians, you might be able to make connections for your songs. You can use musicianship in aid of songwriting in that way. Of course, there are excellent musicians who are also great songwriters; one proficiency does not necessarily preclude the other.

Songwriting is a skill separate from musicianship. Songwriters are students of the world and of how it can be expressed through song. Being able to play a musical instrument or read and write music is not a prerequisite for adopting this lifetime course.

29
....

FREE SAMPLES

*Don't think you can sample from
previous recordings for free*

Songwriters who have their own at-home studio or access to studio time may feel free to sample the sounds from previously released records. Sampling is the process of taking the sounds from a record and using them in your song, either in their original form or electronically manipulated into another form. Samples can range from a one-time use of a small piece of an obscure song, to the looping of one bar of a song throughout a new song, to the use of a recognizable riff or hook from a hit song, to a rewrite of the lyric of an original song which is then treated as a parody.

Sampling is rampant today and very popular with newer songwriters who see it as a cheaper way to get great sounds in their songs. They may think that they don't need anyone's permission to sample, especially if the records they are sampling from are thirty years old, or if they're just using little pieces, or if the original recordings weren't big hits in the first place.

If you are a writer/artist and the product you come up with winds up on a record, you are on the wrong track if you think samples come for free. If you don't get permission and pay up front for the use, you may wind up paying more for those tracks than you can earn from the song.

Any sounds that are embodied in a commercially released recording have two layers of ownership. First, there is the owner of the copyright on the underlying work, which is usually the publisher. Second, there is the owner of the sounds on the record, which is usually the record company. You may think that people won't know you used part of their record because you cut it up and switched it around and looped it, but you will be surprised what people can recognize. Samples need to be cleared on both levels of ownership, and each will want a fee or a percentage of the song, depending on the nature of the use.

If you negotiate for permission before your record containing the samples is released, you may be charged a one- or two-thousand-dollar flat fee

for three seconds' use. If the copyright owner discovers a use that was not agreed to, the same three seconds could cost fifty or sixty thousand dollars in a lawsuit settlement.

Since the use of samples can have such a drastic effect on the status of a song, it is very important to keep track of what you are doing when you use samples. If you are using samples, keep a written record of the origin of the samples' titles, writers, publishers and record companies. This information is all on the label of the record. Also, take note of what parts you sample, the length of time sampled from the original, and how the sample is used in your song. The more information you can supply, the easier you make it for the person who is getting permission for the uses, which is called "clearing the samples."

The area of sampling is on the frontier of the music business. Nobody knows what to do with it, so they make up their own rules as they go along. Madeleine Smith of Songwriter Services in Los Angeles clears samples for many of the top rap producers and artists. She tries to see to it that her writer/artists get some income from their records. This isn't easy when the writer uses three samples and each of the publishers thinks its piece is worth 50 percent of the song. The problem is magnified when the record company releases six different mixes on a twelve-inch or maxicassette, and the writer/artist gets paid only once, while the publishers insist on being paid six times. The money to pay the publishers comes out of the future income of the writer/artist. That's how sampling can cost more money than you can make with it.

Today's musical instrument technology is making it easier for samplers to kick the habit and create their own music, thereby avoiding sampling troubles. However, many writer/artists are still sampling. One Warner Bros. executive stated that he deals with up to twenty sampled products at a time for his label alone. If you're among these samplers, remember, it's not a free ride.

30

MISMATCHMAKING

Don't forget prosody: the marriage between words and music

Unfortunately, something like 50 percent of American marriages end in divorce. Maybe it's due to the times and people's unwillingness to work through the tough challenges that face every relationship. Maybe when they "fell in love" they each fell in love with what they wanted to see in each other, and closer exposure eventually revealed what was really there, much to their mutual discomfort.

Songs are no different. The words and the melody/music get married after falling in love one day; some of the marriages last and others don't. Alan Bergman uses the image of the words sitting on the melody like an old easy chair; they should be that comfortable with each other.

When it works, you have a great song/marriage. For example, take Allan Rich and Jud Friedman's number one song "I Don't Have the Heart," recorded by James Ingram (see chart on next page). The title line melody of the chorus descends and resonates emotionally with the sad meaning of the line as well as with the cadence it would have in actual conversation. "To hurt you" starts a fifth higher than the note on "heart" and comes down on "you" to give the feeling of an apology. The last line of the chorus, "Not the way you want me to" goes higher and ends higher than the title line melody, adding energy and torn emotions to the meaning of the lyric.

This is a songwriter's song, a timeless song that will be rerecorded many times over the years, a perfect example of prosody. When a song has perfect prosody, it means that the message of the lyrics, the feel of the music, and the emotional intensity and pitch of the melody are perfectly meshed. Have you ever noticed the shape of the melody in "The Sound of Music"? You could almost do a dot-to-dot drawing of mountains by connecting the notes. When the lyrics talk about a brook skipping and falling, the melody skips and falls. When the chime flies, it flies on the highest note in the melody. Prosody delivers the message on every possible level at once.

In the heat of the moment when lyric and melody first meet, everything looks good and sounds good, and the excitement of making contact makes the world seem right. As time goes on and things cool down a little, well, maybe the lyric could be stronger here, or the melody more interesting there, and you begin to see where each others' expectations aren't being met.

You can tell when the marriage isn't working. An obvious example would be a hot-blooded song with a lot of words about physical attraction on the dance floor set to a melody with long held notes in 3/4 time. Such a lyric would be better set to a high-energy, fairly rapid-fire melody and feel. If you think this is obvious, it isn't. Would a heavy lyric about a break-up work set to a joyous melody like "Afternoon Delight," recorded by the Starlight Vocal Band? The attitude of the lyric and the melody have to work together, not against each other.

A lyric should be basically conversational; if there are too many inverted phrases such as "waiting, I stood in the rain," it may be difficult to write a melody with a natural flow that also meshes with the meaning of the lyric. We like melodies to flow rhythmically with the accents the words themselves would have in conversation; if they don't, it is because we are intentionally calling attention to that moment. Again, the point is to make the lyric and melody work together for the fullest impact rather than call attention to the craft or lack of it.

We try to make the melody bring out the passion of the lyric like the music brings out the emotional intent of a scene in a film. This means incorporating melodic intervals from syllable to syllable that enhance the meaning, melodic phrases that rise and fall to create pathos or passion, rhythmic phrases that change from section to section to keep the interest up and to keep from boring us with repetition, harmonic progressions that match the melody and lift us into an energetic chorus if necessary, and minor chords to sound sad or angry or major chords to sound positive or happy. Ideally, the melody/arrangement expresses the intent of the lyric so well that you don't need to hear the words to know what the song is saying.

Just like a marriage in which two people have to learn to work together and help each other grow, so words and music help each other fully express themselves, help them be the best they can be and support each other through the hard times before getting a cut. When it's right, the combination of melody and lyric becomes synergistic, more than the sum of its parts. Together they create a new life that feels so natural it seems as if they were created simultaneously in one easy flow.

I DON'T HAVE THE HEART

by Allan Rich and
Jud Friedman

31

LOST, LOST ON THE RANGE

*Don't write a melody that has too wide a range
for most singers*

"The Star Spangled Banner": If you've ever tried to sing this song you know what a herculean feat it is, even though Whitney Houston makes it seem easy. It isn't. It's a very wide-ranging melody—you might sound good on the low notes in the beginning, but by the time you get to the chorus you've blown your reeds and sound like Roseanne Arnold. Perhaps one of the reasons this song survives, besides its political message, is that it gives singers a chance to show off their super vocal chops.

But for the most part, writing songs this difficult to sing is not a great idea. One reason is that you obviously limit the number of singers who would sound good performing it. If you're the artist, you know what your range is, and you can write a song with a very wide range if it suits your voice. But that song will have few outlets with artists who are not blessed with your range.

The range of a melody is a tool like rhyming, song structure, modulations, and so forth. An orchestrator has to know the range of the instruments when writing an orchestration from a film composer's sketch or the instruments might literally not be able to play the written note. The human voice is the songwriter's ultimate instrument. Writing within a reasonable range is using the vocal instrument to its best advantage.

A general guesstimate of range limit is an octave plus five notes for most singers. Those that claim four octave ranges are not talking about full voice alone. They are including falsetto and bass tones that are hard to sing words to while intoning. When we talk about range, we're talking about full voice. Even an octave plus five notes is pushing some singers with great voices.

Sometimes songs get too rangy because their melody is weak: The energy level is shored up by making the melody go high, and while this solves the problem of dynamic energy dropping off at an undesirable place, it creates the new range problem.

You want your singer to sound great all through the song. At no time do you want the performance to sound strained because the singer had to reach for notes. You want to avoid bringing the melody down too low when intensity, anger or aggression is required. You might want the melody lower for intimacy, but upper-middle range when the dance partners are sweating. Rock choruses are often at the top of the singers' full voice so they can scream away. You basically want to keep a singer's voice at that point in his or her range that suits the emotional moment you're creating in the song.

The responsibility for making a singer sound great starts with the writing. Even if the message is great, the feel is terrific, and the melody has strong moments, if the singer doesn't love the way the song feels in the act of singing it, the song will probably be rejected. You don't have to be a singer to know what works for the voice. An obvious corollary is that the song should also be in the right key for the singer, so the energy or intimacy is there where it's needed.

If you are smart enough to have made contact with a particular act looking for songs, find out not only the lead singer's range, but also at which note the singer is forced into falsetto. You could figure this out from previous recordings. Armed with this information and knowledge of quirks in the singer's voice—like where Kenny Rogers gets the growl in his range or Patti LaBelle does her high glissando holding the last note for four (not really!) minutes—you might build something into the melody to take advantage of it.

Of course you have to serve the song, and do whatever you must to make it work the best it can, which includes not being concerned about range unless you're over an octave plus five notes. But consider the average listener's ability to sing along and remember the music; watch people in their cars singing with the radio at the next stop light, and hold fast to the image that they're singing your song.

32
·········

THE LONG AND WINDING MELODY

*Be sure your melodies lead to the hook;
don't let them wander*

When a songwriter brings a song to the workshop with a melody that seems to wander aimlessly and not get home to a hook, we can guess how the song was written. More often than not, the lyrics came first and the melody was written after the lyrics. When the lyrics are written without lines of a definite length and rhythm structure that are grouped in clearly repetitive sections—that is, verses and chorus—the melody written to them will wander as well. The net result is a feeling of being lost in the desert and continuously crossing your own trail, thirsty for some clear, graspable melody.

This kind of writing is perfectly fine, but it's not really songwriting; it's tone poem or song poem writing, where the music is more accompaniment than an integral stand-alone melody wedded to a lyric.

Sometimes wandering melodies result from having been written first, developed along the lines of symphonic, film score, or New Age music that doesn't have the same requirements as popular song structure. This, too, can be very effective for atmosphere, especially if the lyric matches the emotional content of the mood of the music and has interesting imagery. In some cases, the repeated musical theme may be eight or sixteen bars long and may not have a place to put a succinct title.

Sometimes the song fits a song structure melodically and lyrically, but the title line is buried in the middle of the verse or chorus and isn't placed strategically in the music. This situation also leads to an overall unresolved feeling in the song.

Ironically, song structures today take many shapes with new variations being created daily while still holding to the two basic structures: verse/bridge and verse/chorus. Country songs often have the title in the last line of the verse or in the prechorus, or "lift," leading into the chorus as well as in the first line of the chorus. A prechorus/lift is a section different from the verse that sets up the chorus both lyrically and melodically. R&B/pop songs can open with a verse, go to a lift, into the chorus, to an extension of the chorus, back to the verse, lift, musical break, chorus, chorus extension, bridge, and so on. Some rap songs are written to be sung over a continuously repeated bass riff, with the only real distinction between sections being different rhythmic phrasing, harmonies, or extra production on the chorus. Even with all these variations on the theme of structure, the listener is never lost. The repetition of distinctive melodic segments helps us keep our bearings at all times.

Many lyricists hear melodies in their heads as they write lyrics; this is how they create the rhythmic patterns of each line, shape the overall flow of the verse, and match the pattern of syllables, accents and rhymes in subsequent verses using the same melody. When the music person comes along to write a melody to these lyrics, this method will have made his job much easier.

One remedial exercise that can result in a commercially strong song is to write a new song based on the structure of a hit song you love. Here's how to do it: Write new lyrics to an existing hit melody, putting the title lyric in your tune in the same place as it is in the original. In fact, match it line for line, accent for accent, to the best of your ability. Then, bring your lyrics to your collaborator to have a new melody composed for them, without revealing the source of the structure. Or, if you are going to write the new melody yourself, do your best to forget the original melody. No one will ever know what you did, and you will have a guaranteed rock-solid interesting pattern and structure. Composers can use the same technique; they can write a new melody to already existing hit lyrics, then write new lyrics to their new melody.

You may not actually enjoy listening to Muzak music when you get on the elevator or walk through your favorite department store, but one day we were in a K-Mart and heard one of our songs being played sans lyric and we loved it. Melodies require the same focus the lyrics must have; they both have to be great excuses for getting to the lyrical and musical title. Strong songs have strong melodies that can stand alone.

33

THE HOOK LINE IS SUNK

Be certain you have a melodic hook or your title pays off melodically

We didn't say this, and if you ask us to testify to it we won't: The first thing most listeners get into when they're hearing a new song is the music. Much of the time, even though songwriters slave over getting those lyrics just right, it is difficult or impossible to decipher the lyric on the first few hearings. The music has to attract you enough to listen again. We didn't say this, will not admit to saying this, and if you ask us if we said it, we only understand Swahili. (We've heard too many writers use this as an excuse for a weak lyric, and there is absotively posilutely not one good reason for using one weak apostrophe.)

If your listeners get into the music first, it's important to let someone leave your musical presence humming one of your babies. You have to give them something to remember. That something is the hook. It's the part of the melody that strikes your fancy the most. Usually, the title sits right on that part of the melody. You may not remember any other part of the song, but when that part comes around, you can sing it. You can't stop singing it sometimes. You're hooked.

A hook is the perfect image for this part of the song because it sticks out from the song and grabs you. The hook is to the melody what the title is to the lyric. It is the hub of the melody wheel. In the best of all possible songs, all the melody lines lead up to and support the melody of the hook. Without this melodic focus to grab the listener, the song is so much mush, easily tuned out and forgotten.

The right location is important for a hook. Place the strongest melodic moment at a strategic place, such as the first line of the verse, last line of the verse, first and third line of the chorus, first and last line of the chorus, and so forth. If you can find a new place to put it and make it work, go for it. One of our latest songs has the hook/title on the second and fifth line of the chorus, but there's absolutely no melodic or lyrical doubt that it is the title.

Unfortunately, the failure to create a melodic moment around the title is not one that glares by its visibility, but rather by its omission, so you don't "hear" it as wrong. There's just nothing about the song you can remember. Even if there is a lyric title hidden somewhere in the song, it's not set off musically so that anyone hearing it knows this is it. It just sounds like another line in the song, maybe one of the best lines in the song, but not the title.

See chapter thirty-two for a great technique to write stronger melodies and hooks. Imitation is one of the highest forms of compliment and a good learning technique.

You have to repeat something many times over before a child really learns it. We were not made to get everything the first time, despite what your inner critic might say. Treat your listeners like children, with respect and an understanding of their limitations: Repeat the hook as often as you can without driving them crazy or boring them, or at least enough to leave a good taste in their mouths. Then they will be able to hum the hook of your song after just one hearing on the radio.

34

JUST ONE HOOK

Include melodic, rhythmic and instrumental subhooks

You might think, from reading the last chapter, that if you repeat your main hook line the optimum number of times, your listeners will be so irresistibly drawn into your song that their attention will not wander for an instant. That's a fine thought, but the reality is that listeners are superfickle. If you give them a second without something interesting happening in the song, they'll start thinking about their shopping lists or carburetors.

After expending all the time and creative energy required to write and rewrite a great song, you don't want to lose your listeners' attention in the valleys between your main hooks. Now your assignment, should you decide to accept it, is to dress your song up and take it out on the town.

Even when you're sitting 'round the campfire passing the guitar and singing songs, the ears have it when someone starts playing a short lead solo to get you into the song. Those first few notes can be a distinctive signature. You only need to hear the first five notes of "Imagine" to know exactly which song you're listening to. In fact, we can name it in two notes! How many notes of "I Can't Get No Satisfaction" by the Rolling Stones do you need to hear before you're hooked? One? One and a half?

Notice in these songs and others how these distinctive note groups repeat in the spaces between the lyric lines, hooking the parts of the songs together. (There's that word "hook" again.) The best songs have more than one hook going for them. There is the main hook, which is the coming together of the high points in the lyric and the melody. And then there are all these little hooky bass or lead riffs, slides or bent notes, between chorus and verse sections and between lyric lines that keep the listener's interest up and the excitement going throughout the song.

Without these minihooks, your song is stepping out in a plain old housecoat. Sprinkle them throughout your song and you'll do for your song what the fairy godmother did for Cinderella. You'll expose the beauty of your song by dressing it up. The great thing is that you have to dress it up for the demo anyway, so your work won't be wasted down the line. Adding these minihooks helps you see if the song stands on its own as a piano or guitar vocal. We've found in listening to the original demos of many hit songs that these catchy musical minihooks often turn up on the final record release. Today's producers basically copy your demo work verbatim when they produce the record because they don't want to mess with something that works.

This dressing up is even more necessary if the song is not particularly melodic, such as a Janet Jackson, Paula Abdul or Hammer hit. They add punch to a good song that's not particularly unique and needs all the help it can get to present it in a seductive light. The presence of these spicy subhooks also shows a professional mind at work.

You don't have to be an instrumentalist to create these addictive minihooks. You can sing them to communicate them to collaborators or hired musicians.

You can also catch your listeners' ears in other, more subtle, ways. Try to create rhythmic and melodic moments throughout the song that stimulate aural interest. Play with the rhythm, for instance, by singing a phrase in triplets rather than on the beat and making the accompaniment (drums, rhythm guitar, bass on a demo) track with it. Make the bass move in interesting rhythmic variations and with or against the melody to strengthen the moment (don't stick to root position chords even when just playing guitar).

These moments or "soundbites" are calculated and are peppered throughout hit songs in such a way that the listener's attention is directed to the words and melody the entire time. They keep the interest up as the melody is sung and they also bridge the vocal silences. They can be as simple as rhythmic/thematic guitar licks or as technologically dependent as the latest drum samples. The better you dress your song, the more ears you'll turn.

35

·········

IN SEARCH OF THE LOST CHORD

Avoid writing songs with chord structures that are too complex

You know the feeling. You're playing your instrument with some lines of inspired lyric in front of you. The melody you're creating sounds a little like the one you wrote three songs back and your hands are falling into familiar chord progressions. You're not stuck, but nothing you're coming up with is turning you on. You can't tell if anything you're playing is any good. It's time to break away from the all too familiar and do something different to make this song stand out.

So you go out shopping at the Chord Store. Did you know that rappers have been known to license a single chord sampled from a record label's copyrighted recording? One publisher tried to tell a rapper's representative, "We don't own the chord A." But the rapper's rep wasn't taking any chances and insisted on a license for the sampled chord. The publisher gave in and charged a five-hundred-dollar licensing fee, saying, "That's fine with me, we have plenty of chords where that one came from!" We're not talking about that kind of chord shopping, though. We mean when you go

to your instrument of choice and experiment with the possible chord combinations.

You buy an A-flat when you're in the key of C, and go from the A-flat to the C-sharp 7 to the key of F-sharp. This is fine, but unfortunately you're in the middle of the verse. It's different and draws a lot of attention, but is it working toward the intention of the lyric and melody? Maybe you're writing a country song and throw in several major seventh chords, ninth chords, or half-diminished chords. Are they in keeping with the tone of the song? Do they throw it into another genre, like jazz? Sometimes you make chord changes every half bar, which ultimately gives the song a restive feeling, as if it never settles into a groove and has no home key tonic feeling.

There is no question that you must keep yourself interested in your creations, trying new combinations of harmony, melody and rhythm. But as both Tom Snow and Tom Kelly have said, it wasn't until they simplified their work that they started to be successful.

From another angle, some chords and chord sequences are too simple. If you only play rudimentary piano or guitar, there might be a tendency to play all your chords in root position, with the tonic in the bass. Granted, a moving melody and lyric will work a cappella, but by doing some simple chord manipulations you can make a song sound more interesting. Take a I-IV-V-I progression in the key of C and off the top of your head make up a simple melody. Sing the same melody over a C chord, going to an F with an A in the bass, a G with a B in the bass, and back to the C; or C going to an F with a G in the bass, to G7 and back to C; or C going to F with a D in the bass (which is a Dm7 or the II chord in the key of C), to G-sus, G7 and back to C; and so on. Suddenly a world of opportunity becomes available to give more feeling to your melodies. This is one area of study that many of the greatest songwriters today continue to pursue; it adds to their arsenal of skills and opens the doors to doing film scoring down the line.

Between making your arrangements so complicated that they distract the listener's attention from the song and making them so simple they lack harmonic interest, there is a middle ground you can only find by writing song after song. It takes time to find your own lyrical voice in the things you like to write about and particular ways you like to express them. It takes time to find a way to keep your interest up as you search for new-to-you harmonic progressions while balancing the need to serve the emotional intent of the melody, lyric and genre (pop, R&B, country, etc.).

36
·········

DON'T PLAY IT AGAIN, PLEASE
*Make sure your verses and chorus aren't too alike
in rhythm and melody*

Frequently in our workshops we see lyrics that could fit neatly into a rectangle drawn around them on the lyric sheet. The right margin of the words is almost as straight as the left throughout the verses and choruses. For example:

IT'S ALL THE SAME

*When your song
Just goes along
And every rhyme
Is in a line*

*When your words
Can all be heard
To hit the beat
With the same feet*

CHORUS:
It's all the same

*It's just too much
It's much too tame
We're losing touch
Monotony's
A deadly game
It makes us sleep
When it's all the same*

*So syncopate
And variegate
It's not too late
To miss the gate*

*Escape the rut
And show us what
Can happen when
You take off in an exciting new direction!*

© 1991 Pea Pod Music

In our workshops, we see the lyric sheet before

we hear the song. If the verses and choruses are marching along in formation this way on the lyric sheet, a little flag goes up in our heads and written on the flag is "It's all the same." When the writer plays the song, our misgivings are usually confirmed. The verses, the chorus and the bridge all have the same metric pattern, similar melodies, the same chord changes, and therefore, a uniform emotional intensity.

While repetition is an important device for driving home the hook or central idea in the song and for making the song memorable, it does have its limits. When repetition is carried too far, especially within the structure of the song, the song loses its power to grab and keep the listener's attention.

We didn't make these rules about varying the impact of the parts of a song. We learned about them from a cricket at the Exploratorium, a wonderful museum in San Francisco, on one of our monthly treks there to teach songwriting workshops for the National Academy of Songwriters.

There was a cricket in a glass cage with an electrode implanted in its brain. The electrode was connected to a device that displayed the cricket's brain waves. If you knocked on the cricket's cage, the display screen would show the reaction in the cricket's brain, a big jump in the usually regular brain wave line. But if you stood there knocking in the same place, after a while the cricket's brain would not register any reaction. No new information is no information at all.

It's the same with a song. If a song drones on with the same metric pattern, the same melodic range, the same chord progressions, the same emotional intensity throughout, our ears will turn off to it. The professional listener will hit the stop button on the tape machine. Should the song by some miracle get on the radio, the average listener will make a radio station's worst nightmare come true by switching stations.

In the three-minute movie of your song, you need to have a build-up and a climax. Try drawing your own "brain wave" graph of the ups and downs in your song. See how they compare to the diagrams shown in "Common Song Structures," on pages 18 and 19.

Notice that in a verse/chorus structure, the height of emotional intensity in the music and the lyrics should coincide with the most intense part of your message, the title or hook. The title is very often the first line of the chorus and is often repeated several times. In a verse/bridge structure the most intense point is usually the end of the bridge.

Is the graph of your song a flat line? If so, you need to play with it some more to build in some peaks and valleys. We want to be stimulated, excited by songs. One of the best ways to keep a song interesting from beginning to end is to keep new elements coming in with each part of the song's structure.

Here are some ways you can keep your songs from becoming flatliners:

- If the verse has notes of short duration and medium range, open up with some long, high notes in the chorus;
- Vary the length of the melody lines significantly from one section to another; for example, make the verse lines long (twenty syllables) and the chorus lines shorter (ten syllables), or vice versa;
- Vary the length of the sections; if your verse is eight lines long, make the chorus a short four lines;
- Vary the rhythmic accents within the lines of a section;
- Vary the feel of the sections; make the verses rhythmic and less melodic, and become more melodic in the chorus;
- Keep the chord progression interesting by modulating out of the key of the verse into a new key for the chorus.

When experimenting with ways to vary the intensity of the parts of your song, make sure your title sits on the most outstanding point of the melody. Listen to your song as pure melody and chord progressions and be as objective as possible. Does the part of the melody where you have the title stand out from the rest of the song and say, "This is it!"? If not, you may need to move the title to the part of the melody that does.

PART FOUR

....

ONCE WRITTEN, LOOK TWICE

Rewriting Wrongs

37

DON'T SAY NOTHING BAD ABOUT MY BABY

Learn to accept criticism of your songs

We are always amazed by the incredible amount of creativity and care that songwriters put into their work. We know how much it takes to pull lyrics, melody and chords out of thin air. As Thomas Berger said, "Why do writers write? Because it isn't there." A tremendous amount of thought and effort is involved in the creation of a song. It's no wonder that many songwriters regard their songs as extensions of themselves. The song is not just scribbles on paper and notes in the air, it's your baby. You don't want anyone to tell you that your baby's ugly. "Honest criticism is hard to take," said Franklin P. Jones, "particularly from a relative, a friend, an acquaintance, or a stranger."

For many writers, it's a case of "Love my song, love me." This kind of personal involvement with your songs really can't be helped in the early years of writing. Each new song is precious to you. You put your heart into every bit of the song, and you certainly don't want your heart trampled on. Fear of the pain that might come from exposing your song to criticism may keep you from showing your songs to anyone.

For some writers, this whole process is avoided by cloaking doubts and sensitivity in arrogance. These are the ones who show up at workshops expecting everyone who hears their song to fall down on the floor and worship the coming of the world's greatest songwriter, the one who can write no wrong note. After they show the song and the feedback begins, they become outraged that anyone would have the nerve to suggest an improvement to their obviously perfect song. Their defensiveness is a dead giveaway that they have a long way to go as songwriters.

The problem is that it's just during the stage when you are so emotionally involved that you need the most feedback on your songs. We spent years as songwriting students in various workshops and can recall vividly the awful feelings of annihilation that we experienced as our songs were taken apart, rearranged and rejected a thousand different ways. Our minds were screaming, "Our baby! How can you do this to our baby?" In such moments, it is important to write down what people are saying to you because your emotional distress makes it difficult to remember what went on during the time your song was in the hot seat.

As unpleasant as this may sound, it is a valuable experience and well worth living through. It does get easier. Through the process of seeking out and using feedback, you grow as a writer. You get used to looking at your songs as separate from yourself, and you don't take criticisms about your songs personally.

Where can you find feedback? Feedback can begin at home if you have a friend or relative whose opinion you value. The person you need has to be able to express what's good about the song, what message she got from the song and where the song was confusing. The person who loves you so much that he can only make glowing compliments is not the one you need for this process.

The wonderful songwriting team of Ray Evans and Jay Livingston, who wrote "Que Sera, Sera," "Mona Lisa," "To Each His Own," "Secret Love," and the themes to *Bonanza* and *Mr. Ed*, wrote another song you probably know. Originally it was called "Tinkle Bells." Ray brought it home to get feedback from his wife. She said, "Don't you know what tinkle means?" It had never occurred to them. So Mrs. Evans was the midwife at the birth of the song we sing every December, now known as "Silver Bells." Without her, the song could have gone down the toilet.

Some relatives and friends may take the opportunity of being asked for feedback to put you down personally. Once you discover this is happening, tell that person in no uncertain terms that you do not want to hear his or her opinion. And don't ask for it again. Being a songwriter is tough enough without asking for more trouble.

A more formalized source of feedback on your songs is the songwriting workshop. There are songwriting groups all over the country, and the National Academy of Songwriters is forming a network of these local groups. You can contact NAS to see if there's a songwriting group near you. Community colleges sometimes offer workshops like the ones we did for Santa Fe Community College. If songwriters have not already formed a group in your area, you could take on the project yourself. Post notices, take out free ads, develop a mailing list, meet regularly to share songs, perhaps get a local club to sponsor a songwriters' night. This is exactly how the existing local songwriter organizations got started. NAS is also developing guidelines to help you get your local events organized. In California, call NAS at 213-463-7178. Outside of California, their toll-free number is 1-800-826-7287.

A great feeling of community develops in a songwriting workshop. We're all writers striving for similar goals. We share the same difficulties and desires. If the workshop is run with a respectful attitude toward everyone involved, the creative shot in the arm is phenomenal. When a workshop is done right, the participating songwriters grow to love each other. Each song becomes a group collaboration with the participating songwriters suggesting rewrites as if the "baby" in question were their own.

Unfortunately, some people seem to enjoy hurting other people, and they occasionally show up in songwriting workshops as participants or even as leaders. If you sense that such a destructive person is a participant in the workshop, talk to the leader about making some ground rules clear so negative behavior is not allowed to continue. If it's the leader of the workshop who is making nasty, cutting remarks, it's time to move on to a situation where you can get respectful, supportive feedback.

NAS also has a song review service for members who do not live in Los Angeles. You send your tape and lyric sheet, and they reply with feedback on the song. The cost is $12.50 per song. This service is available to NAS members only.

It's part of your growth as a songwriter to develop a sense of where you can get intelligent and informed feedback on your songs. Even so, the song is your baby, and you may choose to ignore any and all suggestions to change it. That's your right as the creator of the song. After collecting feedback from several sources, you may use some of the suggestions and toss the rest. That, too, is your prerogative. Eventually, the feedback process ceases to be a painful exposure of your innermost soul to insensitive criticism. As you mature as a writer, you see that you have an endless supply of songs and that each one is not a matter of life and death. You come to value the process of getting feedback as a tool that you can use to fine-tune your songs.

38

·········

STRANGER IN A STRANGE SONG

*Check to see that your message is clear—
not hidden between the lines*

When we write a song, we have a whole lifetime of meaning behind it. Everything we are at the moment when we write it comes into play. We know what we're talking about intimately. Naturally, we assume that everybody else should know what we mean.

Anyone who has tried to communicate complex emotions, even to those closest to us (or maybe especially to those closest to us), knows how hard it can be to be really understood. This is even more true when it comes to strangers. A stranger to your song doesn't know you well enough to guess at what you're trying to say. Your meaning has to be perfectly clear to the listener without the benefit of consulting your autobiography or your assumptions.

Don Curry impressed us with the skill he brought to a song he shared in our Santa Fe workshop:

COWBOY IN THE WESTERN WORLD

*It's seven a.m. and the industrial world
Grinds out its dreams the American Way
The cloudy currents of the interstate
Stretch from Miami to the Golden Gate*

CHORUS:
*I want to make it in the Western World
I want to rise to the top and spread the word
I want it all and I'm never gonna fall
I'm just a cowboy in the Western World*

*The winds are shifting in the face of time
Running to the deadline just around the bend
With morals drifting, slipping out of view
The future's in the hands of me and you*

CHORUS: *repeat*

*Nobody told me that it couldn't be done
The moon was out of reach and belonged to no
   one
Don't even ask if you have any doubt*

*When you reach for the stars
That's what the game's all about*

CHORUS: *repeat*

© 1991 Don Curry

Don paints a remarkably strong picture in his first verse. You can almost see the smog drifting across the continent as the country wakes up and begins to grind its early morning gears. Let's start with lines one and two: great image, very unique, sets the scene as early morning and the shot as a wide-angle aerial view of the United States. So far so good. Lines three and four: another very interesting way to say that morning is arriving in industrialized America. We're ready for some new information. We were definitely hooked by this verse and ready to buy whatever Don was about to sell us in the chorus.

When we listened to the chorus, we figured the message was that the singer sees this industrial animal as the bronco he is going to bust by rising to the top in the business world. Okay, we'll buy that, too. The enthusiasm in the first line of the chorus leads us to believe that the singer approves of what's going on and wants to participate to the point of being on top of it and running the show. The phrase "spread the word" usually means that someone is excited about something positive and wants others to know about it. There is nothing in the words as they stand so far that would lead us to believe that something is wrong with this picture.

But with the second verse, we started to wonder. Now the picture is starting to change, and it sounds as though the singer doesn't approve of what's happening in the world. The second verse says, in effect: Times are changing, the pressure is on, morals are decaying, and we have to do something about it. How does the chorus, which we have assumed is positive and enthusiastic, fit into this turn in the lyrics?

Now we are strangers lost in a strange song, and the third verse, instead of putting us back on track, leads us even further down the path to confusion. It is in this confused state that we try to deal with deciphering the message of the first line, "Nobody told me that it couldn't be done." This line is a good example of how words can play tricks. It could either mean that he feels he can do what he aims for because he has been told that it is possible. Or it could mean that the thing actually can't be done, but no one informed him of that fact. Since we are currently lost, we have no context to refer to that will make us feel sure which way to take the line. The next line builds on this confusion, because it could mean either that we can't make claims on the moon or, as an extension of the previous line, that since no one told him that the moon was out of reach and unclaimable, he could make a claim on it.

Since we are in doubt about what is going on, we won't ask about the next three lines. Our reaction to Don when the song was done was: "Great creative writing! But we don't know what you're trying to say. What's the message?"

He replied that he meant to say that the singer wants to become very successful in the business world so that he can look down from the top of the pile and tell everyone how wrong it all is. Don felt that he had expressed that in the phrase "spread the word" in the chorus. We never would have guessed that he was trying to say that.

How can you tell if your listeners are going to get lost when your song makes perfectly good sense to you? We have a self-check technique that we call being a stranger to your song. Put your song in front of you and then put aside all of your preconceptions about what it means. Pretend you never read these words before. Read the actual words that are printed on the paper without reading any meaning into them beyond what is actually contained in the words. Imagine yourself walking up to a stranger in the street and just saying those particular words from that particular lyric line. Would the stranger know exactly what you are talking about or would he look at you as if you are talking a language he doesn't understand?

Take your song one line at a time and give it this test. Each lyric line is like an element in a mathematical equation. Each line must not only make sense on its own but must also be a logical part of the whole formed by all the lines added together.

Examining the song in this way, for the sense of each line, we can see that the trouble with Don's song is in the chorus, which set us up for something positive. Don's intended message is not there in black and white and that is where it has to be. You cannot expect your listeners to fill in the blanks or to hear that you have your tongue in your cheek. We think the song would be better served by being definite in the first line of the chorus about the intent of the song. The chorus should also flesh out the reason for choosing the title. What does the cowboy concept have to do with all this? If the chorus truly stated the writer's concerns about where all this industrialization is leading us, the second verse would make a lot more sense.

We would still be a bit lost in the third verse, however. Don needs to put each one of those lines to the "stranger" test. They can all be taken either positively or negatively, and that doesn't serve the purpose of the song, to communicate the writer's message.

Our thanks to Don, who did an outstanding job on this song, for allowing us to take it apart line by line like this. You need to do this to every song you write. Being able to remove your own prejudices and preknowledge of what you think the song is saying and to see what it actually is saying is a very necessary skill in your bag of songwriting tricks. You have to be a stranger to your song to see it for what it really is.

39
· · · · · · · ·

TWO DIFFERENT SONGS, YOU'VE WRITTEN TWO DIFFERENT SONGS

Be sure the verses and the chorus aren't about two different things

Sometimes, perhaps in an effort to distinguish the chorus from the verses, songwriters go overboard. The resulting song has separate sections, all right, but with great gaps of meaning between them. Candace Magner's "Sing Your Song" is an example of a song that came to a fork in the road and went both ways.

SING YOUR SONG

Take a trip out in the coutry
Take a spin around the town
Or take a walk and look around
And if you're lonely, fly away—
You'll meet a friend another day

    CHORUS:
    Sing your song loud and lovely
    Sing it sweet, or sing it fine
    Sing it up or sing it down
    And if you're lonely, do it right,
    Sing it every day and night.

You know me, I'm a country lady,
And I know you for a country man,
And I'll come to you whenever I can,
And if you're lonely, you come to me
And I'll set your mind and your heart at ease,
    'cuz I

    CHORUS: *repeat*

© 1990 Candace A. Magner

The chorus in this song is very focused. It is about singing and singing only. But the verses have nothing to do with singing. Candace has the start of two or possibly three different songs here,

as the verses don't have much in common with each other either. Starting with the chorus, she can write new verses that can easily be created out of a laundry list of reasons to sing: when you're happy, sad, scared, in love, or out of love. Since she has the word "lonely" in the chorus, she might build the verses around a good-bye situation. The leaver is going on a trip and will return, but it will be a long time, so the leaver advises the leavee to sing while she's gone to relieve the loneliness.

The structure of a verse/chorus song is almost like a logical equation. We took logic in college and all we remember about it is: If p, then q. If you say, for example, that all broccoli is green, then if this is broccoli, it must be green. Such is the value of a higher education.

In the verse/chorus structure, the verses are the "if p" part. They give the underlying background information that supports the message of the chorus. The chorus is the "then q" part. The chorus gives the summation of the message, the main statement of the song. The verses support the chorus, and the chorus fulfills the verses. Together, they're undeniable. If they are divided in their impact, the song falls apart.

The best trick is to have each verse lead inexorably to the chorus, but each in its own fashion so that the chorus takes on a slightly different twist in meaning with each passing verse. Remember that you are creating your own little world in each song. Sticking to the point of your chorus consistently is the gravity that will hold your song world together.

TOO MUCH IS MORE THAN ENOUGH

Don't include song parts or lyrics that don't add to the forward motion of the song

When Abraham Lincoln said, "He can compress the most words into the smallest idea of any man I ever met," he couldn't have been talking about a songwriter. Songs are like diamonds, concentrated and crystal clear. Or you could say that writing a song is like wringing out a dishrag: You have to squeeze and twist until you get every excess drop out.

Consider this song, presented at a workshop in Santa Fe:

SUMMER STORMS

Summer storms and memories
seem to get the best of me
and I'm hoping that this wine
will help get you off my mind

I'm drinking to forget the past
keep my world from spinning so fast
but when I get it spinning slow
your memory just won't go

I see your eyes shining bright
those warm summer nights
We loved all summer long
like storms without rainbows

As the storm starts blowing in
I think about what might have been
had it all gone a different way
where would we be today?

Not meaning what we say
our words seem to fly away
and before we can take them in
they're carried off by the wind
and turn to tears running down my face
those memories we can't erase
We loved all summer long
like storms without rainbows

Memories I just can't let go
I wish I could somehow know
that all the mistakes I've made
are worth the price I've paid

Afraid to ask for what we need
we think that others should plainly see
and not knowing what we want
our dreams turn to ghosts
that haunt when the nights are warm
carried by summer storms
We loved all summer long
like storms without rainbows

© 1990 DeEdda Freyer

This was one of DeEdda's first songs and the very first time she had shared a song with other people. There are a lot of great images in the song that tell the story in an interesting way. She sticks to the central idea of the lost love, and all the lines clearly relate to that theme. This is a very good early songwriting effort. It took a lot of courage to show it in the workshop. We congratulated DeEdda on a job well done.

Now, using what you learned about song structure in chapter eleven, what would you say is the structure of this song? The opening four-line section does not repeat verbatim, so we can't call that section a chorus. The three longer sections, which have eight lines each and end with the same two lyric lines, feel like verses in a verse/bridge construction. There are two more four-line sections that follow the structure of the opening four lines. Looks like we have three bridges in this song. That's two bridges too many.

It's quite common for writers to come up with too many parts to a song. At a certain point, the song takes on a life of its own and requires that you make difficult choices in the interests of letting the song be the best it can be. This requires a certain amount of ruthlessness that you can only develop by writing so many songs that each one ceases to be precious.

It's fine to have too many parts; you can simply remove the parts that serve the song the least. In this case, we recommended that DeEdda eliminate the second and third four-line sections. They don't move the song forward significantly because they are the only parts of the song in which the singer indulges in vague reminiscing. All the other lyrics use actions and pictures to express emotions, a great lyric writing device. We asked DeEdda to look at the song as a straight-ahead verse/bridge construction. It would open with verse one: "I'm drinking to forget the past . . ." Verse two would follow: "Not meaning what we say . . ." Then the current first four lines would make a fine strong bridge while keeping us drinking in the moment: "Summer storms and memories . . ." And "Afraid to ask for what we need . . ." would be the last verse, possibly followed by a repeat of the last two lines as a coda.

Speaking of the last two lines, they are the hook of the song. The title of this song is really "Storms Without Rainbows." Please don't cry because we cut those two extra bridges out. If they're strong enough, they can find a nice home in some other song.

Even in its cut-down version, this is a song of many words. They are well chosen, though, and we wouldn't recommend trying to edit this song down any further. In general, though, when writing lyrics it's best to keep that dish rag in mind. Keep squeezing and twisting until every word is power-packed and no word is just along for a free ride. One of our most favorite songs is Willie Nelson's "Crazy." You can count the number of words in that song on you fingers and toes but the emotional impact of that song is like a locomotive with a full head of steam.

Fewer words with more meaning are the hallmark of a great lyric. Study the hit "I Don't Have the Heart," written by Allan Dennis Rich and Jud Friedman and recorded by James Ingram. The chorus is:

I don't have the heart to hurt you
That's the last thing I want to do
I don't have the heart to love you
Not the way you want me to

Look at how much is said in those few words. The first "I don't have the heart" carries the usual meaning of that idiom in our language: I don't have it in me to hurt you. This establishes the singer as a good guy, a sympathetic character who doesn't want to hurt the singee. The second "I don't have the heart," however, twists the meaning wonderfully. This time it means that he doesn't have enough love in his heart to respond to the love coming from the singee. See how much emotional content and conflict they've packed into only seventeen words?

Songwriters are free to study all of the best examples of their craft. You can easily study the use of words and structures in the songs that you love most. This is a different experience from just cranking up the radio and singing along. Write down the words, look at the structure closely, and name the parts. Decide for yourself what makes the song great. Chances are you'll find that the best are those that do the most with the least.

41
·········
NEVER SAY REWRITE
Be willing to rewrite

Picture yourself in your special writing place. You open up, go within, listen to your muse, or whatever. Words, melodies, chords come to you and you capture them. There is something holy about this picture. Some songwriters become convinced that what comes to them in this manner should not be tampered with at all. "It came to me exactly like this," they say. "It's meant to be this way."

The myth that songs come to songwriters in final, completed form is perpetuated by Hollywood. We've seen hundreds of movies that show childbirth but never one that truly conveyed the experience. Movies depicting the birth of songs go to the opposite extreme. Hollywood makes having a baby look awfully hard and writing a song look way too easy.

The best songwriters in the world spend countless hours fine-tuning every note and word in their songs. We have a friend who collects Beatles recordings. Somehow, he got a work tape of John Lennon in the writing process of "Strawberry Fields." Listening to Lennon play the song over and over, making changes each time, talking to himself about what's right and what's not, is inspirational. It's guaranteed to make a "Never Say Rewrite" songwriter sing a different song.

As the saying goes, "Songs are not written, they're rewritten." The rewriting process starts concurrently with the writing process. It's no insult to your muse to try for something better than what is first presented to you. It's a rare songwriter whose muse is so totally cooperative as to deliver perfect songs on demand. That's why they call it "courting the muse." We have to spend some time being nice to our muse, gratefully accepting what is offered but not necessarily keeping it all.

We have so many distractions and confusions in life, we can't expect to have a clear, open channel that only delivers perfection. We're going to get a lot of junk in the process of getting the good stuff. When junk comes, it's up to us to smile and say, "Thank you for sharing that with me," and then

let it go. It's counterproductive to judge ourselves negatively for having less than wonderful ideas. These are just things we have to get out of the way so we can get down to the treasure beneath the junk.

Perhaps it is the fear of having to admit that everything we think of is not wonderful that makes some of us want to believe that we mustn't tamper with the muse. Remember the old margarine commercials in which Mother Nature tastes something and swears it's butter? When she's told otherwise, she disappears in a furious cloud of smoke shouting, "It's not nice to fool Mother Nature!" Songwriters who don't want to fool with their muse are fooling themselves. Pretending to be perfect only rules out the trial-and-error process of true growth.

Some songwriters don't get to the "Never Say Rewrite" point until later in the game. They work and rework their songs to a certain level. At that point, they make the demo and bring it to a workshop or pitch it to publishers or producers. The listener who says, "I don't understand that line," or "I think you have too many verses," or anything of the kind might as well be talking to a brick wall. The songwriter in question believes the song is perfect, and anyone who has another opinion is just wrong, that's all. This attitude does not win friends in the music business. Being willing to consider constructive rewrite suggestions is the hallmark of a professional.

If you stand by your conscientious objection to rewriting at any stage of the game, you may eliminate your song from the running in a recording project. The rewriting sometimes goes on right up to the minute the lead vocals are being put to tape in the studio. This is one of the meanings of the phrase, "It ain't final 'till it's vinyl." Perhaps the phrase will continue to have meaning even though vinyl records have now gone the way of the dinosaurs.

We're absolutely not saying that you should make rewrites against your will or rewrites that you cannot live with creatively. Only you can know where to draw that line. It is a problem, though, if you draw the line so early in the game that you box your creativity into a corner. It's also a problem if you don't draw the line at all, as we shall see in our next songwriting song.

42

KILLING IT GRADUALLY WITH REWRITES

Don't rewrite a song to death

When a publisher or producer expresses interest in a song, it's music to a songwriter's ears. "A song I wrote could be heard by millions. It could change the world! What a concept!" As your mind rushes ahead to your Grammy acceptance speech, you can barely hear the "But . . . ," from the other side of the desk over the roar of the crowd. "But" can be a real kick in the . . . head. As a professional songwriter, however, you're going to duck as the "but" whizzes by your head and come up smiling and eager to hear what the person has to say. At least that is how you will act after you've tucked your tender ego away some place safe.

Here's what could happen when the songwriter answers the existential question "to rewrite or not to rewrite" with endless rewrites. The publisher says, "I love your verse, but it doesn't have a strong chorus." So the writer takes this song and rewrites a new chorus. Then the writer takes it to someone else and that publisher says, "I love that song, but I don't like the lyrics to the second verse." The writer then rewrites the lyrics to the second verse and does another demo on the song. Then the writer takes it to someone else who says, "That song needs a bridge." The writer takes that same song, writes a bridge, and redemos the song. The song gets worked over and over and over, and somehow something—whatever was good about it to begin with—gets lost in the wash.

You may cut your song off from real opportunities by being unwilling to rewrite at all. But there's such a thing as being *too* willing to rewrite. You can rewrite a song to death. It's like killing the goose that laid the golden egg. If you take the song too far apart, you may lose the initial spark that inspired you to write it.

Only you and your collaborator, if there is one, can make the decision about where the rewriting stops. You are 100 percent responsible for the song, and you own 100 percent of the song. *You* have to live with the rewrites. A good rule of thumb is to make your best judgment about whether you really feel that the rewrite has improved the song. If the answer is yes, go for it. Otherwise, forget it. If you decide not to rewrite, and the publisher is not interested in the song without the rewrite, all is not lost.

Remember, you are a songwriter. That means that you write songs. You don't just write one song and then stop writing until you've "made it" with that song. Believe it or not, we have met songwriters who have chosen this illogical course of action. If you're reasonably sane, you realize that this is just one song. You will write many more. Tell the publisher that you've made the effort but you're not happy with the rewrite. Perhaps this is not the right time or place for this song. Sometimes it's easier and more fruitful to try to learn something from the critique of the song and then write new songs. Let the publisher know you appreciate the interest and you'd like to come back with new songs written with the feedback in mind. This way, even though this song didn't work out, you can keep the door open for the next song. If you do go back to the same publisher and your new song reflects what you learned, you will boost your credibility as a songwriter and begin to build a positive relationship with the publisher.

Pursue this relationship by bringing in your new and always better songs. Don't worry about angering the publisher. If the publisher doesn't respect your prerogative as a songwriter to make the final decision on the song and can't recognize your sincere attempt to establish a positive relationship, you don't really want to deal with that person. Leave the scene gracefully. There are lots of really good people in the music business. If you're lucky enough to be dealing with one of the "good guys" (male or female), act accordingly. If possible, try to get an idea from the person of what projects are open to outside songs so that your next pitch can be geared to them.

Just because the song in question didn't feel right with the suggested rewrite, you don't need to abandon that song, either. That was just one person's opinion. Try pitching the song to several other customers. If everyone says the same thing about it, you might reconsider the rewrite. But if you believe in the song just the way it is, stand by it. Many songs that you hear as hits on the radio were rejected by over a hundred music business professionals before someone heard the potential of the song. Only you know what's best for your song, and only time and persistence will tell.

PART FIVE

TWO HEADS, OR MORE, ARE BETTER

Collaboration Misconceptions

43
....
DOING IT ALL

Don't think you can/must write it all yourself

Ever see a one-person band in the flesh? A friend of ours, Don Davis, has been cited in the *Guinness Book of World Records* for playing the largest number of different instruments at once. Horns, whistles, drums, cymbals, fretted and fantasy instruments loom behind and over him on a giant backpack. In front, he wields a huge accordion. More contraptions are strapped to his legs and suspended in front of his face. He can't be beat when it comes to numbers of decibels produced by a human being. But, friends, don't try this at home. Don is a professional one-person band. You may put your growth as a songwriter in jeopardy if you attempt to write, play, and sing everything alone.

Creation in isolation has its good points. There's nothing like the courtship that goes on when it's just you and the muse. But if you only write alone, you miss out on a wealth of learning opportunities. We highly recommend collaboration as a songwriting learning tool. Billy Steinberg learned more about himself when he started to collaborate: "I didn't feel that I was stronger at writing lyrics than I was at writing music. I just thought I did both. I had really been sheltered as a songwriter. I had never co-written and I had never been around people with real musical gifts. I knew I wasn't a great guitar player but I wrote songs with my limited knowledge of chords. After a few years of working with Tom [Kelly], I started to realize that his musical talents far exceeded mine. Then I realized that I was also good at lyrics."

Note how long it took this realization to dawn on Billy. The slow business of show business requires infinite patience. Beware of wanting to do it all and make it all happen *now*. It will break your heart. Also, note that he had no way of knowing that someone else could be so gifted or even of what his own gift was until after the experience of working closely with someone else.

We saw a nature program on public TV about hummingbirds recently. The show was overflowing with amazing facts about these flying jewels, but the image that floored us the most was the picture of a very special hummingbird. Over millions of years of evolution, this bird has developed a bill of a particular length, curve and twist to exactly fit a flower that has the same depth, curve and twist in its nectar-holding flower. The feeding birds zip from flower to flower pollinating and thus ensuring the survival of the flowers. The flowers can't exist without the birds, and the birds can't exist without the flowers. They're a perfect match of gifts.

Believe it or not, you, too, are the result of millions of years of evolution, and your creative fit is just as perfect. It's our job, as creative human beings, to realize and identify what that means for each one of us. We each need to dig into ourselves to identify the particular seed of creativity we have planted in there and already growing. A good place to start looking is your childhood. What did you really love to do as a kid? Chances are, you loved doing it because it was the expression of your gift. Some are gifted with the variety of talents that it takes to "do it all" or most of it. Prince writes, produces, performs, and dances to his songs. He may not be your style, but his talent is undeniable. Most of us have been given more specific gifts.

Billy's collaborator, Tom Kelly, told us, "The odds of somebody writing music and lyrics and hitting a home run on both ends are really pretty slim. There are some people that do it, but there are a lot more people that fall short because they try to do it. It's best to be able to recognize your strengths and really concentrate on them. Collaborate with somebody who can fill in the voids."

We'll talk about the pitfalls of collaborating in later chapters. For now, let's just look at the bright side. Here are some of the advantages of collaborating:

- Making a date with someone else ensures that your writing session won't be put off while you engage in avoidance activities such as cleaning out the attic.

- Collaborators can provide instantaneous feedback, a new angle, a great lyric line, a beautiful melody, funds for making demos, music business connections, musical talents, recording equipment, enthusiasm and commiseration.

- If you are lucky enough to find a steady collaborating partner, you can experience a rich, rewarding and unique relationship. Since collaboration requires exposing your most vulnerable creative underbelly in the presence of another human being, trust and respect for each other are mandatory.

- The closeness of collaborating can be scary, but it can also be very educational. It provides an opportunity to learn from your co-writer and to learn about yourself as you relate to your co-writer.

Another form that "doing it all" takes is the writer who also wants to be the artist singing the song she or he wrote. This is a worthy goal, but it loses its value if it causes a case of tunnel vision and self-limiting decisions. Case in point, Billy Steinberg's illuminating story: "I had a band and I kept doing these demos to try to get a deal as an artist. But all these A&R people would say, 'We have such and such an artist on our label and we'd like to have him cut this song.' I was always disappointed because I was calling up to hear them say, 'We want to sign you to make a record.' At a certain point, the light bulb went on. I realized I'm really not a great singer, but I am a good songwriter. I was very stubborn; I didn't want to see that."

The moral of his story is: Take a good, honest look at yourself. Only after Billy began to concentrate on his strengths did he become an extremely successful songwriter. If you're thinking about simultaneously wearing the distinctly different career hats of writer and artist, check out how they fit by looking in the mirror the world provides you. Ask yourself serious questions, such as:

Am I willing to live the lifestyle a career as a recording artist would require?
Can you handle the inevitable rejection you will experience trying to get your career going? Can you handle long periods of separation from your spouse and family while you do a concert tour to promote your record?

Do I have an outstanding talent as an artist?
There's a saying going around the music business, "They're not signing talent. They're signing hairdos." You may have a great hairdo now. You may even get signed for it. More power to you for having fun and earning money at the same time. Nice work if you can get it. But we believe that talent will out. If you're in this for the long run, you have to believe in yourself and your talent. You have to put that belief to the test by really scrutinizing the truth about yourself.

Do I want to be a recording artist more than anything?
You're going to need a real hunger for expressing yourself as an artist to make it through the obstacle course you're going to face. If you know in your heart that you couldn't stop it if you tried, you can surrender to your destiny gracefully. If you're being driven by the sheer pleasure of doing something you love, there is no way you can fail, no matter what level of fame and fortune you do or do not reach in the world.

If the answer to any of these questions is maybe, you don't have to give up your dream of being an artist. You may want to put it on the back burner while you concentrate on your exquisite skill as a lyricist. When you become a successful songwriter, you will have credibility and be presented with opportunities to expose your previously hidden talent.

Discovering what your gift is and how you are to give it to the world is an ongoing process of honest self-examination. What do you really enjoy doing most? What do you feel you're really best at? With the answers to those questions, you can go bravely forth into the world and seek others to add their best to your best.

44
·········

DIVING IN, CRAWLING OUT

Have an agreement with your collaborator before you start working on a song

You're convinced that collaboration is the way to go. Now all you have to do is find your perfect match. How do you find collaborators? A songwriting workshop is an ideal place. They afford a unique setting that allows you to get to know the person and the songs he or she writes before you suggest a possible collaboration. *All* of our collaborators are people we have met in songwriter workshop situations. Local clubs that feature original music are good places to do your collaborator hunting. Teaming up with an artist or a band that can provide a ready-made demo recording group and immediate live outlet for your songs is a wise move. Some songwriters' publications, such as the *Musepaper*, published by the Los Angeles Songwriters Showcase, have columns in which collaborators post their searches for writing partners.

Don't overlook schools as a resource. Many professional musicians and songwriters started out in high school bands. The creative writing studies and the music departments of your local junior college or university probably have bulletin boards on which you can post an "I'm looking for a collaborator" announcement. If you are attending school, ask the teachers in those departments to recommend some outstanding students to you.

Find out if the songwriters in your community have organized to create some gathering point, such as an open mike night at a local club or monthly educational meetings. If these things don't exist in your community and one of your gifts is a knack for making things happen, you can get help from NAS (National Academy of Songwriters, 6381 Hollywood Blvd., Suite 780, Hollywood CA 90028; phone 800-826-7287) to start forming your own local songwriter organization. They have written step-by-step instructions on how to produce your own songwriters' event and will send it to you on request. Please include a self-addressed, stamped envelope with enough postage for a three-ounce reply.

Cut to the scene of your first meeting with your collaborator. Somehow, you met and agreed to try a collaboration. Now, do you sit right down at the keyboard and noodle until your new co-writer starts spontaneously singing the lyrics and melody over your riff? Isn't that the way it always happens in Hollywood movies about songwriting teams? Real life, as usual, is a different story.

It's a mistake to rush into writing right away. For the time during which you will be creating a song together, it will be like a mini-marriage. If you don't allow yourself time to get to know and trust each other, you may have the opportunity to experience the true meaning of "Marry in haste, repent in leisure." It's extremely important to have an understanding before you both invest your time and creativity in writing a song. Otherwise, you may find yourself crawling out of a confusing and painful experience with your confidence in tatters.

It's best to make a date to talk to your potential collaborator. Even if it is someone you know from a songwriting workshop, don't assume you know what she or he has in mind. Now is the time to share enough information to let you feel safe to write with each other. Both of you should talk about the kinds of songs you love to listen to and write. Talk about your songwriting histories and goals. Talk about the kind of equipment you have for demo making. Talk about your songwriting habits and your idea of how the collaboration you are now contemplating will go.

A fruitful collaboration is based on mutual trust and respect. You can't expect your collaborator not to get on your nerves once in a while, but for the most part, you should be comfortable with each other. It is essential that you admire each other's writing. Use this talking time to develop a friendly rapport. If you are in the same political and philosophical ballpark, you will have more confidence in each other's ability to write together.

It's important to find out how well your collaborator knows the business aspects of music. Sharing information on this level can be a mutually educational experience. What contacts in the music business does each of you have? Does your potential collaborator have direct access to a recording artist? What are your pre-existing contractual situations and opinions regarding the ownership of the publishing of the song? And last, but very far from least, there should be some sort of agreement between you as to how the ownership of the song will be split.

Will you be starting from scratch on an entirely new song? We think it's disrespectful and demoralizing to write a song and then try to pick it apart to see who wrote what percentage of it. If you're in the room together and you're both working on the song, the song's the thing. You're both giving your all. You both have equal responsibility and deserve equal credit for the song. For us, it's important to make it clear at the outset of writing the song that everyone who collaborates on it divides ownership of the song equally. We indicate this by writing in "50 percent (or 33⅓ percent, or 25 percent) words and music" under each writer's name on the copyright registration form. All expenses incurred in demoing and pitching the song are equally shared, and all income received is equally distributed among the writers. We believe this kind of business agreement is the basis of a trusting and respectful writing relationship with our collaborators. As we've said, trust and respect are absolutely necessary in the collaboration. Without them, we cannot drop our defenses enough to create spontaneously.

If you were presented with a completely arranged melody and asked to write the lyric, you might expect to be identified strictly as the lyricist. That means that you wouldn't get income from the song when it's recorded as an instrumental or in foreign translation. The standard procedure is to separate the lyricist's and composer's income streams. But we like to credit both writers with "50 percent words and music," even when the complete lyrics are written first by only one partner in the collaboration. Without those particular words, we wouldn't have found that particular melody.

Does the other writer have the melody and the chorus lyrics written and want you to write just the lyrics for the verses? This situation calls for an adjustment in the percentage of the song, because one writer has already done more than half the work. It would be best to have a frank discussion of the matter and agree up front about the value of your contribution to the song. It's far better to be in agreement before the writing is done than to fight about it after the fact. While you're busy arguing, another song will find its way to the producer you were going to approach. Arguments among collaborators after the song is written often result in songs that spend the rest of eternity in limbo because none of the writers want to deal with each other.

If you talk before you write, and you find out that you come from different universes and couldn't possibly get along, there is nothing lost and experience gained. You have to feel equal to your collaborator. If he or she is miles ahead of you in skills, knowledge and/or contacts, you may be unable to function effectively because you feel inferior. Putting the shoe on the other foot, if you feel you are far superior, you won't have enough respect for your potential collaborator. Each of you needs to feel secure in your gifts and eager to pool your different but equally valuable talents.

Those hurdles overcome, you're ready to start writing together. You will be creating a piece of property, like a plot of land made out of the magic of your creativity. Anyone who wants to use your property will have to get your permission and pay you for the privilege. (Permission to record a song is only necessary for the first recording. After that, users will still have to pay you mechanical royalties as set by law, called the statutory rate, but will not have to ask permission to record the song. However, most users would rather negotiate with copyright owners for a lower mechanical royalty than statutory rate.) In other words, you're going into business together.

Some time during the writing of the song or, at the very latest, as soon as the song is completed, you need to enter into a collaboration agreement. This is a written contract between or among you that should contain the following information:

1. Title of song
2. Names of songwriters
3. Nationality of songwriters
4. Year of birth of songwriters

5. Percentages of words and music credited to each songwriter

6. Full addresses and phone numbers of songwriters

This information is needed to fill in the blanks in the PA copyright registration form for your song. It will make life easier for whoever will fill out the form if all this information is already gathered. This is also a good time to talk about who will be filing the copyright registration, what the business address will be, and where the files related to the song will be kept.

In addition, a collaboration agreement might include language to the effect that:

- All writers share equally, or in proportion to their percentage of ownership, in the expenses of demoing the song.

- No money is to be spent without the consent of all writers.

- Writers are to notify the other writers in the agreement of any changes of address. (This comes in handy when ten years down the line, someone wants to record the song.)

- No agreement is to be made regarding the song without the consent of all writers. (However, you should provide for breaking this rule. See chapter forty-eight, "Missing Persons.")

- Consent among the collaborators to agreements regarding the song may be given orally or in writing. (You specify which.)

- No changes are to be made in the song without the consent of all the writers. (Saves you from the nasty surprise of being written out of the song.)

- If any writer becomes dissatisfied with the collaboration prior to its release or assignment to a publisher, the writer may withdraw his or her contribution to the collaboration freely, providing he or she makes no further claims on any subsequent collaboration on the song. (Separating out one individual's contribution may be difficult and troublesome.)

- If a dispute arises over the collaboration agreement, the collaborators agree to submit to arbitration by a lawyer of unanimous choice or by the American Arbitration Association.

This is a document that you can create yourself. A lawyer would be able to write a more complicated agreement that covers many more subtle bases, but if money is an object, some kind of agreement is better than no agreement at all.

All writers sign and date the collaboration agreement, and everybody gets a copy. Then everyone lives happily ever after, right?

Wrong again, collaboration breath! Read on and weep!

45
....

IT'S NOT MY JOB

Take responsibility for the complete song, even if you "only wrote the lyrics/melody"

Sometimes one member of a collaborating team will come to our songwriting workshop to get feedback on a co-written song. Let's say it's the lyricist. We'll play the song, and a songwriter participating in the workshop might say, "I think the melody was too upbeat for the subject matter. There's no prosody (emotional agreement) between the lyrics and the melody." Mr. or Ms. Lyricist often replies, "Oh, but that's the melody. I didn't write the melody."

What's wrong with this picture? Why doesn't this lyricist feel responsible for the music? The lyricist may not be able to play one note on the piano, but he wouldn't be a lyricist if he didn't have musical instincts. Why not be a poet, a novelist, a screenplay writer, if words are your gift? Why choose songs if there isn't something in you that loves and understands greatness in songs?

What happened in the collaboration to make the lyricist disown the melody? Wasn't he allowed to give input on the writing of the melody? How can you create together if you can't relate honestly to each other? Now, we come to the heart of the matter. Communication. You want to communicate to the world through songs. But first you must overcome the communication barriers that come between you and your collaborator as you write the song together.

Avoid all the pitfalls from the outset by doing as we suggested in the first section of the book. Talk about the title, the intention, the mood, the setting, the situation, and the characters in the song. Free associate ideas of who the singer is and why she is singing. Consider which artists you think would relate to the message of your song. Listen to some of their current songs to get a feel for their musical style. Discuss the structure. Does the idea want to flow into a verse/chorus or verse/bridge form? As you have these discussions, you are building up to the trust it takes to show your creative underbelly.

What happens when you open up, become completely vulnerable, make a suggestion for a line in the song, and your collaborator says, "Yecch! That stinks!" in disgust? Your creativity slams shut like a clam; you're hurt and angry. You vow never to collaborate again. We thought we had discovered one of the secrets of life when we learned through repeated experience that extremely painful situations always turn out to be opportunities to grow. Then we found that it's no secret. In research conducted at California State University, more than 87 percent of people studied said that a painful event (death, illness, breakup, or divorce, for example) caused them to find a more positive meaning in life.

So when your collaborator makes a stabbing remark, look upon it as a golden opportunity for you to practice your assertiveness skills. You will be doing yourself, your collaborator and the song

a favor if you simply say that you feel that it's not productive to cut each other down. If the line isn't to your collaborator's liking, there are ways to say it without attacking. For instance, "That's not quite there yet; I think we can get a stronger line. Let's keep trying."

Arthur Hamilton, who wrote the fabulous song "Cry Me a River," related a story about his collaboration with Barry Mann. Barry is co-writer of "You've Lost That Loving Feeling," "Somewhere Out There," and "Sometimes When We Touch," to name a few of the monumental songs he's contributed to over the last thirty years. You may have heard him singing, too. Barry is the writer/artist who brought us the immortal "Who Put the Bomp?"

Arthur talked about a lyric he had given to Barry. After working separately on the melody, Barry invited Arthur to hear what he had done. Barry played the melody and sang the lyrics, then turned to Arthur and said, "I'm having a problem with this spot right here. It's probably my fault, but I just don't think the words and melody go together." Arthur saw immediately that the melody did call for a change in the lyrics. In the end, Arthur wound up rewriting two entire lines of lyric because of the changes in the word or two where the lyric and melody weren't meshing. Arthur was thrilled by the sweet and gentle way that Barry suggested the change. The point is that it's not what you say, but how you say it. Truly great songwriters know better than to be arrogant.

It's really a matter of respect. If you respect the ability of your collaborator, you will not criticize the occasional awful suggestion. We all have trash that we have to get out of the way before we get down to the good stuff. If you react negatively, you start to function as the too-early editor for your collaborator, and the result is the shut-down of the creative flow. If you make the mistake of putting your collaborator down, you can make amends by apologizing and cleaning up your act. That kind of an attack is often, if not always, caused by the attacker's insecurities and defensiveness. Examine yourself honestly. Stop blaming your collaborator for your frustrations with the song. Give yourself the reassurances that you need to carry on with confidence.

If you keep clear and direct communication lines open throughout the writing process, every iota of the song will be agreed to by all the writers. By agreeing to this word, this note, that rhythm, that feel, each writer is responsible for that part of the song, even if it clearly came from another writer in the team. You cannot simultaneously keep score on who wrote what note or which word and be spontaneously creative. You are all responsible for the total song. If there's a part of the song that you really can't own, it's up to you to make your feelings known. Then what?

We'll talk about collaboration impasses in the next chapter.

46

LET'S DO IT MY WAY
Don't insist on your way when a collaborator disagrees

You're collaborating with a new partner. The song is coming along pretty well. You have the title, the first verse, and part of the chorus written. You're both working on finishing off the chorus lyric, and you've both tried a lot of possible lyric lines on each other. None of them have made either of you jump up and down and shout. Suddenly, your co-writer exclaims, "Eureka!" You eagerly listen, wanting it to be the answer to your search.

Despite an enthusiastic presentation of the line, you're not thrilled with it. You do your best to respectfully express that you think a better lyric could be just a line away. You suggest some more work on the line. Your co-writer gets all bent out of shape, claims it's the perfect line, and insists there's no way you're going to find a better one; you've already spent enough time on it, and you should just go with this line.

Now is the moment of truth. You discover that, in all your prewriting talk, you forgot to lay a very important ground rule. The rule is this: Not one jot of lyric or melody goes into the song without all the writers' agreement. And giving in to pressure does not qualify as agreement. Pressure has no place in a creative collaboration.

Likewise, if you're the writer who is offering a line that is not greeted with great joy by your collaborator, you need to learn to accept that gracefully. You might state a few calm reasons why you think it fits perfectly. If, after giving it a second look, your collaborator isn't turned on to the line, you need to let it go.

We attended a workshop given by Marilyn and Alan Bergman, world-class lyricists whose collaborations have won them Oscars and Grammys galore. "The Windmills of Your Mind," "The Way We Were," the theme from the movie *Tootsie* and "What Are You Doing the Rest of Your Life?" are among the standards they have written. During the workshop, they spoke at length about their policy of mutual respect. If the lyric line doesn't make them both absolutely happy, it's tossed without a second glance. There are a hundred, a thousand more where that came from, and one of those yet unconceived lyric lines *will* make them both happy. We heard these words of wisdom fifteen years ago, and we've never forgotten them.

With this philosophy, the Bergmans are expressing their complete confidence and trust in each other. They know that they have what it takes to keep at it until both of them are totally satisfied. The thought of running out of ideas never occurs to them. Of course, they've been writing lyrics eight hours a day for umpteen years, and their skills are razor sharp. They find the lines they're looking for faster than we do. That only means that we have to be more patient with ourselves as we stumble around learning to walk the songwriter way.

It's fantastic when a song comes fast and easy.

Some songwriters are known for creating lyrics at lightning speed. The late Sammy Cahn, lyricist of "All the Way" and "High Hopes," whose "Love and Marriage" is used as the theme for TV's "Married with Children," wrote lyrics as fast as his collaborators could play the melodies for him. Most of us, most of the time, however, take a bit longer. Some songs take weeks, months, even years to come together.

We had a strange experience while writing a song with Harold Payne. Contrary to our usual procedure, we had written the melody first without a title. We knew where the title fit on the melody, so we three worked separately on finding the perfect title. It may have been two or three days of writing and some four hundred rejected titles later when Pat came up with an idea she liked and typed it on her computer. She looked down and noticed that Pete, who was working at a desk beside her, had just written the same title down on his piece of paper. She turned to him and said, "Oh, you like that one?" thinking that he had seen it on the monitor and copied it. He replied, "Yes, I just wrote it." As we sat staring at each other wondering at this coincidence, Harold burst in from the backyard, saying, "I've got the title." It was the same title. Working independently, we had all written the same title at the same time. This had to be the title we had been looking for all those hours. There's a saying that applies to this situation: Don't give up before the miracle happens.

Suppose you realize your error of omission and take an intermission from writing to discuss the basic ground rules of the collaboration. You could say something like, "I understand you feel strongly about the line, but I think we should have a basic rule in the collaboration that we both agree fully to every line in the song, or the line is not in the song. Let's try a few more lines, and if we really can't find anything better, we may still use it." What happens if you work and work and work and still you don't find something? You can choose to:

- Accept the lyric that your co-writer loves and you're not so crazy about and move on to completing the song;
- Take a break from the song and come back to it another day;
- Take two aspirins—songwriting is a dirty job, but somebody has to do it.

When your collaborator develops a hard head after you've written a dozen great songs together, it can be an even bigger headache. We had that experience recently, and it was devastating. The writing went so well at first. We were all excited by the process and the product of our collaboration. Then, all of a sudden, something went wrong. Our collaborator started to insist that there was one right way for things to go, and of course, it was the way she or he had in mind. We tried to reinstate the "everybody must be happy" rule, but it fell on deaf ears.

The songs that followed also fell far below the quality of the previous songs we had written. We are now faced with ending a relationship for which we had high hopes. Can this collaboration be saved? We don't know because we're still dealing with this as we write. We do know that it's pointless to try to create when the relationship between collaborators has deteriorated from a democracy to a tyranny.

P.S. The collaboration lives on. We agreed to disagree on some points because we value the relationship more than we value being right all the time. We also got better at insisting that we try all ideas, instead of allowing anyone to preemptively edit the ideas before they're tried. And we're writing better than ever together.

47
········

I TAKE THAT BACK

*Don't try to change your collaboration agreement
after the song is written*

Once upon a time we had a collaborator. And the collaborator was a very nice person with strong connections to an institution based on teaching the power of love. We had a long acquaintance with this person through our mutual involvement in several music business organizations. We all thought it was a very good idea to collaborate.

We talked about our business understanding before beginning to write; we all agreed that this would be a three-way collaboration and an even three-way split of ownership. So we sat down to write, and the writing went very well. We were enthusiastic about the song, ideas flowed freely, and we completed the song with no problems.

We went on to write song number two together. Again, the writing went smoothly, with everyone contributing continually in the process. After song number two, the collaborator called for a meeting. We don't want to give away this person's identity, so we'll use the name Sean, which could belong to either a man or woman.

Sean said, "Look, I think I'm contributing more to this collaboration than you are. I think I deserve half of it, and you two should split the other half." You could have knocked us over with a guitar pick. We had trouble believing what Sean was doing: Sean was trying to "take back" the deal we had all agreed to. When we understood that Sean was serious, we felt betrayed and angry. That ain't no way to treat a collaborator! The collaboration was over immediately. The two good songs we wrote together have gathered dust on our shelf ever since.

What if you do feel that, on one song or another in a collaboration relationship, your actual contribution was more than your percentage? If the writing relationship is a good one, you need to think about the long run. Perhaps two or three songs from now your contribution will be less than your percentage. We feel strongly that petty quibbling over who wrote what is anathema to a collaborative relationship. Write a few more songs together,

and if you feel strongly that you're doing most of the work, talk to your collaborator. You won't be able to go on with the relationship with this feeling of inequality.

Honesty is the best policy, but a little bit of tact goes a long way. First, make it clear you are not talking about changing the deal on the songs you have already written together. Even if you did not put your agreement in writing, you are honor-bound to live up to it. You need to let your collaborator know you value the relationship.

Tell your collaborator that you feel you are consistently contributing a greater part of all or most of the songs you have written together. Ask your collaborator if he thinks this is happening, too. If the answer is yes, you can breathe a sigh of relief and talk about what kind of deal you feel would more fairly reflect the way songs are being created in your collaboration. If the answer is no, you've got trouble in collaboration city, but it can be overcome if both of you are committed to the relationship.

You could always choose to continue the relationship on an even-split basis. But if you resent this arrangement, your writing will suffer. You could both agree to write the next song, observe who contributes what, and decide accordingly how it should be split. We hate this idea, but maybe you can make it work. We don't think you can do math and songwriting simultaneously. You could agree to modify your writing process so that it becomes more clear who is doing what, or so that the work is shared more evenly.

Collaborators bring much more than their writing skills to the songwriting process. They bring recording equipment, music business connections, business skills, office facilities, vocal talent, musicianship, inspiration and enthusiasm. Be sure you add in all the factors when you start crunching numbers—you wouldn't want a good collaboration that could last a lifetime to get lost in the crunch.

48

MISSING PERSONS

Know how to deal with a song when there's interest and you can't find your collaborator

On a day like any other day, you get a call unlike any other. The caller wants to record your song. You sent a record company a tape two years ago, and unbeknownst to you, they have been holding it for consideration. Since this is the first time this song will be recorded, the record company needs you to issue a mechanical license. A mechanical license is a piece of paper that says they are permitted to mechanically reproduce your song on a cassette or CD, and they have to pay you *x* amount of each copy sold.

Your problem is that you wrote that song with Sam Songwriter four years ago. You never knew him well, and you have no idea where he is now. If you have no collaboration agreement with Sam, you're out of luck. Sam owns the song just as much as you do. You can't issue the license without his agreement.

To avoid this awful situation, you must include some provision in your collaboration agreement for each of you to act on opportunities for the song, in case you cannot get in touch with each other. Even if you're best buddies and never lose touch, it's useful to have such a provision for those times when one of you is traveling around the world and hard to reach.

The collaboration agreement should state that all collaborators on the song will notify each other of changes of address. Put your old collaborators on your holiday card list; they will at least know where you are at the end of each year. The planet seems to be spinning much faster these days, and I guess a few people fly off the face of the earth each year, because cards bounce back undelivered from a couple of our old friends each December. Despite the best intentions to stay in touch, this provision in your collaboration agreement doesn't guarantee that you'll always be able to find old Sam Songwriter.

The provision to deal with your missing collaborator should state that, if unable to contact or locate the other collaborator/s, any of the writers

on the song has full power of attorney to make an agreement regarding the song. For the power of attorney to be binding, it must be notarized.

When you are dealing directly with a record company like this, you are acting as your own publisher. Another way to deal with the situation of missing collaborators is to form a publishing company owned by all the writers. Then all of you sign a publishing contract to that company for that song. As co-owners of the company, each of you will have the power to do business with the song. For more about being your own publisher, see chapter seventy-four, "One Hundred Percent of Nothing."

If you thought ahead and were prepared when that call came, you are now able to issue the license on the song that you and Sam wrote. The song is recorded, released, and winds up on an album that does fairly well. In a year or so, money starts to come in for you and Sam. Now what do you do?

Even if you didn't go through the formality of forming a publishing company with Sam, you are one in fact. Money from the record company will come to you as Your Name and Sam Songwriter Music Publishing. Half (or whatever percentage you agreed on) of that money belongs to Sam. You need to keep an accounting of the money received and the money that belongs to Sam. There is no law that says how you have to keep this money for Sam, but you need to be ready to show him the accounts and give him his money should he hear about the recording and find you.

There is no answer to the question of what to do if Sam never shows up. It seems reasonable to us that some of Sam's money could be spent on locating him. Since you should have Sam's social security number on the collaboration agreement, you might be able to use that information to find him. If you know Sam loves to read *Rolling Stone* magazine, try a personal ad in their classified section.

Another missing persons problem that songwriters run into is the case of the disappearing publisher. What happens when you sign a single song contract with Pat Publisher and then Pat vanishes? If you signed a contract without a reversion clause, you have a problem. That means you gave Pat complete ownership of the copyright and all power to do any business with the song for the length of the copyright.

This is only one of the reasons, but it seems to be sufficient, that we advise you to insist on a reversion clause in any publishing contract. The reversion clause states that the ownership of the song reverts to you after a stated period of time if there is no commercially recorded release. The time can range from six months to two or three years.

If the problem is that you can't find the publisher, it stands to reason that the reversion of the ownership of the song should not depend on your being able to find the publisher to give notice that the time is up. Make sure your reversion clause has language that provides for the situation of the disappearance of the publisher. It can say something to the effect that ownership of the song reverts to the songwriter upon written notice sent to the publisher by registered mail. The reversion clause should also state that if the publisher refuses to accept your certified mail or if the publisher moves without providing a forwarding address, the attempt to give notice by certified mail will be considered the legal equivalent of giving notice.

Our purpose in this book is to give you an overview of the pitfalls along the songwriting road. For a more detailed explanation of the legal aspects of songwriting, read Kent Klavens' *Protecting Your Song and Yourself* published by Writer's Digest Books. For help in locating missing persons, check out some Sherlock Holmes from your local library for sleuthing tips.

Providing for the possibility of losing track of your collaborators or your publisher in your agreements with them may make the difference between a hit song and a dead issue. Don't forget to take care of this important little bit of business that can mean a lot.

PART SIX

GETTING IT ON TAPE

Demo No-No's

49
·········

NO UP-FRONT FEEDBACK

*Don't spend money on demos before getting
informed feedback on the song*

After your song is written, the next step is to make a demo; that's short for "demonstration tape." The demo will be the only embodiment of your song that the publisher, producer or artist will hear. In most cases, you will not be there in person to present the song. The demo will have to present itself. It will have to be strong enough to stand on its own without your being there to say, "This part needs horns," or "The record would have backup vocals here."

There are a million ways to go wrong in the demo-making process. In the chapters that follow, we'll cover a variety of preparation mistakes and ways to avoid or undo them. Some of the most important things you need to do to get your songs down on tape are the things you do *before* you go anywhere near a tape machine or recording studio.

Taking first things first, the song is the thing. No amount of horns, backup singers, or money poured into a demo is going to make a weak song strong. Too often in workshops we are presented incredibly elaborate demos of songs that are shining examples of all the errors we've covered so far in this book. The lyrics are confusing, the melody is monotonous, the character the singer is representing is an unsympathetic lout, and so on.

We literally wince when such an empty demo is played because we hate to tell a writer that she just wasted three hundred dollars, or whatever she spent making the demo. It hurts us to have to point out this painful truth. The writer could have spent half that money on taking a songwriting workshop and then made a much better demo with the other half of the money. The only thing we can recommend to the songwriter is to create a file like the one we did when we bought a lemon of a car from "a little old lady from Pasadena." The label on the file read "$400 Lessons We Have Learned."

To save yourself the pain of creating your own "very expensive lessons learned" file, do not spend penny number one on a demo until you have some informed feedback on the strength of the song. Review chapter thirty-seven to refresh your memory about where you can find this feedback. Don't just ask your mom—you know she loves you too much to see your flaws or those in your song. Get feedback from several people whose opinions you value.

A good demo can cost a lot of money, and it can be money well spent. But before you start spending, stop to listen to your song. A very good thing to do before you make a demo is to make a pre-demo. A pre-demo is the demo you make at home with whatever equipment you have on hand. If all you have is a little cassette deck, just sing and play into it and make the best recording you can.

If you have synthesizers, MIDI, drum machines, DAT recorders, and so forth, your investment in that equipment is a testimonial to your seriousness. You can make your own elaborate demo at home with a minimum of further cash expenditure. However, do not discount your most irreplaceable and therefore valuable asset: your time. No one gets more than twenty-four hours each day. You can spend a long time making a terrific in-home studio demo of a song that could have been terrific, too, if you'd sought some feedback and done that necessary rewrite.

Make every effort to have the pre-demo at least suggest the sound you will be going for in the ultimate demo. Use your guitar or piano to play the rhythmic hooky riffs that you imagine will be played by horns later. You can use your voice to indicate musical ideas you "hear" for instrumental solos or fills. Try to capture the feel that you want to express in the demo. The amount of thought and creativity you put into your pre-demo will have a big effect on the quality of the final demo. The demo-making process is really a decision-making process. The more decisions you make before the meter starts ticking in the studio, the less money you spend and the less stress you experience.

A pre-demo is a handy tool. You can play it to your esteemed feedback providers. You can give your ears a rest from the song for a day or two, then play the pre-demo again. Does the song grab your interest and hold it all the way through? Do the emotions in the song build and pay off? Is the melody memorable? Is this a message the world needs now? This is the moment of truth. You have to distance yourself from the song and look at it with a really critical eye. Ask your song, "If I spend three hundred dollars making a demo of you, will you pay back on my investment?"

If you honestly think the answer to that question is no, it's time to get your hand out of your wallet and get back to work on the learning process of songwriting. Maybe this song is as strong as it's ever going to be. Maybe the idea wasn't that strong in the first place. It wasn't a wasted effort, because you learned so much while you were writing. Maybe it's time to write another, better song and put this one in a file marked "Lessons I Learned for Free."

This is not an easy thing to do. Songwriters want to be heard. We want the world to sing our songs. We want that so badly that sometimes we think we can make it happen if we only spend enough money. The only thing we really gain by spending money without a lot of thought first is more space in our wallets.

If, when you play your pre-demo, the feedback is totally positive and your most critical listening of it still leaves you knocked out, you're ready to start thinking about your demo. Your pre-demo comes in handy again. Give a copy to the vocalist with a lyric sheet so he can become familiar with the song before the recording date. Give copies to the musicians who are going to play on the demo session. Give a copy to the producer or engineer you will be working with on the demo. Or send a copy to the mail-order demo service to help them know what you're trying to get at with the song.

Notice we said "a copy." Never let your original out of your hands. It will find a way to get lost. Treat your pre-demo as you will your demo. Mark all items with a copyright notice (©, the year, and your name or your publishing company's name) and your phone number.

When you create a song, it's like creating a piece of real estate. The song is the land itself. It is the basis of the value of the property. The demo is the house you build on the land. If you build on sand, the house will fall. You have to make sure your song is as solid as a rock before you start construction on top of it.

50
· · · · · · · ·
POISONING THE PRODUCTION WELL
Don't have an overbearing or put-down attitude in the studio

D-day has arrived. (Demo day, that is.) You've booked the studio. It's your song, your money, and you're in charge. You're drunk with the power of the moment. You tell the musicians what to do. You tell the engineer what to do. If anyone makes a mistake, you let them know you don't like it a bit. Your money is being spent and mistakes take time.

You put your coffee cup on the top of the mixing console, your feet up on some outboard gear, and say to yourself, Today, I am a producer, and I say what goes.

This doesn't really happen, you think. Well, the picture we've painted is mild compared to what has actually happened in recording studios: fist-fights, food fights, and even gun fights. Coffee in the console, smoke and sparks in the air, engineers being held hostage — these are the things that happen when people forget to check their egos at the door of the recording studio.

When you are the producer, your attitude sets the tone for the session. If you are encouraging everyone to do their best instead of insisting that they toe your line, you will get a much better performance. If your attitude is overbearing, if you criticize and put down the people you are working with, expect the worst. You'll get it, because you're poisoning the production well. No one can be creative while being put down.

Remember when you wrote the song. You had to open up to a sensitive place in yourself to reach the emotions you needed to put in the song. The people you hire to record your demo are having the same experience. In the same way that you didn't need your inner critic or a criticizing collaborator then, they don't need your criticism now. You need to make the recording session a safe place where everyone can be free to open up and give their creative best.

Old-fashioned manners can go a long way. "Please" and "thank you" should be mainstays in your vocabulary. Be sure to emphasize what's going great. A suggestion for improvement does not have to be couched as a criticism of what's been done.

But what if someone really is making a lot of mistakes and giving a bad performance? You cannot afford to pay for someone else's bad day. Try calling a ten-minute break and asking to speak to the person privately. Ask if there's something wrong or something you can help with. You probably can't help, but just the offer may be enough to lift the person's mood.

If there's no improvement after the break, you may have to accept that you cannot work with the person in question. If you hired the person on the recommendation of the studio, they may accept some financial responsibility if it's clear that person is not performing. They want your business, so they want you to be happy. Consult with the engineer. You can be sure the engineer is hearing what's really going on. It's the first item in their job description.

Engineers are a special breed. If you are going off the deep end, they will suggest the saner route once or twice in a mild way. If you are insistent, they will clam up and do as you say. Their job is to serve the producer, even if they think the producer is wildly incompetent. They won't fight you if you're determined to do it your way.

If it's the engineer that you're having trouble with, speak to the studio owner. If the engineer *is* the studio, you've just learned not to make demos there. You will have to decide whether to make the best of a bad situation or to get out while you're ahead.

You may be paying the bill, but don't forget that what you're paying for includes the expertise of the people you have hired. Megalomania and defensiveness will get you nowhere fast. Open communication and respect for everyone involved will get you everything you need.

51
....

TOO MANY DEMOS SPOIL THE WALLET

Don't make too many demos at once

The only thing worse than a songwriter blowing a lot of money on a demo of a song that isn't ready is a songwriter blowing lots and lots of money on many demos of many unready songs. We've had songwriters in workshops tell us that they've sent off twenty songs at once to a mail-order demo service. At a hundred dollars per song, or even fifty dollars a song, that's way too much money to spend at once, for several reasons.

First, demo-making is an educational process. How can you learn from your mistakes when you make them all at once? If you make one or two demos at a time, you can learn from the mistakes you make on those. That way, demos number three and four can be better than one and two. You have to give yourself time to process the information.

Second, sending a huge quantity of songs to a mail-order demo service cuts you out of the process. This is your education you're paying for; don't miss out on the field trips. Even if you feel totally incompetent to make your own demo, it is preferable to get your body into the studio and watch the process if you can. Musicians and engineers do have to take breaks, and you will have the opportunity to strike up relationships that may be mutually beneficial. Perhaps you'll find a collaborator. Maybe one of the musicians is a member of a band that needs material. A good friend of ours wound up marrying the owner of the studio. All she went there for was tape copies! So you never know what connections you might make in a studio. Whatever it is, it wouldn't have happened to you sitting at home staring at your de-

pleted checking account balance.

Third, it's highly unlikely, no matter how good a songwriter you are, that you have twenty hits on your hands at once that need to be demoed right now. You are far better off concentrating on the one or two most powerful songs you have. Take your time and do a bang-up pre-demo. Study the songs currently on the charts. Who do you want to pitch these two hits to? Tape their latest songs off the radio to study their vocal range and "image." Tape songs that have the feel you want on your final demo. Audition vocalists and choose the one you think will best serve the song. Research your recording options; for instance, some studios offer discounts if you buy blocks of time, and some give better rates when business is slow.

If there is no studio close enough for you to be physically present at the recording, use mail order as a last resort. If you're unhappy with the results, at least you'll only be unhappy with two songs, not twenty. We'll cover the subject of how to get the best demo possible from mail-order demo studios in chapter sixty-one, "The Demo Is in the Mail."

Emptying your wallet is not going to make you a better songwriter. Filling your mind with experience will. Don't let any opportunities to learn pass you by. There is so much to learn. That's the great thing about songwriting; it's a never-ending learning process. You can get a lot more learning out of doing fewer demos at one time. It's the difference between wolfing down a meal and savoring every bite. The latter is a more exquisite experience, and it's better for your digestion.

52
....

TOO MANY PRODUCERS SPOIL THE DEMO

Don't let everyone else make your demo decisions

On your obstacle course to songwriting success, you've managed to avoid sinking in the mud puddle of confusion. You've finely focused your ideas and expressed them clearly and with passion. You've asked for input and rewritten as you felt necessary. You've chosen two or three of your best songs to demo. You've asked around and booked a studio that several other writers have highly recommended. The engineer and the musicians are warmed up and ready to roll. What could go wrong now? Plenty.

As the songwriter hiring the studio and the musicians to demo your song, you are officially the producer of that recording session. What does a producer do? We asked Quincy Jones that question. His reply: "There are thousands of decisions to make about the right musicians, the engineer, the studio, the perfect tempo, the right key, the arrangement, the instrumentation, the mood, the feel. Basically, you're trying to bottle lightning all the time."

These thousands of choices can be overwhelming. It's highly likely that the situation will cause decision overload—this is when your eyes roll up in your head and little "tilt" signs appear where your irises used to be. You feel the lights going out in your brain, like a scene from a movie on the New York City blackout. On the outside, you try to look cool. The band plays on to the end of the song, and when everyone looks to you for your opinion, you turn to the engineer and say, "What do you think?"

There's a variation on the old light-bulb riddle that's going around the music business:

Joker: "How many record producers does it take to screw in a light bulb?"

Jokee: "I don't know. How many?"

Joker: "I don't know. What do you think?"

You start collecting opinions. Before you know it, the drummer is producing the drum part, the guitarist is producing the guitar part, the bass player is producing the bass part, the vocalists are producing the vocals, the engineer is producing everyone else's productions, and you're not producing anything but a cold sweat. The confusion compounds if there are several collaborators stirring up the works as well.

The only antidote for this affliction is to know that the purpose of the demo-making process is to realize *your* dream for the song. If you have collaborators, part of preparing to make the demo is to come to a consensus about the direction you all want the song to take. You must agree before you get into the studio either that the same respect and "everyone must be happy" ground rules apply in the demo recording as in your collaboration process, or that one of you should take the lead in the production of the demo. Since every tick of the clock in the studio is usually echoed by chimes of the cash register drawer opening up and swallowing down more of your hard-earned money, the pressure is on. Even so, this is not the time to pass the buck. Someone has to be in charge of the vision for the song. As the songwriter who is paying for the demo session, that honor is yours.

It is one thing to ask for the engineer's opinion or the musician's opinion or the vocalist's opinion. It is another to let them start running the show. As lost as you may feel, it's your responsibility to let the people you are paying know that you value their input but that, ultimately, the decisions are yours to make.

It's a fact of songwriting that the only thing you have to "sell" is your opinion. It's your unique point of view that makes you irreplaceable. Making all the difficult decisions in the writing and demo-making processes is the method by which you educate and refine your opinion. Exercising your decision-making muscles is the only way to build them up. At first, expect your demos to miss the bull's-eye of your hopes for how they should sound. Most producers at the top of the music business charts can think of changes they'd like to make long after their songs have become hits.

Ask successful producers how they know when the recording is right; their answer will probably feature the phrase "gut feeling." They know in their guts when it's right. They were not born with these informed intestines; they developed them through trial and error and by learning from the great talents that went before them. You, too, can have smart guts, and the way to get them is this: When the music stops, you might ask your engineer, "What do you think?" But the answer is just one of the variables you will consider when you ask yourself the most important question of all: What do I think? Then, tune into your own gut reaction.

If you are very new at demo production, and making so many decisions in rapid succession seems an impossible task to you, it may be time to hire someone to act as producer. It will still be up to you to communicate to the best of your ability your idea of how the demo should sound. If you do hire someone, you have to let that person do the job. Of course, you will need to express your opinions about how things are sounding as you go along, but don't drive yourself and everyone else crazy by engaging in a power struggle with the producer during the demo session.

Remember, you're not only paying for this person's experience as a producer, you're paying for your own education. The recording studio is the graduate school of songwriting. Make like a sponge and soak up every bit of information you can. Before long, you will know enough about demo production to take on the exhilarating and challenging job of bottling lightning.

53

BIG-BUDGET BLUES

Don't spend too much money on one demo

The demo is an extremely important part of the songwriting process. It's the only way to have your song heard by people in the music business. Someone might come to a club and hear you sing your song and say, "I love it." But the next sentence will invariably be, "Give me a tape." You cannot overestimate the importance of a good demo. Although there are still a few people in the music business who claim they can "hear" a song through a poorly produced demo, they are rare birds. There's no getting around the necessity of making the best possible demo of your song.

You know this to be true, so you hire the philharmonic and a star vocalist who charges several thousand dollars. Don't laugh! Just such a multi-thousand dollar demo found its way into our workshop. One of the writers was a brewery heir for whom money was no object.

Many writers cannot afford these extremes. All things are relative, though; we've heard a bunch of way-too-expensive demos over the years. There's nothing like going broke to get a person discouraged about being a songwriter, however. The big-budget blues can get you down so low, you don't feel like singing anymore.

When is a demo too expensive, and how does it get that way?

A demo gets too expensive when it's not a demo. Remember, the purpose of the demo is to display the song. It is not meant for commercial release. The more elaborately produced recording that becomes the record is called a "master." The master is mechanically reproduced onto the tapes and CDs that are sold in stores. If you are trying to record a master when you should be making a demo, you will definitely spend too much money.

You will also spend too much money if you spend too much time in the studio. Make as many decisions as you can before you get into the studio and the clock starts ticking your money away. If possible, get a rough demo of the song to the musicians and vocalists before the session.

You will spend too much money if you hire a studio with many more tracks than you need. A good 8-track demo studio is all you need. More tracks in a studio mean more money per hour and more time in the studio filling up all those tracks. Unless you can get a super deal on 16 or 24 tracks, you will be paying for more complexity than you can use on a demo.

Demos can get too expensive without your spending a dime in a recording studio for hire. Many songwriters build demo studios in their homes. This is a great idea if you know when to stop buying equipment. However, some songwriters get hooked on accumulating every new gadget that comes out, and their home studios become black holes that suck in every available dollar. If you intend to use your home studio strictly for demo making, you can do what you need without going nuts in the recording equipment store.

It's a different story if your intention is to produce the finished product in your home. Composer Ray Lynch recorded his *Deep Breakfast* album at home and sold twenty-five thousand copies from his dining room table before being picked up by Music West Records. Songwriting can be a cottage industry. If that's your intention, your investment in sophisticated equipment is warranted.

What are the essential elements of a good demo?

By far the most important element of a good demo is a great vocal. If you can get a special singer to deliver an emotionally convincing performance of the song, you've got 80 percent of what you need in the demo.

The basic tracks usually call for a drummer/drum machine, keyboard/synthesizer or guitar, and an electric bass. "Sweetening" the basic tracks with horns or strings (acoustic or synthesized) is optional. With today's technology, you can make a demo that sounds like it has a full complement of musicians with just one talented person, a sequencer and synthesizers/samplers.

How much money should a writer spend on a demo?

You can get a good demo made in an 8-track MIDI studio for two to three hundred dollars. Half of that should be spent on the lead vocalist. Top-of-the-line singers, who are often up-and-coming artists themselves, are well worth it. Their gift of making every note and word sound heartfelt will add tremendously to the impact of your demo. We're not talking about mail-order demos here. You'll find them in a later chapter.

What are some ways to cut demo-making costs?

Collaborating cuts costs by spreading the cost of hiring outside studios among the collaborators. Collaborating with someone who has a home studio is a good way to cut costs. Make sure you bring something to the collaboration as well, so friction doesn't develop because of unequal contributions. For instance, you can supply the recording tape.

Shop around before you hire a studio, as rates and services offered vary. Ask about lower prices for "down" time; some studios are eager to sell certain "undesirable" time slots. Some studios are also willing to make deals for lower prices if you hire them for several blocks of time. Make sure you find out what equipment and services are included. Is there a separate charge for the engineer? If you have to pay for the tape, how much will it cost? Perhaps you can bring in your own tape and save money.

If you are hiring a studio, the best way to economize is to do as much preparation as possible before you enter the studio. Have your chord sheets clearly written and copied for everyone who needs one. Know what "feel" you're going for and be ready to communicate that to the musicians and vocalists. A good way to do this is to play a tape of an already successful song with the desired "feel." Make sure your lead vocalist has a copy of your rough demo well in advance of the session so she can be familiar with the song. When the session starts, get down to business and keep focused and positive. This is some of the best fun you will ever have with your clothes on. Enjoy it.

54
·········

JUST JAM IT

Have a clear idea of the feel and sound you're going for in the demo

Once upon a time, there were four musicians: a drummer, a bass player, a piano player and a guitarist. These musicians were being paid a substantial fee by a songwriter. The songwriter figured that if the musicians could charge so much money, they should be able to perform magic. The songwriter called the musicians together in a recording studio and said, "Play and make beautiful music together." And they lived unhappily ever after.

Believing in the fairy tale that musicians make music by magic is a good way to enlarge your demo-recording studio bill. It can seem like magic among the top-of-the-line musicians working in music industry centers who make their living as studio musicians. These musicians can read charts and are ready to start laying down tracks within a half hour of encountering a song. You can expect to pay each of these top musicians fifty to one hundred dollars for each song.

Even if you are dealing with musicians of this calibre, you can't expect them to know how you want your demo to sound. You must let them know what you want. This presumes that you have first decided what you want. Here are some questions to answer that will help you decide:

- Which artists would I like to record this song?

- Is this a pop, rock, R&B, country, New Age, jazz or inspirational song?

- What records have the feel I would like in this song?

- What tempo do I want for this song?

- What instruments do I want on this demo?

Once you have answered these questions for yourself, you can tell your musicians the answers. You must provide them with chord sheets. A chord sheet is not the same as a lead sheet or sheet music. You need not write down every single note. Just indicate rhythms and chord changes.

An example of the kind of chord sheet we use is shown on page 90. In Nashville, they use a dif-

ferent style because the musicians play by numbers. The vocalists are given lyric sheets with numbers—for example, 1, 2, 3, . . . 8—above the lyrics to indicate the pitch of each melody note. The numbers of the chords are written below the lyrics, or just written out on a sheet of paper for the musicians. The chord numbers can be in Arabic (1, 4, 5, 1) or Roman numerals (I, IV, V, I).

It helps to play pieces of several records that have the feel you want for your demo. As our friend Harold Payne wrote in a song, "Music speaks louder than words." This is true when it comes to communicating your song, too. Playing the song on the spot is one way to show the musicians the song. It's even better if you have a rough demo to play. The rough demo process gives you time to work out the little touches that add to your song, such as hooky riffs between the vocal lines.

After communicating as much as you can, sit back and let the musicians add those things that never occurred to you. They didn't get to be top studio musicians for no reason! They will have special gifts to offer, and you would be foolish to get so stuck in your own ideas that you aren't open to their suggestions. However, don't lose sight of the fact that you have the final word.

Not everyone in every town is lucky enough to have access to musicians this talented. Unless you are sure that the musicians you hire are very fast and very good, it will probably be worth your while and save money on studio time if you arrange to have a rehearsal a day or two before the actual recording date. This will give you time to work out the arrangements of the songs before the recording studio clock starts ticking. Rehearsing is necessary if you are dealing with a group of musicians who are not used to playing with each other, that is, musicians who are not members of the same band. Bands already have their musical communication lines in place. Individual musicians have to spend a little extra time setting up those lines of communication.

Unless you are an excellent musician yourself or your intention is to be a writer/artist/musician on your own recording, don't play on your own demo. You will have enough decisions to make without having to worry about your performance as well. It's fine to get in the studio with the musicians and play the song with them a couple of times to show them some of your ideas, but once they have the ball rolling, let them run with it.

If you take time to decide what you want in your demo and you communicate that clearly to the musicians you hire, you have a much greater chance of being happy with the results. You are asking for trouble if you expect it to just come together magically, but do leave some room for the magic that can happen spontaneously in the studio.

55

SELF-SUNG DEMO HERO

Avoid singing the demo yourself; hire a dynamite singer

Clothes may or may not make the person, but lead vocals definitely *do* make the demo. We know you love to sing your songs. We love to hear songwriters singing their songs. The National Academy of Songwriters produces a concert series called "A Salute to the American Songwriter." It's magical to hear the writers of the fabulous songs you live and die by singing their own creations. You come to view these people as national treasures for the contributions they have made to our culture.

In that situation, it's endearing that some of these people can barely sing. You love them all the more for getting up in front of so many people to display their vulnerability and love for what they do. But when these writers make demos of their songs, you can bet they don't sing on them. Barry Mann can sing (who can forget him on "Who Put the Bomp?"), but when he and Cynthia Weil made the demo for "Just Once," they hired a hot demo singer. The demo singer was James Ingram, and that demo was his ticket to a record deal. Our friend Ben Weisman, who has written fifty-two platinum-record songs for Elvis Presley, once played a demo of a song he wrote and Elvis recorded. The demo singer was a session guitarist named Glen Campbell. Take a tip from the writers on top: Don't sing on your own demos.

Of course, it's a different story if your goal is to be a writer/artist, and you intend to be the one who ultimately records your songs. If you can honestly listen to your own vocal performance on the song and judge it to be outstanding, by all means sing on your own demos. But if you have to admit that you're just an okay singer, go out and hire yourself some dynamite. It will be well worth the investment. An outstanding lead vocal is the single most important part of your demo.

If you write songs for other artists to record, you need to do your homework. Every song has a personality. The song itself calls out for a certain type of voice to sing its message. Who should record the song you have written? Male or female? Big, raspy growl or light, young tone? Are there long, high notes that require an advanced mastery of breath control? Have a clear picture of the vocal sound your song requires.

Now, to find the perfect singer. Ask around among your songwriting friends. Listen to singers in clubs and choirs. Ask for samples of their singing skills on tape. Singers who want to make money doing demos should be ready with such tapes. Get to know as many singers as you can for future reference, as each of your songs will call for a different voice.

When you've chosen the singer for the current demo, give that person a rough demo and lyrics of the song you're about to record. Allow sufficient time for the singer to get to know the song.

At last you are in the studio, ready to record the all-important lead vocal. Before the singer sings one note, you need to focus on the emotional content of the song. As the producer of the recording session, you are very much like the director on a movie set. You let everyone know what's happening in the story and how you want them to act. Talk about the situation of the song, about the feeling you want the singer to go for, about the dynamics (loudness and softness) of the various parts of the song. Talk the entire song out before you try to record it the first time. Don't expect to catch the song on the first take. The singer will be warming up to the song and getting comfortable in the recording situation.

After the initial take, talk about what you loved in the performance *first*. The singer needs encouragement and support in order to take the risks involved in an outstanding performance. After you praise the performance, point out areas where you'd like changes. Try a second recording. Again, praise first, then ask specifically for certain changes. Once you get a basically good take, you can "punch in" the particular lines that you feel need improvement.

Just remember the Golden Rule when you're dealing with your singer, and you will get the best results. When someone is putting their creativity on the line, the last thing they need is a disparaging remark. Don't say, "You're flat," when you could just as easily say, "Let's try that line again," and demonstrate, either by singing or playing on an instrument, the notes in question. Only an atmosphere of trust and respect will allow an outstanding performance to come through your singer. It's up to you to provide that atmosphere.

When you have that excellent lead vocal on your demo and compare it to your own rough demo, you'll be glad you hired someone else to sing it. Having a "set of pipes" is a wonderful gift; so is the gift of being able to write great songs. They don't necessarily come in the same package. Part of the pleasure of being a songwriter is giving others an opportunity to express their gifts through your songs. Everyone benefits. You have a great demo. The singer has a great work sample. And if the singer happens to be an artist who is shopping for a record deal, this demo may be a ticket to the top of the charts for both of you.

56

....

LITTLE VOICE LOST

Put the vocal up front in the mix

Musicians love to hear themselves play. You can't blame them. If they didn't love it, they wouldn't be doing it. If you're a songwriter who is also a musician, you know what we mean. You put a lot of creativity and work into the chords and melody of your songs. Then, when it's time to make a demo, you're the one who plays the keyboard, the guitar or the bass. Your performance of the music is extremely important to you. You have every right to be proud of what you create and to want everyone to hear it.

But sometimes this desire to be heard can cloud your judgment when it comes to mixing down the demo. You want so much for everyone to notice that terrific chord change—or that great lead guitar lick, or that fantastic drum track—that you can't find it in your heart to pull back the faders on those tracks. It just sounds so great to you.

You know the vocal is important. You may have gone to the trouble and expense of hiring a great singer to do the lead vocal. Still, that doesn't make you want to put your music in the background. It can all be up front, can't it?

The answer is *no*. In a demo, something has to be up front and something has to be in back. And the something that has to be up front is, without a doubt, the lead vocal. If the lead vocal is overpowered by the musical instruments, the melody and the lyrics are lost to the listener. In a demo, that's the same as saying the song is lost.

Many people are familiar with the famous Japanese film, *Rashomon*. Three characters in the film tell the story of the same event, which they all experienced together. However, each one tells an entirely different story. The point is that we see things the way we want to see them. We also hear things the way we want to hear them.

A musician/songwriter may hear more than enough vocal interfering with the music in the demo. That songwriter is surprised when others respond to the demo with, "I couldn't hear the vocal," or, "I think the vocal should be more up front." If you have had this experience, you have some psychological factors working against you. You can remedy the situation by putting the vocal much further up front than you think it should go, thereby getting it where it needs to be. Or you can

ask for feedback from other people in the mixing process and rely on their less prejudiced perceptions.

Musician/songwriters aren't the only ones who need to be aware of the placement of the vocal in the mix. Many nonmusician songwriters get so entranced with all the new toys in the studio that they lose sight of the essence of the song. Unless a song *is* an instrumental—a song with no lyrics— the essence of the song is its message. The message is conveyed by the music, yes. The emotional feel of the arrangement communicates the message as well. But the bulk of the message is contained in the lyrics and the melody. It is the vocal delivery of that message with all of its emotional content that sells the song. If you bury that vocal, you're selling your song short.

Picture the song as it is being performed by Whitney Houston, for example. The curtain rises and the orchestra begins to play. Now, where is Whitney? Is she sitting down among the violin players? Is she back there with the kettle drums? Oh no, she's right up front and center, glittering in a skintight gown. All eyes are on her and all ears hear her voice towering above the musical instruments. That's the right place for the singer to be, both on the stage and in your demo.

57

·········

THE KEY'S THE THING

Be sure to lay the tracks in the singer's key

It used to be that all demos were made by live musicians. A person banging away on an actual drum set, another whole person playing bass, and a guitarist and/or piano player were needed to lay down the basic rhythm tracks. Back in the bad old days, we learned one lesson the hard way. We had a song and a friend who is an excellent singer (she went on to tour with Ray Charles for years). She agreed to sing the demo for us. We laid the basic rhythm tracks in the studio, then invited her in.

We discovered, to our great chagrin, that we had recorded the tracks in a key that didn't suit her voice. She tried singing it high; it was too high. An octave lower was too low. Finally, she went for the higher octave, but the demo was never right. She couldn't hit some of the notes with the conviction that we needed. You only need to waste a couple of hundred dollars like this once. It's not a lesson you forget.

Some demos are still made the old-fashioned

way: they *play* it and record direct to tape. Also, simple piano/vocal demos or guitar/vocal demos are based on tape recording the tones produced by the musicians. In these cases, it is crucial to choose the correct key for your vocalist before you record the first note on tape. And it's a more subtle choice than just, "Can the singer hit all these notes?"

If you're going to make a great demo, you want a great vocal performance. You have to tell the vocalist exactly what kind of emotional atmosphere you want to create in the song. Knowing the singer's high note, range, or the note where falsetto voice kicks in is not enough. If you want a certain lyric line to be expressed forcefully, you have to know if the singer can go beyond just hitting the note to pushing it, punching it, growling it, screaming it, or whatever it takes to deliver the emotion you choose.

The only way to know these things is to test the song with the singer *before* you go to tape. Quincy Jones is not the only producer to tell us that choice of key is a make-it or break-it proposition for a song, but his word alone is good enough for us. If you are using live musicians, get the musicians and the vocalist in the studio together to pick the key. If this isn't possible, get a tape of the song to the singer and try to communicate verbally the kind of performance you want. Describe the vocal quality you want in the song. Point out the areas where you want the most intensity and ask the singer to tell you what key he thinks is best.

Some of the worry about choosing the key has been eliminated by modern technology. Today, many songs start out as information in a computer. MIDI sequencer technology frees you from worry about key because you can change the key with the push of a button. If you are using MIDI sequencer technology, you can create the basic rhythm tracks and store them on disks or hard drive. When your singer comes in, you just push a button to try several keys until you find the right one.

After the perfect key for your singer is selected, the basic tracks information in the computer is put on tape. You then record the singer on the tape. It's best to have the lead vocal before you start to build the rest of the tracks. Then, add your backup vocals and any "sweetening" (that is, additional arrangements with synthesized or acoustical instruments) you want. Remember, your musical setting needs to highlight and accent (maybe even praise) the vocal performance, not bury it.

58

....

GIVE ME A BIG BREAK

*Don't put long instrumental breaks
in a song demo*

Songwriters love songs. We all have our favorites, and we can't help but emulate the songs we think are the best. We go to concerts and see the bands in action: They begin with a long instrumental lead-in as the audience roars in recognition and the lead singer bows in response; the lead guitarist wails away on a long solo; the drummer takes a minute to show off in midsong; the song ends with many repetitions of the chorus as the lead singer improvises variations. We buy tapes or CDs and listen to and thoughtfully study what's going on in these five- to seven-minute songs. And we get some very wrong ideas about how to present a song.

Then we engage our local demo studio and call together the musicians. We ask for a long instrumental lead-in, a couple of solos midsong by the lead guitarist and drummer we've hired, and choruses ad infinitum until the demo is seven minutes long. All this, of course, takes extra time and money, but it's worth it, isn't it? Now our song sounds like our favorite band.

The trouble is, we've probably just bought a one-way ticket to the eject button on the publisher's tape deck. Time is at a premium for everyone in our mad, mad world. Ask almost anyone about their time and they'll tell you how busy they are, how much they have to do, how they can't get around to doing a zillion things they think they should.

A publisher or producer's time is like that to the tenth power. The good ones want to give songwriters a chance, and they really make an effort to listen to the mountain of tapes on their desks, around their desks, under their desks. Every minute is golden. When they pop in a cassette, eager to hear a hit song, and you make them wait through a minute or even thirty seconds of wheel spinning, you are not winning your way into their hearts. By thirty seconds, you should be through the first verse and into the hook. They want to be knocked out of their chairs and *fast*.

The same is true of long, midsong instrumental breaks and long end-of-song productions. If you are a songwriter showing a song with the intent of getting an artist to record it, give them the song, the whole song, and nothing but the song. Get in fast, get to the hook fast, get it over with as soon as you have demonstrated the key elements in the song. Catchy, quick instrumental riffs should be included; long instrumental solos should not.

Many of the greatest rock 'n roll classics of the fifties were under two minutes long. Those songs are packed with so much fun that two minutes feel like forever. Check out the Leiber and Stoller classics "Charley Brown," "Alley Oop," "Love Potion Number 9," and "You Ain't Nothing but a Hound Dog" for sterling examples of how to get to the point quickly, stick to it, and make it in a big way. Use them as models for making your song

demos and leave the extended productions to the producer of the ultimate commercial recording.

You enhance your chances of having your song recorded if you use your demo to show the song in its most concentrated form. The professional listener will appreciate the subliminal message you send when your demo is short and sweet: "I appreciate and value your time."

While you have your stopwatch out, try timing the songs you hear on the radio. This is not the same world as the concert hall or the album you listen to at your leisure in your home. For a radio station, songs are vehicles to get the audience from one commercial to the next. Some stations like to brag about how many songs they play in a row. These are short songs, usually around three minutes in length. The radio stations don't mention that between these blocks of songs they play just as many or more commercials back-to-back.

Radio makes songs into commercial successes. If you sell a million records, you do it because people heard your song on the radio and liked it enough to pay for what they can just as easily get for free. But the money you earn from selling a million records is just a fraction of the money you earn from performance royalties for radio airplay. A close study of the types and lengths of songs used on the radio station that you want your songs to play on would be an excellent investment of your time.

The entire picture changes if you intend to sell yourself as a performing artist, especially as a self-contained band. In that case, you *do* need to show off your potential as a live performing group. You're selling more than the song, you're selling yourselves as an image, a lifestyle. You're selling *your* expertise as musicians, *your* ability to carry off an extended performance on the song. Even so, remember that time is money at record companies, and use your judgment about how long you draw your songs out in your presentation.

When you're in the demo studio, keep time on your side.

59

A BIG OVERPRODUCTION

Keep your demo uncluttered

Letting a songwriter loose in a demo studio is like letting a toddler loose in Toys 'R Us. There's no end to the toys that can be gathered and played with. Samplers and synthesizers enable us to create full orchestras right in our own bedrooms or garages. It's such fun, why don't we add this, and that, and that!

When a songwriter gets carried away in the studio, the result is something like what an artist gets when she mixes all the colors of paint together: mud. When everything sounds the same because all the parts of the song have every possible instrument going at once, the ear takes a little nap. It says, "Wake me up when something new and different happens."

The song demo can be viewed as a work of art in time. For convenience, let's break the song down into three-second pieces. If the average song is three minutes long, we should have sixty of these three-second pieces. You could draw a line graph of what's going on in each of these time intervals with the height of the line determined by the number of instruments playing. If everything is going on at once all the time, your graph will be a straight line.

Variety is the spice of life and of demos. A straight line doesn't offer variety. A graph with peaks and valleys does. To make your demo interesting, you need to add a pinch of guitar lick here, a bit of drum pattern there, a background vocal in this spot, a hooky lick on a saxophone right there. These little touches can be repeated as appropriate.

Don't let even these light touches get in the way of your lead vocal. The lead vocal is the gem in the center of your setting; the licks, riffs, rolls, and solos are the little stones surrounding it that are meant to show off the centerpiece in the best way.

You are less likely to get carried away in a studio that you have hired by the hour. That situation has the built-in restraint of the ticking clock and access to feedback from the engineer and musicians you hire. But left alone in your home studio, it is easy to let yourself go. You paid good money for all these toys, and you want to use them.

You need to separate the playing that you do to please yourself and the playing you do to serve the demo. This requires a level of objectivity that is sometimes difficult to achieve. Asking for feedback from someone you trust and whose opinion you value is a way to get around the problem of subjectivity. Play your demo and ask if there is any place in the demo where your listener's interest lags. It helps to hear your song through another's ears.

It also helps to listen to the radio and take note of the way songs are arranged. The songwriters who come to our workshops are always amazed when we play tapes from our collection of original demos of hit songs. You can literally hear the record in the demo. The riffs, the arrangements, the vocals—they're all there. They're in a less finished form, but definitely there. So what you hear on the radio is usually what was on the demo.

When you're making a demo, use a light and tasty touch. The important thing is quality, not quantity, of sound.

60
·········
CAN'T STOP NOW

Don't continue to work when the session is going badly

Let's say that you've done your homework; you've planned and prepared your demo recording session. You've hired the musicians and the vocalist. You've supplied them all with rough demos of the song/s, and you've given them an idea of the kind of feel you want. You plan to record three songs, so you've booked the studio for six hours to record the instrumental tracks. The musicians arrive in the studio on time, and you go right to work.

The session starts off fine, and you're happy with the way things are going. After three hours, you realize that you only have one song down and two to go with half the time left. You start to panic and get impatient with the inevitable delays. You pressure the whole situation and call an end to all coffee breaks. You find out that the studio is available for a couple of hours after your session is supposed to end, so you push on past your time.

Now you're dealing with tired, harassed, and even angry musicians. The engineer is starting to mutter unpleasantries. The situation has gotten out of hand, and it's your responsibility. This is what happens when you get so fixated on how you think things should be that you can't see how they really are.

The same thing can happen when you book the session to record the lead vocals. Expect to spend about three hours on each song on the lead vocal alone. Remember, the lead vocal is the most important ingredient of your demo. If you don't push the singer to take some risks, you won't get an exciting performance. But if you push the singer too long or too hard, you will destroy your chances of getting a salvageable performance.

From start to finish, recording sessions are 100 percent emotion. As the producer of the session, whether it's in a hired studio or in your own home studio, it's your job to be sensitive to the emotional tone of what's going on. If it doesn't feel good while you're doing it, chances are it won't sound good.

Even after you have the tracks down and the musicians and singers are gone, you still run the risk of doing your songs a disservice if you rush the mixing process or push past the emotional and physical limits of the engineer and yourself. Many songwriters who are new to the recording process are shocked to find that the mixing process takes as long as laying the tracks. That is, if it takes two or three hours for the instrumentals and three hours for the vocal, expect to take six hours to do the mixing. These time estimates presume you are working with competent professional musicians and vocalists.

In fact, some songwriters are shocked to the point of disbelief. Whenever we do a workshop in another city, we interview local people who work in the music business. We want to show the participating songwriters that people in their own hometown are actively involved in making music. In Santa Fe, we invited James Townsend, a singer/songwriter who had produced his own cassette album and who was selling it locally and getting airplay on local radio stations. We asked him, "What was the biggest lesson you learned in this process?" His immediate response was, "The mixing took much longer than I expected."

The day before, we had interviewed the owner of the recording studio where the album was cut, Max Highstein. Max explained his approach to such projects. He talked about how he sits down with the songwriter and discusses the kind of music the songwriter has in mind. Then he gives the songwriter an estimate of how long it will take and how much it will cost.

So we asked James, "Didn't Max tell you that the mixing would take a long time?" James said, "Yes, but I didn't believe him." If you haven't been through it, it *is* hard to believe. But believe us, we're not exaggerating. Laying down the tracks is only the beginning. The recording is really made in the mix.

Mixing entails sitting down listening to the same song over and over and over again as you: get the sound of each and every instrument exactly the way you want it; build a frequency balance among all the instruments; compress or limit the vocal and place it prominently in the mix; pan tracks left, right, or center; adjust volume levels; and generally whip the song into a cohesive sound image that is constantly interesting. It is exhausting work and requires a tremendous amount of concentration.

There is also the physical reality of fatigue. Your ears do get tired of listening; the nerves don't fire as well. To minimize loss of hearing sensitivity, we recommend that you do your mixing at low sound levels. If it sounds good when the volume is down low, it will sound good when it's loud.

Any creative process is really a series of decisions. Recording a demo involves nonstop decision making. Each of us has his own level of tolerance for this kind of intense mental work. It's up to us to stay in tune with ourselves and those we hire so we know when to take a break. A quick walk out in the fresh air may be all you need. Or you may need to come back another day. When the session is not going well, it is far better to call it a day than to antagonize everyone involved.

There comes a moment in the demo-making process when the most important thing to know is when to stop.

61
·········

THE DEMO IS IN THE MAIL
Make the best of mail-order demos

We've had songwriters tell us that they have sent off ten or twenty songs to a mail-order demo service, along with a great big check, only to receive a great big disappointment in the mail a couple of weeks later.

Making demos of your songs is an important part of the learning process we call songwriting. Because there is so much to learn in the studio, we recommend that you participate personally in the process. If you think that's impossible because you live far away from any recording facilities or because you feel you are not technically inclined enough to do your own recording at home, think again.

There is probably a recording studio near you no matter where you live. Magazines that cater to the recording studio industry publish annual directories that list entities in business as recording studios. In *Billboard* magazine's *International Recording Equipment and Studio Directory*, studios are listed in every state except North Dakota.

Wherever there is a radio station, there is recording equipment. Some local cable TV stations

make their facilities available for free to the public. Perhaps you can approach your local radio station about the possibility of using their audio recording facilities.

Networking and collaborating with other songwriters can put you in touch with people who do not operate official recording studio businesses, but who are willing to help you record your project. The proliferation of easy-to-use, in-home recording studio equipment has made the process possible even for those of us who are all thumbs when it comes to switches and knobs. With a little money and a little more experimentation, you, too, can record your own demos—at least your own rough demos.

If, after researching your possibilities, you still feel that you want to have your demos made by a studio that does mail-order demos, you're going to need that rough demo. When you order a demo by mail, you are not there to give any input during the process. Therefore, you need to make your input up-front as clear as possible. Making a rough demo with at least an indication of the feel and the parts you want included will go a long way toward ensuring the final product is something you can live with.

How do you find a mail-order demo studio? Be sure your source is a legitimate songwriter-servicing organization, such as NAS's *Songtalk* magazine or the Los Angeles Songwriters Showcase's *Musepaper*. Call your nearest songwriters' organization for recommendations. Don't confuse a legitimate mail-order demo service with a song shark. A legitimate mail-order demo service will *not* promise to make you a star, release a record of your song, or charge you an exorbitant fee.

Mail-order demo services will send you a sample tape of their work on request. Some charge a five-dollar fee for the sample tape, which can be applied to your demo bill if you decide to use their service. These demo services will offer you a choice of instrumentation. The more instruments you want, the more the demo will cost.

We know of a wonderful mail-order demo service that delivers excellent full rhythm section demos for $125. That's reasonable, because the going rate is closer to $175 for a fully produced demo. We've seen ads for piano or guitar/vocal demos for as low as thirty dollars, but we wonder what quality you could possibly be getting. At that price, the demo maker has to record the song in one take to make any money.

It's a rare song that will impress the professional listener with just a piano or guitar vocal demo. That's because these days, most professional listeners have no imagination. They want the finished product, or as close as you can get to it, handed to them on a silver platter. If you do have to go with a simple guitar or piano demo, you absolutely have to have a dynamite singer to do the lead vocal. We doubt the thirty-dollar demo maker has a knockout voice, or he wouldn't be sitting at home cranking out cheap demos.

Research several mail-order demo services by phone or mail. They will gladly furnish you with information about their recording equipment, instruments and services available. Some demo services specialize in certain styles, such as country. Ask the demo service what styles of music they do best. Check with them about what information they need from you. Ask for a sample tape of their work.

When you have made your choice, send as much information as possible about your song and how you want it demoed. The more you communicate, the better your chances are of getting what you want. Your package should include:

- A rough demo of the song
- A neatly typed lyric sheet
- A chord sheet—a lead sheet is not necessary
- Instructions about the feel you want in the demo, including references to recognizable songs, and possibly a recording of a song that you want your demo to sound like
- Your choice of male or female lead vocal
- Your choice of instrumentation
- A money order for the cost of recording the demo; projects paid for by personal checks are not recorded until after the checks clear the bank
- Send the package certified mail (return receipt not necessary) so you can trace it if the post office loses it

We recommend that you try a mail-order demo service on only one song at first. If you don't like the product, you can change to another service for the next song. If you send a bunch of songs at once, you may be stuck with a bunch of demos you don't like.

We hope your mail-order demos have the zip you want.

PART SEVEN

ALLOW ME TO PRESENT MY SONG

Pitching Package Pratfalls

62

....

NO WAY IN

Don't seal your demo package with a roll of tape and a thousand staples

We've opened countless tape packages while helping NAS with their song review service and various song competitions. You wouldn't believe the lengths some writers go to in packaging their tapes for mailing.

One package started out with an 11×14-inch padded envelope that was secured by twenty or thirty staples. Having fought past that, we were greeted with a similar envelope, only smaller. Frazzled and covered with mangled staples, we found the tape inside the smaller envelope. It was wrapped tightly in seven layers of plastic bubble wrap, secured by full-mummy wrap of fiber-reinforced packaging tape.

By now we had cultivated a distinct dislike for the song inside, whatever it was, and an even deeper dislike for the songwriter, whoever he or she was. Dedicated listeners that we are, we hunted up a pair of scissors and cut our way through this last barrier. Finally, panting from our efforts, we got the tape in the deck and got what we expected, a song that contained most of the mistakes in this book. If only the writer had taken as much care in writing the song as in wrapping it up.

This is just one of many stories about impregnable tape packages we could tell you, stories about styrofoam, rubber bands, boxes within boxes, duct tape and more. Professional listeners at publishing companies and record labels deal with hundreds and hundreds of tapes, as well as thousands of other details in their jobs. They simply don't have the time to struggle through bizarre packaging barriers.

Building a fortress around your tape is an expression of tremendous insecurity. It sends a message to the listener that you are terribly worried about this tape. It must be protected by many layers of nonbiodegradable materials. As much money as possible must be spent to ship it. It tells the listener in no uncertain terms that you do not care one bit about making his or her job a little easier by allowing easy access to your precious

tape. In short, it plainly states that you do not have a professional attitude.

If you've been building the unbreakable tape package, now's the time to stop. You need to relax your grip on your songs. You want other people to hear them. Show that you have some consideration for the listener by making your package easy to get into. The best presentation package is the simplest: a brief cover letter, a lyric sheet, a cassette tape (without the plastic box) in a letter-sized envelope with a little piece of tape across the flap of the envelope in case the glue doesn't hold.

The inclusion of a self-addressed, stamped envelope (S.A.S.E.) for the return of your tape is optional. We found that most publishers didn't return the tape anyway, so we were out the cost of the envelope and the stamp. We decided that including the S.A.S.E. sent a message that we assumed the listener would want to return our tape. We prefer the message that the listener will want to keep our tape. So we stopped including the S.A.S.E.

Hounding the listener for the return of your tape is a sure way to earn his or her eternal animosity. We think of demo tapes as our calling cards—bread on the waters of the music business. Let them go (keeping a record of where you sent them for your information and for tax deductions); you never know what will come back to you. Here's a story to illustrate the value of letting go:

A songwriter we know had decided to quit trying. She packed her recording equipment in boxes and put it in storage. While she was putting things away, she came across some demo tape copies and sent them off to a couple of people, just to get rid of them. The owner of an independent record label in Nashville liked her songs and called her. The last we heard, she had a record on the country charts and had married the record company owner.

It's not the wrapping around your tape that establishes it as precious; it's what's on the tape. Put your utmost effort into the writing of the song and the production of the demo, but when it comes to packaging the tape for mailing, make it easy on yourself and the potential listener.

63

NOT MY TYPE

Don't send handwritten lyric sheets

One of the essential parts of a tape presentation package is the lyric sheet. Every lyric sheet tells a story about the songwriter who sent it. There's the frantic tale told by the lyric sheet that's been scribbled in pencil on a page from a spiral notebook, then ripped out and thrown in with the tape. Doubtless the songwriter was in a big hurry to get somewhere else and just threw the package together on the way to more important things.

There's the lyric sheet that's ever so neatly printed in teeny tiny letters, done with a teeny tiny pen, presumably by a teeny tiny songwriter.

Have you heard the one about the lyric sheet that's hand-printed semilegibly on hotel stationery? It's even more interesting when some of the words are crossed out and rewrites are added for that extra plot twist.

For those whose tastes run to horror, there's the frightening tale of the invisible lyric sheet. This is a tale of two possibilities: There is no lyric sheet at all in the package, or there is one, but it is the twenty-fifth generation copy of a light original that has slipped into a dimension somewhere between visibility and a blank sheet of paper.

The more sophisticated lyric sheet stories always involve a dramatic device called a typewriter (or for computer buffs, a word processor and printer). Even with these, songwriters will find a way to make their lyric sheets difficult to read. Some of these are the lyric sheet war stories, where the words are typed in one long run-on sentence. This margin-to-margin smokescreen of words camouflages the song structure.

Others go to the opposite extreme. They want so much for the reader to know each and every component of the structure and how it relates to the whole. They label every few lines—Verse I, Verse II, Prechorus, Chorus, Bridge, Verse III, Prechorus, Repeat Chorus, Repeat Bridge, Repeat, Repeat, and so on—until there are more part names on the sheet than lyrics.

Some songwriters like to create an air of mystery. They'll leave clues but don't want to give away "who done it." Their lyric sheets are cleanly typed and beautifully copied. However, the only identifying feature on the lyric sheet is their publishing company's name, which may or may not be registered with a performance rights society. An interested publisher may not be interested in trying to find out who the writer is and how she or he may be contacted.

Some songwriters like to spell *everything* out. They insert handwritten letters over their typed lyrics indicating chord changes: F, C, G, F, C, G, and so forth. Sometimes the insertion of chord names partially obscures the typed lyrics, calling for an extra deciphering effort. Imagine how a publisher welcomes this. Even when confined to the space between the lyric lines, the chord names create a cluttered, confused look on the lyric sheet.

We're not making up these stories, faithful readers. We have examples of every one of them right before us as we write.

Make sure that everything your lyric sheet has to say about you is good. It should say, "Here is a person who cares enough about songwriting to type the lyrics out so that the structure of the song is clear. This songwriter wants to be contacted if there's interest in the song; here is a name, address and telephone number. This songwriter knows something about the music business, because here is a copyright notice.''

For all those songwriters with sad lyric sheet tales to tell, we wrote a little song. It's called ''Example of a Lyric Sheet'' and it goes something like this (actually, it goes exactly like this):

EXAMPLE OF A LYRIC SHEET
by Fred Music and Sylvia Lyricist

All lyric sheets should be typed
On standard sized paper (8½ × 11-inch)
With the title and the authors at the top

    THE CHORUS SHOULD BE IN CAPITAL LETTERS
    OR INDENTED, OR BOTH;
    IN VERSE/BRIDGE STRUCTURE
    THE TITLE SHOULD BE IN CAPS

Include your name, address and telephone number
At the bottom of the page
Under the copyright notice

    CHORUS: repeat

The bridge reminds you to completely circle the ©
In the copyright notice; (parentheses) won't do

    CHORUS: repeat

©Fred Music and Sylvia Lyricist
    (or you may use your company name)

Fred Music and Sylvia Lyricist
100 Hit City Lane
Recordville, USA 10000
(111) 111-1111

Okay, so it doesn't rhyme, but it does show how a lyric sheet should look. Your lyric sheet says who you are to the publisher or producer. If it's less than professional looking, the listener may take one look and say back to it, "You're not my type."

64
·········

READ THIS LEAD SHEET

Don't send the lyrics on a four-page lead sheet

We are often presented with songs in our workshops that have been written out on six or seven sheets of paper full of hand-drawn musical staffs. The song is fully written out in musical notation, every note in every chord is there for all to see, as are vocal harmonies, chord names, dynamics and, buried in the midst of all this, the lyrics. Of course, to fit below the proper notes, the lyrics must be hy-phen-a-ted.

Henry Mancini told us that he used to hand-draw all his staffs in the very beginning of his career. But he did that only because he didn't know he could buy paper with staffs already printed on it. So you are in great company with your hand-drawn staffs. With today's technology, even handwritten notes on printed staffs are obsolete. There are computers that will produce laser printouts of ready-to-print sheet music at the touch of a button. The problem is, no one in the music business wants to see your staffs, hand-drawn or printed.

You want your song to be taken seriously. You might think that creating a complicated lead sheet will impress the professional listener with your seriousness. The listener will be impressed, all right — impressed with how much time and energy you wasted and how out of touch you are with how songs are being pitched in today's market. Pitching fully written lead sheets went out with the days when songwriters actually went into music publishers' offices and played their songs on pianos. Practically none of the professional listeners that you pitch to today can read music.

Putting your song in lead sheet form does more than waste your time. It makes your demo presentation package harder to handle. Instead of a nice, neatly typed one-page lyric sheet, the listener is now fumbling with three or four pieces of paper that either fall apart and fly to every corner of the office or are taped together in a way that is reminiscent of a road map and impossible to refold.

Publishers and producers don't want to have to sift through sheets and sheets of paper and endless hyphens to follow the lyric. They don't care one bit about your skills in writing down a musical arrangement. They just want to listen to your tape and be totally knocked out by your song. They want a nice, clean, uncluttered lyric sheet to glance at while they listen. So, save the trees by limiting your demo tape presentation to one pithy cover letter, one lyric sheet, and one outer envelope. You might even check into recycled paper and save a tree.

You used to need a lead sheet to register your song with the Copyright Office in Washington, D.C., but that has changed. Now all you need is a copy of the song on tape. We like to include a lyric sheet with the tape on our copyright registrations, but it isn't required.

Don't let your urge to impress lead you to do unnecessary work. Concentrate on putting all of your energy into the important tasks, writing the best possible song and making the best possible demo.

65

SAVING THE BEST FOR LAST

Don't put your best song at the end of a twelve-song demo tape

There's something we want to say in this chapter, but we don't want to say it just yet. We're going to beat around the bush for a while. It doesn't really matter what we say here, because we're going to say something very important later—much later, in fact. We just want you to wade through a lot of words first. Maybe it will be boring. You might even get a little mad at us for putting you through all this. We really don't care about that. You've got plenty of time, haven't you?

We could keep this kind of much ado about nothing up for a great number of paragraphs, maybe even pages. You'll have to be patient with us. We'll get around to the point sometime. We are taking the time and trouble, after all, to write all this stuff, and you owe it to us to read it whether you think it's good or not.

Here we are in paragraph number three. This isn't our best writing, but we expect you to keep slugging away at it. There's going to be something great at the end, so just keep reading. We'll get to it eventually. How would you appreciate it if you didn't have to go through some trouble to get at it?

Have you ever noticed that your mind begins to wander when you're getting bored? Bet you have the urge to shut this book right now and go do something else that would be more fun. Do you think life is about having fun? Where would this world be if everyone thought that?

Okay, joke's over. Wasn't very funny, was it? What we've been doing here is trying to give you the emotional experience of the publisher or producer who is sent a tape with a half dozen or a dozen songs on it. The songwriter who puts this tape together feels the need to give the listener an overview of the collected works of Me, Myself and I. By some unfathomable leap of calculation, the songwriter figures the ideal order of these songs is to put the worst first and the best last.

As a result of this scheme, the listener incurs the expense of purchasing a wig—having pulled out every hair on his head long before the best song comes around. Those are the listeners who care enough to try to wade through the entire tape. Most professional listeners can't afford to care that much about someone who obviously doesn't care enough about the listener's time to be selective. They will listen to snippets of the first few songs, make a judgment, and toss the tape into the circular file for recycling. The masterpiece at the end will never be heard.

First of all, there should never be that many songs on a demo tape. You are far, far better off sending only your single best song. Impress the listener with your selectivity, not your fecundity. At the very most, put three songs on your demo tape. If your package is easy to get into and your songs are about three minutes long, you're still asking for fifteen minutes of the listener's time. Considering the kinds of pressures people in the music business have to deal with, that's asking a lot. When you send only your very best two or three songs, you also send a message that you know the value of the listener's time. If the listener likes something on the tape, she can always ask for more.

Even if you only send your best three songs, don't save the very best for the last. Remember how we talked about grabbing the listener by the ears in the first few lines of the song? The same is true for the line-up on the demo tape. If you have your absolutely hottest song first on the tape, you increase the chances of having the second and third song heard. If the first and second songs aren't knockouts, the listener will probably not have the patience for the third.

You may think this is heartless, cruel and irresponsible behavior on the listeners' part. Try to remember that they're only human. They have indigestion, fights with their spouses, car accidents on the way to work, and plenty of job-related stress. Your demo tape can make their day if you knock them out with a song. They want that more than anything.

Unfortunately, they rarely get what they want. Usually, listeners have to go through at least a hundred tapes to find one that interests them. Their patience wears thin. Remember how you felt when you read the first part of this chapter? Admit it; you were beginning to resent us for wasting your time and attention. So you know how the listener feels when a songwriter doesn't care enough to put the best song forward.

66

CERTIFIED UNACCEPTABLE
Don't send songs by certified or registered mail

After all the time, effort, creativity, blood, sweat and tears, not to mention money, you've put into your demo, there's no way you're going to trust your tape to the perils of the regular U.S. Postal Service, right? You're going to walk that baby right up to the counter and fork out whatever sum it takes to send it certified, registered, return receipt requested, insured, special delivery, priority mail. Little do you realize that you have just turned your demo package into a super bouncing ball. It will end up back on your doorstep, unopened. It may even beat you home from the post office.

Mailing your tape by anything but regular first-class mail spells p-a-r-a-n-o-i-a to the person on the receiving end. It indicates that you want proof for the infringement lawsuit you are planning to institute against their company and their songwriters. Michael Jackson and Lionel Richie are constantly having to deal with what they call "nuisance" lawsuits by songwriters who claim that they wrote "Thriller" or "Three Times a Lady." You can fill in the name of any successful songwriter and song title in the previous sentence.

This is now so prevalent that doors are slamming shut all over the music business. The professionals are driven, in self-defense, to protect themselves from the amateurs. Many people who used to listen to "outside tapes" have stopped doing that. These litigious songwriters have made it harder for all the rest of us who are trying to get our toes in any door that's even slightly ajar. We'll talk about how to transform your demo from an "outside tape" to an inside pitch in the next section on making connections.

If you can't bear the idea of releasing your tape into the wind, rain, snow and dark night of first-class mail, you might draw inspiration from stories we've heard of unusual demo deliveries. One songwriter landed in a helicopter on the front lawn of an artist's home to deliver a demo. Another songwriter cornered Donna Summer in the ladies' room at a disco club; even more interesting, this songwriter was of the male persuasion. We've heard of demos arriving at publishing offices encased in beautiful antique boxes. Someone who knew the passion of Arista Records' president Clive Davis for a certain ball club packed the demo with a baseball signed by all the members of the team.

Creativity counts in demo delivery. Even if you can't afford a helicopter, you can do something to make your tape stand out from the others that are piled on some desk somewhere. Most of those envelopes are of the just plain white or mild-mannered manila varieties. Spice up your demo presentation with color-coordinated envelopes, stationery and tape labels to make them stand out from the crowd. Anything you can do to make your outer envelope and its contents more attractive and appealing to the eye will count in your favor. Publishers are people, too. They get bored looking at all that white and beige.

Be sure not to get too cutesy. You want to look professional. Get help, if you need it, in choosing your "image." The typeface you choose on your personalized stationery can make a statement about you and your music. Do you write New Age music? Consider having your name, company name, and so on, done in calligraphy. Aiming for the top of the pop charts? Look into having your stationery typeset in a hot modern typeface. If you have a publishing company name (see chapter seventy-four, "One Hundred Percent of Nothing," for more information on this), a coordinated logo printed on your envelopes and stationery will make your package stand out. Get help from a friend who is an artist. You can pay your friend a handsome fee after you have your first big hit.

After you have done all this careful creation of an outstanding and unique presentation package, you will still probably have to stick on a regular first-class stamp to cover the latest postage price hike and drop your dreams in your local mailbox. Talk about an act of faith. Seriously, we find this the perfect moment to say a little prayer, releasing the results of our efforts into the universe and congratulating ourselves on having done our best.

67
....

GUESS WHO WROTE THIS
Put your name and phone number on all parts of your presentation package

More than once—and once is already one too many times—we've heard an announcement like this at the California Copyright Conference: "We have a tape here; the song title is . . . , but there's no name or phone number on the tape. We want to record the song. If you know who the writer is, please contact us." The producer of film music making the announcement is hoping that someone among the music business attorneys and publishers assembled there will recognize the song title. The producer will not be able to record the song unless its writer is located.

We know writing the song was no big deal, right? As Gene Fowler said, "Writing is easy. All you do is stare at a blank sheet of paper until drops of blood form on your forehead." Making the demo was a breeze, wasn't it? You couldn't wait to separate yourself from all that cash. So, it doesn't matter that here you have someone actually interested in recording the song, and they can't tell who the writer is. What a catastrophe! We can hardly think of anything worse.

Don't ever let this happen to you. It's so easily avoided. Every piece of your demo presentation package must have your name and phone number (including area code) on it: your cassette, your lyric sheet, and your cover letter. That's all.

Disaster averted.

PART EIGHT

MAKING DISCONNECTIONS

How Not to Get Your Songs Heard

68

PITCHING PARANOIA

Avoid coming across with a defensive attitude, afraid of being ripped off

Recently, a young self-contained band asked us to advise them on how to proceed with their careers. They've been working around town and have started to generate a "buzz." This has nothing to do with honey bees. It means that people are getting excited about the group.

The group feels that any day now someone is going to approach them with a contract, and they're afraid that they will be taken advantage of because they are young and naive in the ways of the music business. We suggested that they come to the workshop at NAS to get some feedback on their songs. Their response was that they were afraid to show the songs, because they hadn't registered them with the Copyright Office yet.

We wonder where the buzz is coming from if they're afraid to show their songs, but we're getting used to holding two contradictory thoughts in our heads at the same time, so let's bypass that mystery. Let's try to solve the conundrum of how a songwriter is to get songs out in the world when he thinks they will be stolen as soon as they are shown.

First of all, your songs are protected by the copyright law as soon as you put them in a fixed form. That means as soon as you scribble them in pencil on a scrap of paper or sing them a cappella into your minicassette machine, you have created a piece of property that belongs to you and you alone. If someone steals that property, you can take that person to court and sue him.

If the song is stolen before you have registered the song with the Copyright Office in Washington, D.C., you will have to complete that registration before you can bring the infringer to court. Some of the money you might have recovered will not be recoverable if you wait until this late in the game to register your song with the Copyright Office. Next, you will have to spend a lot of money to bring the suit to court, and you will have to prove that the infringer had access to your song

and that the infringing song is substantially the same as your song.

Copyright registrations currently cost twenty dollars per song. That can mount quickly to a tidy sum, especially if you are prolific. Since we are our own publishers, we do register all the songs we are currently pitching with the Copyright Office. If you are a songwriter who is pitching songs to publishers, chances are your single song publishing contract will provide that the publisher do the paperwork and pay the fee for the copyright registration.

To obtain song registration forms, called PA forms, call the Copyright Office at 202-707-9100 anytime, day or night. They will send you a limited number of forms, but all you need is one, since they can be photocopied. The forms come with directions for filling them out.

For a more economical way of registering your songs with a disinterested third party, consider the song registration service offered by the National Academy of Songwriters. Write to: NAS, 6381 Hollywood Blvd., Suite 780, Hollywood CA 90028 for information on their song registration service.

It's easy to say that you have protection under the copyright law. The reality is that your protection is only as good as your lawyers and the amount of money you are willing to spend on a lawsuit. Look at George Harrison's "My Sweet Lord." We'll never forget the first time we heard that and said to each other, "Hey, George Harrison wrote new words for 'He's So Fine'!" Somehow, he had no idea that was what he was doing. The copyright owners of "He's So Fine" had to bring him to court, where the judge decided it didn't matter that George Harrison didn't know what he was doing. He must have heard the original song and unconsciously remembered and repeated it. The court ruled that he had to share his royalties for "My Sweet Lord" with the copyright owners of "He's So Fine."

Steve Allen admits that melodies run through his head in such rapid succession that he can't tell whether they're his or playbacks of other people's songs. He, too, had a song published that he later found, to his embarrassment, was entirely someone else's melody. Once he realized this, he gave the other writer half the royalties.

Are there people in the music business who are lying in wait to pounce upon your songs and steal them? We don't think so. There are song sharks. Those are the creeps who advertise that they will get your song recorded, then hit you up for money. They may even produce a piece of vinyl with your song on it. A stack of these will only add to the clutter in your closet. Never pay anyone to publish or "make a record" of your song. This is different from paying for time in a recording studio to record a demo or master of your song.

In the legitimate music business, people are too busy to bother with stealing from songwriters. If you write a hit song, they want to be your friend because you are going to make them lots of money. It doesn't make sense to kill the relationship with the songwriter who writes the gold record.

If you're still afraid of being ripped off, take a tip from the great country songwriter, Tom T. Hall. He said that early in his career he considered it a compliment to be stolen from, because it meant that someone thought enough of his writing to steal it. A similar idea is expressed in the movie *The Red Shoes*: "It's much more disheartening to have to steal than to be stolen from."

You must go forth boldly with your songs in full display. Shout them from the highest hills. Sing them in your church, synagogue, community meeting room. Give your tapes to friends, family, co-workers. Get them out in the world where they can be heard. Don't hold back one iota. You never know where the connection is going to come from. If you keep your songs hidden, you are guaranteed not to make that connection. No one is going to go into your closet and dig around, looking for a hit.

No one can steal your ability to write songs. That talent is uniquely yours in the universe. It is perfectly safe.

Are there people in the music business who will hand you contracts that contain clauses in fine print that can be very detrimental to your career and your income? You bet your life! Still, you have nothing to fear. No one is going to force you to sign anything. Never, never, never sign anything unless you have been advised by an attorney specializing in the music business and you understand the basic meaning of what you are signing. The National Academy of Songwriters has a panel of attorneys who charge a set low fee to members for initial consultations.

Contracts are not written and signed on the spot, they are negotiated. They go back and forth while attorneys on either side adjust the deal according to the clout of the parties involved. You don't have to worry about being taken advantage of if you follow the simple rule of always being represented by someone who has only your interests in mind.

There's a definition for fear that we like: False Evidence Appearing Real. There is nothing to fear but fear itself. If fear is keeping you from getting your songs out, we hope we've helped. If you can't shake your fear, we recommend the A.R.T.S. program to heal the cause (see chapter three).

69
········

STAYING IN THE CLOSET
Don't be afraid to pitch or show your songs

Some songwriters fear being ripped off so much that they never actually show their songs. Other songwriters keep their songs secret because they are embarrassed or afraid of criticism or ridicule. If you're not showing anyone your songs, it's obvious that you're a closet songwriter.

You are not alone in the closet. You would be surprised how many people have written songs. Sometimes it seems to us that everyone in the world has a song stashed somewhere around the house.

To combat fear of being ripped off, we recommend registering your songs with the Copyright Office or depositing copies in the NAS Songbank. It costs $20 to copyright a song. To receive forms and instructions from the Copyright Office, call their 24-hour hotline at 202-707-9100. It will probably cost you less than a stamp if you call at midnight. Ask for form PA, that is the form used to register songs. The NAS Songbank costs $10 for the first song and $6 for others registered at the same time ($6 for the first, plus $2 for additional songs for NAS members). Call NAS at 1-800-826-7287 (outside California) or 213-463-7178 for further instructions.

With evidence of your ownership in hand, you can seek legal recourse should anyone steal your song. Basically, you do not have to worry about people stealing your songs. Other writers are too busy writing, and legitimate music business people are far too inundated with great songs to risk their reputations and their legal fees to defend a copyright infringement suit.

Fear of ridicule is not so easily overcome. Unfortunately, our first attempts at creativity are often invalidated by our parents. "That's nice," they say, "but you can't make a living at it." Or they may launch into a full-scale lecture on what makes a really good song (poem, drawing) and why ours isn't. The tender bud of our creativity is nipped right off.

Some songwriters react by going underground. We continue to create but don't show anyone. Others of us shut down, stop creating and eventually become convinced that we're not creative. Some of us go on creating, even though the process is painful because the original external critic has now taken up residence in our own head. Therefore, we find ourselves constantly dissatisfied with what we're writing. No matter what form the damming of our creativity takes, it spells trouble in our lives.

The desire to write songs is a gift that is meant to be shared. When something happens that dams up the flow between the desire and the expression, the energy backfires on us. It gets diverted into activities that are not good for us. We find ourselves overeating, using drugs or alcohol, obsessing about sex, spending money compulsively, gambling, overworking, or being preoccupied with the past and future.

If we are lucky enough to wake up to what we're doing, we may still think we'd be fools to try songwriting. We buy into society's devaluation of creativity: We're too old, it's too late, we're not good enough, it's not practical.

All this results in either not writing at all, writing song fragments and never finishing anything, or writing complete songs but never really recognizing what we've done or showing it to anyone. The pain of the original blow to our budding creativity is awakened every time we approach the songwriting process. The pleasure that was the motivation for the original songwriting impulse has become inextricably entwined with pain.

If this sounds familiar to you, there is help. The A.R.T.S. program that we referred to in chapter three deals with these very common experiences. Much of the healing available through this program comes from being in contact with other people who are experiencing the same problems. With this solid base of support in the safety of a communal closet, every one of us can go out into the world with the courage to share our art.

Many of us were negatively conditioned in our childhood. Did you ever hear of Pavlov's dog? Pavlov discovered that if he rang a bell every time he fed a dog, eventually the dog would salivate at the sound of the bell. That's positive conditioning, because the dog got a reward when the bell sounded. Similar experiments have been done with negative conditioning. Suppose every time an animal heard the bell, a slight electrical shock was delivered to the floor of the cage. Eventually, the animal jumps when the bell sounds, with or without the shock.

The fear and shame that we feel about our creativity was learned. We were not born with it. Something shocking happened to us, probably thousands of times, in subtle ways we can't remember. Most of us grow up receiving constant messages from our family and from society at large that art is not an important and necessary part of life. Once we realize that we need to connect with our creativity to lead relatively sane lives it's up to us to recondition ourselves. We need to teach ourselves that it is all right to be creative, to share our songs. The first step is to share a song in a totally safe environment.

That's what A.R.T.S. provides. You can start your own A.R.T.S. meeting. You only need two people to start. Call 212-873-7075 for help. If that idea doesn't appeal to you, you can just open the closet door a crack and let in one special person. Choose someone you know you can trust. Explain that you want to share a song and that you want positive support for it, no criticism! (This is part of the rule read at the beginning of each A.R.T.S. meeting.) If you have chosen your supporter correctly, you will experience the unconditional respect you need to take the next step.

For many of us, it's difficult or impossible to make the simple statement, "I'm a songwriter." We think we're frauds. We can't be songwriters because we are not getting rich from writing songs—in fact, we're spending money on it, not earning money. We aren't songwriters because no one else will record our songs. We aren't songwriters because we don't deserve to live our dream.

Many of our recommendations in this book have to do with getting your song out through the established commercial methods. It's natural for songwriters to want to teach the world their songs. The reality is that our chances are slim. Songwriter Sue Schiffrin talked about this hard reality at a UCLA seminar on "Women in Songwriting": "There's a statistic and I'll tell it to you because I know it and I'm still writing songs in spite of the fact that I know it. They say that of all the songs that are written, 1 percent of those songs get recorded and 1 percent of that 1 percent get to be hits. The odds are against you."

Arthur Hamilton, who wrote "Cry Me a River," was moderating that seminar. He made the perfect rejoinder: "Never face the facts." Don't let the impossible odds get you down. You are still a songwriter even if you don't beat them. If you really want to make it as a full-time songwriter, you will need endless persistence. But your songwriting is just as valid if songwriting is not your career.

If you are currently a closet songwriter, gently recondition yourself over a period of time so that you can open the door wide and walk out into the sunshine. Then share your songs at every appropriate opportunity. You never know who could be in the audience.

Sting talked about the early days of The Police in an interview in *Rolling Stone*. The group would play their hearts outs, no matter who did or didn't show up to listen. One night, there were only two people in the audience. The Police played as if they were in a packed stadium. It turned out that the two people were disc jockeys who got turned on to the group and promoted their music on their stations. The two-person audience turned into a major breakthrough for the group.

The people in your community need to hear your songs. In 1970, we wandered into the Florida Keys and wound up spending Christmas in a campground. It was our first experience with the world of motor homes and travel trailers, and we were impressed by the warm welcome everyone gave us. They just loved to show off their rigs. We were inspired to write a song called "You and Me and Christmas, Fiesta Key." Now you will never hear this song on the radio or elsewhere, but it was well worth the writing. What an explosion of joy hit us when we sang it to the people there.

You need to know that the only requirement for being a songwriter is wanting to write songs. Songwriting is a tool for personal expression and growth. You need to let those songs out, and the world needs to hear them. This is true for the one song you sang in the closet to your one friend as it is for the biggest selling song in the world.

70
....

TO WHOM IT MAY CONCERN

Don't send songs to a company without a specific person's name

You have a song you think would be great for a particular artist. You're a fan of that artist, and you have several of her albums at home. You see that the albums were on XYZ Records, so you pop your tape in an envelope and address it to A&R Department, XYZ Records. You think they will be kind enough to direct your tape to the appropriate person in the company. Think again.

First, that record company is probably getting one to three thousand tapes a week from unsolicited sources. By addressing your tape to an anonymous A&R person, you just qualified to be in that pile. Most likely there is a person hired just to sit all day and hit all those envelopes with a rubber stamp saying "Unsolicited Material—Refused Unopened."

Second, just because your artist has a couple of albums out on a certain label doesn't mean that she is still recording on that label. Even if she is still on the label, she may be out on tour now. She won't be looking for songs until after the tour when her next recording project is planned.

If your tape package is going to be opened at all, you have to make phone contact with a real-live-flesh-and-blood person who says, "Yes, send a tape." Get that person's name! It doesn't matter if it's someone's assistant or secretary. Getting one toe into that outer office is an inch closer to getting into the inner sanctum.

Ask first if they are looking for material for that particular artist. They may say that she is on tour and they won't be looking for another three months. Then it's up to you to call back in three months, talk to that same person, and see if the time has become ripe for you to send your tape. Showing that person that you are professional enough to follow through at the appropriate time will put a few points up on your side of the scoreboard.

Once you get the go-ahead, ask your contact if there is something special you should write on the outside of the envelope. Companies often have a code so the people in the mailroom can distinguish between the unsolicited tapes and the tapes that have the secret password. Don't forget to say, "Thank you." This could be the beginning of a long and profitable relationship between you and this person. A year and three pitches from now, your lower-level contact may just get a promotion. That's when your patient nurturing of this relationship can really pay off.

You're not pitching your song to some anonymous department at a record or publishing company. You're dealing with people who appreciate recognition and consideration as much as you do. It's up to you to show your awareness of this reality by taking the time to make person-to-person contact and find out what you can do to better your chances of having your song heard.

"How and who?" you ask. Reach out and call someone. Ask for the A&R department at the record label and talk to whoever answers the phone. State your business in a straightforward way. If you have a tendency to mumble and stumble over your tongue, write out a script, rehearse it and read it. Ask for the name of the appropriate person to talk to.

Record labels also have a department called Artist Relations. The people in that department can give you the name, address and phone number of the artist's producer, manager and agent. That's if you ask them in a nice, businesslike manner. It's good to have your self-publishing company's name to drop at moments like this, so you sound like an employee doing a job.

When calling publishing companies, ask for the Professional Manager. That's the job title of the listeners in the larger companies.

ASCAP and BMI help developing songwriters because they want you to join their respective organization and not the other one. If you can get to one of the music business centers (New York City, Nashville, Los Angeles), make an appointment to speak to a Membership Representative at

ASCAP and/or BMI. You can play them a song or two, and they will probably give you some names of publishers to contact.

Songwriters' organizations can also point you in the direction of listeners who might be open to meeting with you or listening to your songs. Both NAS and LASS (Los Angeles Songwriters Showcase) publish information about individuals who are looking for specific kinds of songs.

Writer's Digest's *Songwriter's Market* is a good starting point for making connections. But don't just send your tape off to a company because it is listed in the book. Make the extra effort to make personal contact to be sure you're not wasting your time and money by sending the wrong song at the wrong time to the wrong person. To turn all those wrongs into rights, you need to communicate directly with the person (or her assistant) who—you hope—will love your song as much as you do.

Relationship is the name of the game when it comes to making the connections that get your songs recorded. Songs sent through the mail rarely are. Most songs get recorded through some personal contact, however farfetched. Steve Kipner, who wrote "Let's Get Physical," got his tape in the door while delivering sandwiches to make ends meet. Allan Rich, who co-wrote "I Don't Have the Heart," passed a tape to a producer when he sold him a pair of shoes on the Venice Beach boardwalk. Billy Steinberg's girlfriend's brother, a drummer for Linda Ronstadt, got Billy his first major cut. Al Kasha, Oscar-winning co-writer of "We May Never Love Like This Again" and "The Morning After" from *The Poseidon Adventure*, shared a story in his workshop of how he got next to New York's *Late Show* producer by going to the same barber, among other things. Once they had several relationships in common, Al presented the producer with the idea for a new *Late Show* theme in a way that made money for both parties.

Music is a person-to-person business, so pick up your phone before you lick that stamp.

71

·········

ONE PITCH AT A TIME

Don't pitch to only one potential recording situation at a time

Some songwriters who are new to the game believe they would be cheating somehow if they sent a particular song to more than one prospective user at a time. This *is* true in other creative fields, such as children's book writing. It's considered a major breach of professional etiquette for the children's book writer to make multiple submissions. That rule can be bent slightly, but only if you let everybody know in your cover letter that you're doing it. Then the publishers treat your manuscript with less respect.

When we learned about this, we could hardly believe it. How can you function as a writer when you can only pitch to one person at a time and that person may take up to a year to respond? It doesn't make sense to us. We're used to a totally different attitude about submitting material. In the songwriting business, there are no such limitations on how many people you can pitch your song to simultaneously.

What do you do if two or three of them respond at the same time and want to use the song? (We should have such problems.) In this case you will have to investigate the nature of each situation. Maybe one is just a publisher who likes the song and wants to give you a single song contract on it. Number two is a producer who wants to record the song with a new artist. The third one is a producer who wants to put a hold on the song for a major artist and wants to share in the publishing, too.

Publishers come in all shapes and sizes. There are one-man shows and multinational conglomerates. There are catalog collectors who are just building up the size of their catalog, and there are active song pluggers. They offer single song publishing contracts ranging in length from one to twenty-five pages.

If you are contacted by a publisher, the first thing you want to do is review a copy of the single song contract they are offering you. That will tell you a lot about the company. Check to see if they automatically insert a reversion clause. Consult with a music business attorney to get a full understanding of what the contract means. There are good contracts and bad contracts, or contracts that are more or less favorable toward songwriters. Ask your attorney to tell you where this contract falls in the good/bad spectrum and why. You may decide to pass on a publisher on the strength (or weakness) of the contract alone.

That is not to say that you have to accept the first contract they send you. The publisher may or may not be willing to change the contract. You or your attorney should call the publisher to see if negotiation is possible. If the contract is unacceptable to you, and the publisher won't change it, notify the publisher that you aren't willing to sign the song under the terms of the contract. Chalk it up as another educational adventure in songwriting.

If the contract is acceptable or the publisher is willing to negotiate it into acceptable form, you still need to decide if you really want to sign it. If you pitched to the publisher because you saw the company name in some directory, but you don't know much about the company, now is the time to find out.

Ask ASCAP and BMI about the publisher. ASCAP will tell you only if the publisher is a member. BMI will tell you how long they've been a member. Both performing rights organizations will confirm the publisher's name if you give them a song title that is supposed to be in the publisher's catalog. Your local or national songwriters' organization may know something about the publishing company. Ask your contact at the publishing company to tell you a little about the company's catalog and

their intentions with the song. Do this in a friendly, information-gathering manner, not as a suspicious challenge. You might ask how large the company is and if the person you are talking with will be the only one pitching the song. You are considering going into a business partnership with this person and this company. You have the right to know about your partner.

In the good old days when publishers nurtured and trained songwriters, paid for the recording of demos, and were song pluggers in a market where artists were artists and writers were writers, the usual deal was fifty/fifty. The songwriter would sign over ownership of the copyright to the publisher. The publisher would get as many artists as possible to record the song, collect all moneys (except performance royalties, which go directly to the writer from ASCAP or BMI), and then give 50 percent of it to the writer.

Today, the songwriter is expected to be self-nurtured and trained, demo producer and song plugger. Publishers sometimes just do the paperwork, which is called administration. Songwriters who have track records (history of hit songs) also have their own publishing companies and wield sufficient clout to maintain partial (or complete) ownership of their copyrights, which means they collect more than 50 percent of the royalties (or even 100 percent of the royalties).

Songwriters with no track record usually don't have the clout to participate in the publishing income. However, if you make the connection for the recording of a song, even if it's your first cut, you may be able to make a more favorable deal than the traditional fifty/fifty. We do not recommend that you do these delicate negotiations yourself. Unless you possess the knowledge and skills required, have your music business attorney cut the deal for you. See the next chapter for more on how to handle your give and take with a publisher.

The second offer from the producer with the new artist holds some attraction. You never know; his artist may be the next big hit, and you'll be in on the ground floor if you go with this one. When you pitch directly to the producer or artist, you are your own publisher. You are entitled to two streams of income, one as publisher and another as songwriter. If this is a new producer with a new artist, they probably won't ask to share in your publisher income. At the very least, there's a potential for you to come out of this deal with nothing lost and a very good demo gained.

A producer with a lot of clout and an artist who is a proven success present a different set of variables. Often they will ask to have a hold on your song. That means they want to record it, but they won't be recording for a while. They want you to refrain from pitching the song to anyone else in the meantime. For more on holds, see chapter seventy-six, "Hold It, Hold It, Never Let it Go."

A producer with clout will also often ask to share in the publishing income. Then it becomes a question of whether you want to share the publishing income, how much you'll share and under what circumstances. Again, if you are lucky enough to have these kinds of dilemmas, we recommend that you consult the best music business attorney available to you.

Pitch your songs to as many possible recording situations as you like. There is such a thing as going overboard, though. Read on to see what we mean.

72
· · · · · · · · ·
SHOTGUN PITCHING
*Pinpoint your pitches; don't force the wrong song
on the right contract*

You think you've written a great song, and you want everybody in the world to hear it. So you get a music business directory; Writer's Digest's *Songwriter's Market* and *Billboard*'s *International Buyer's Guide* are two very good ones. You can even buy a music business data base to install in your computer. Then you can press a button, have your printer spit out labels for every name on the list, pay somebody to do high-speed tape duplication in bulk, and mail the cassette to everyone.

There might be a good reason to do that, but pitching your song isn't it. If you want to get your song recorded, you need to aim it like a dart, straight at the bull's-eye of the artists most likely to record it. With shotgun pitching, you waste your time and money sending your tape to the wrong people, and you don't endear yourself to the listeners who must waste their time dealing with your tape.

Aiming a song at an appropriate artist is called "casting" the song. Just as casting the actors in movies is an art that gets recognized in the credits,

casting your song to the right artists takes skill and creativity.

Each artist has an image, a personality they express as an artist. This may or may not exactly coincide with who they actually are. It isn't something accidental, though. Artists hire personal managers who advise them on focusing their image, among many other things. Included in the concept of image are the kinds of messages the artist will choose to express.

Harry Connick, Jr., said in an interview on TV, "I would never say, 'I Want Your Sex.'" Anyone even slightly familiar with his image would know that. He sings high-class romantic ballads in a style reminiscent of Frank Sinatra. He presents himself as a very sincere and humble person. Don't send him your hard-rock screaming diatribes or your down-home country truck-drivin', beer-drinkin', honky-tonk songs. This guy's into champagne and moonlight.

Many times we write with a particular artist in mind. But the creative process likes to surprise us; the direction of the song may make a U-turn in midwriting. Even if the finished product does seem to fall into the intended artist's ballpark, we have a casting session for each song after we finish writing it. The result is a list of artist names that is kept in the file with the song. The list grows as other names occur to us or are suggested to us.

To cast your songs accurately, take time to study the artists you think might sing the message contained in your song. Consider the overall tone and the songwriting credits of the artist's last few albums. Would your song fit in with them? Can you really see that artist getting into singing your song? Can the song be demoed in that artist's style and feel?

Most important for you, does the artist record songs written by outside songwriters? For most artists on the pop charts, the answer to this question will be no. Don't waste your time and theirs pitching to these closed situations. If the answer to all of the above questions is a considered yes, proceed to make a demo and research the approaches to that artist.

The artist is surrounded by people who give input on recording projects. The personal manager, the producer, the A&R person at the record label, and sometimes the agent and the attorney are among those who officially or semiofficially perform this function. The names, addresses and phone numbers of the first four on that list are available from the Artist Relations department at the artist's record label. Call them and ask for the information in a very businesslike manner, introducing yourself as president or professional manager of Yourveryown Music Publishing Company, or whatever you call yourself as a publisher of your own songs.

Next, call the contact and ask about the artist's current status. Are they looking for songs now? If not, when will they be? Is the artist taking a special new direction or about to change his or her image? If they are open to listening to your tape, to whose attention should you send it? Is there something special you should write on the outside envelope? If they are not open to receiving your tape, even though the artist is looking for material, explain that you have a song that would be perfect for the artist. Ask them to refer you to a publisher with whom they have a relationship, then pursue that contact using them as a reference.

Don't take offense at anyone's reluctance to provide you with information. These people are being paid to function as a moat around the artist's castle. Often, their first inclination is to say no. Remain businesslike, friendly and insistent but not to the point of being obnoxious. There is more than one way to approach an artist. In fact, if you can get your tape to several of the artist's contacts, do so.

If one of your fantasies is to be a detective, you can live it out in aid of your songwriting. The artist also has an unofficial network for song input: hairdressers, doctors, dentists, band members, fitness instructors, roadies, second cousins, etc. If it's geographically feasible, any contact you can make with someone in this unofficial network may lead to the possibility of pitching directly to the artist. If the artist is coming through your town on tour, make it a point to go to the concert and see if you can make a contact with someone in the artist's entourage.

There is a difference between getting your tapes to as many potential outlets as possible and just sending them out helter-skelter. Carefully aim each one at a particular target. You may not hit the mark, but at least you tried and learned something in the trying.

73

I'LL GIVE YOU EVERYTHING

Don't be willing to sign everything and anything away at the slightest interest by a publisher

You've done your homework. You've captured the idea and chipped away at it lyrically and musically, like Michelangelo uncovering the shape in the marble bit by bit. You've sought feedback and rewritten. You've gone through the creative maze of the demo-making process. You've researched and made enough contacts to have the door open just wide enough for you to slip your tape in. Then one day, while you are sharpening your pencils, putting out the garbage, doing the dishes, anything but facing the endless challenge of songwriting, the phone rings. It's Joe Producer and he wants to record your song. What's your reaction?

When that call came to our house, it was from Philadelphia International, the label created by the songwriter-production team of Kenny Gamble and Leon Huff, best known for bringing us the O'Jays, Lou Rawls and Teddy Pendergrass. They said that Patti LaBelle wanted to record "Body Language," a song we had written with Harold Payne. We had pitched the song directly to them, doing business as Pea Pod Music, after calling them and requesting that they be in a tip sheet we were working on at the time. The caller wanted to know if their company could share in the publishing. Overcome with excitement, Pat blurted out, "Yes! Yes! Yes!" Wrong, wrong, wrong.

First of all, this was not a decision she could make on her own. That song is a piece of property created by three people, each of whom owns an equal share in it. No decision can be made on it unless and until all the owners agree. Second, as songwriters, we are not the best people to negotiate these deals. We are victims of our eagerness to have our songs exposed. Furthermore, there are people who have been in the business end of music for a long time and know a lot more than we do about the small print that can mean big differences. We highly recommend that you have such deals negotiated by a lawyer who specializes in the music business.

Your friendly local lawyer who helps you write your will and plan your estate will know nothing about this. Music business law has its own language, and you need someone who can speak it for you. You must go to a specialist for a deal as potentially important as a song being cut by Patti LaBelle. Our friend and collaborator, Harold Payne, is a wonderful artist who has earned his living as a singer/songwriter for twenty-five years. When this offer came, Harold was under contract to a personal manager. Since the manager was going to earn a percentage of whatever Harold earned while under contract, we turned the negotiation over to his manager. Although he isn't a lawyer, we knew him to be a legitimate and honest person experienced in making these kinds of deals in the music business. And because of his relationship with Harold, he was motivated to make the best possible deal for us.

Why all this wheeling and dealing? Why isn't a simple "yes" or even an ecstatic "Yes! Yes! Yes!" the appropriate response to the situation? There are way too many variables for a simple answer to suffice. When you write a song, you create a copyright. Literally, that means the "right to copy." Actually, it's a bundle of rights that no one can touch without your permission. There's the right to make the first recording of the song and reproduce it mechanically via tape, vinyl or CD. There's the right to synchronize your song to a motion picture or a television show. There's the right to use a bit of it with different lyrics as a TV commercial, the right to put it in a musical teakettle, the right to print it up on sheet music and sheet music books. There's also the right to have it performed on the radio, on TV, in music videos, at ball games, in elevators. What if an entirely new form of delivering music to consumers is invented next week? Your rights for the future need to be protected in the deals you make today.

Then, take all those rights and do them over again for the foreign markets. There's a great big world out there clamoring for American music.

There's also a world of international copyright law and constant litigation going on to clarify the meaning of the laws. As editors of the California Copyright Conference newsletter, we have had the great opportunity of covering their monthly dinner meetings, at which the latest developments in matters affecting copyright are discussed by panels of experts. Copyright law is a universe of knowledge. If you learned everything you needed to know about this subject, you would have no time to write and record your songs.

This is not to say that you needn't bother your pretty little head about it. You do have to study the basics of the legal aspects of songwriting. You need to understand what you're signing, even though you've had your lawyer take care of it. An excellent source of legal information is the Writer's Digest book *Protecting Your Songs and Yourself*, written by our friend and attorney Kent Klavens. Kent founded the NAS legal panel, a good source of music business attorneys who charge an especially low fee for NAS members.

The contracts that songwriters are very often offered are called "single song contracts." These usually come from publishers who want you to assign your bundle of rights to them. In return they are supposed to pitch your song to recording situations and make money, half of which will eventually pass down to you as writer. We are describing a very complex situation so simply that the description is barely accurate, but bear with us.

A publisher will often tell a writer that the single song contract is "standard." There is no such thing. We've seen single song contracts ranging in length from two to twenty-five pages. One of the first contracts we were offered was of the very long variety. We took it home and studied every dot and comma of it. We consulted with Helen King, who founded Songwriters Resources and Services (now the National Academy of Songwriters) out of her own wallet and her compassion for the plight of songwriters. We decided we needed to have a few small changes in the contract. We made an appointment with the publisher and showed her the changes we wanted. Her response was an attack: "I paid lawyers hundreds of dollars to write that contract! You don't know anything about this! I won't change a thing." We retreated

to our closet and came out two or three months later.

One of the bottom-line changes we were asking for and we recommend writers insist on is a reversion clause. Without it, you have signed away your song for many, many years, during which time it may sit gathering dust in the publisher's file. When a publisher owns a lot of copyrights, it's called a catalog. Buying and selling catalogs is big business. It has nothing to do with you and your precious song that you sweat blood over. A reversion clause is language in the contract that says, "If the publisher/producer fails to record a commercially released version of the song in x amount of time, ownership of the song reverts automatically back to the writer(s)." Don't get lost in the shuffle; let your songs come back to you if the publisher is not getting anywhere or doing anything with them.

We won't go into all the details of the single song contract, except to say that all of the various rights mentioned above can be dealt with separately, and deals can be structured to vary according to the status of the song on the recording. For example, you might agree that if the song becomes a single, the copublisher can have 50 percent of the publisher's mechanical royalties (payment for the sales of records, tapes, and so on) on that single only . . . or on all future recordings of the song, or for the next five years. If the same song turns out to be just an album cut, the deal may stipulate that the copublisher will receive 25 percent of the mechanicals. The point is, it takes experience to be able to sense the appropriate level of give and take between the two parties in the deal. The operative word is clout.

Clout is Michael Jackson wanting to record your song. Now there's a situation to say yes to. But when his representatives asked a writer we know to give them some of the publishing on a song Michael wanted to record on the *Thriller* album, she said no. Of course, after the album sold fifty zillion copies, she realized the error of her ways.

On the other end of the spectrum, there are writers who could never even get an offer to say yes or no to. Case in point, Billy Steinberg: "I went to publishers with my songs for years and I didn't have any luck. No publisher was interested in making me any type of an offer. I also went to record companies because I was looking for an artist deal. I think if any publisher had offered me a deal for the rest of my life for $10,000 to own my publishing, I would have signed it for sure. I would have signed anything. I didn't end up owning my own publishing because I was so shrewd. I ended up with it because no one wanted it."

So, when your phone rings and it's Mary Pub-

lisher calling, say, "I'm glad you're interested in the song. Why don't you send me a copy of your contract and I'll have my lawyer look at it." If it's Joe Producer, ask briefly about his intentions for the song, and then say, "Great, I'll have my lawyer/manager/copublisher call you." Then sit back, relax, and enjoy the roller coaster ride.

74
ONE HUNDRED PERCENT OF NOTHING
Don't be inflexible in negotiating rights

At the opposite end of the songwriter pole from those who are ready to give away all their rights at the drop of a contract are the writers who insist on hanging on to everything, no matter what. These songwriters act as their own publishers and pitch their songs to artists, A&R people or producers. When they get a nibble on a song, if they think even a little bit of their bait is going to be lost, they yank their lure right out of the water. Songwriters who have a lot of clout can pull this off. Most of us cannot afford to.

Inflexibility in negotiating the sharing of some of the rights and attending royalties on a song is called the 100 percent of nothing syndrome. Sadly but truly, many decisions about whether or not to record a song are made not on the merits of the song but on the financial possibilities of the deal. If you are not willing to deal away some of your rights in the song, you will exclude your song from deals where the users of the song insist on sharing in the income of the song.

These users do have a point. Without the exposure that they are willing to give the song, the song would make no income. True, you could find someone else to record the song who would not insist on sharing in the publishing royalties. You also might not find someone else.

If you take the song to a publisher, the publisher will definitely demand a percentage of the income on the song. The usual amount is 50 percent, but songwriters with clout can negotiate for some share in that publisher's half. If you think that the publisher can do something for your song that you cannot do, then it is worthwhile to share with the publisher. If you act as your own publisher, you give yourself additional pieces to play in the negotiation chess game. Some of these pieces need to be sacrificed in order to win the game.

These pieces are the various rights in the song: mechanical, performance, and sheet music royalties, synchronization fees, and other uses of the song. You can negotiate with the user of the song piece by piece, with percentages shared varying depending on the nature of the recording. We say "you" here because you own the song. But because these negotiations are complicated, we advise that you hire someone experienced to conduct them for you.

In the last chapter, we gave an example of piece-by-piece negotiations regarding the mechanical royalties. Here's a variation on that theme, using performance royalties: You could agree that the producer of the song gets 50 percent of the publisher's performance royalties for three years after the release of the song. Or you could agree that the producer of the record or the artist's publishing company gets 100 percent of the publisher's performance royalties for the first year and 50 percent for the two years after.

Getting songs recorded is tough enough. Don't make it tougher on yourself by being inflexible in negotiating for royalty shares. This is called paying your dues. Getting your songs recorded is the name of the game.If your song is out there, you're a winner. After you have a successful track record, you will have the clout to be more insistent and selective about the deals you make on your songs.

75

NO SIR, THAT'S MY BABY

Don't be reluctant to let go of a song because you're saving it for your "artist deal"

For the songwriter who wants to be a performing artist, the moment of truth comes when someone else wants to record a song you're saving for yourself. Tom Kelly puts the question this way: "Is somebody else going to do this song better than I can or should I hang onto it myself?"

Billy Steinberg remembers when he answered that question incorrectly: "I had a band called Billy Thermal and we were signed to Planet Records. At the same time, Kim Carnes and her producer, Val Garay, wanted to record a certain song of mine, 'The Price I Pay.' I made a decision that I was saving this song for my own record. My own record was never released and never came to anything. If I had agreed, the song would have been on the album with 'Bette Davis Eyes.' It would have made me some money and it would have been a feather in my cap at the time, but I chose not to give them the song.

"I don't know if that decision would have been the wrong decision for everyone in that situation. If Edie Brickell had given 'What I Am' away, where would she be now as an artist?"

Our guess is that she would have come up with another song to launch her career as an artist. If you are lucky enough to have interest in your songs, we think you should let them get out there and build your credibility.

It is extremely difficult to get an artist deal with a record label, and it is wise to do anything you can to make it easier or to give yourself more clout in the negotiations. Having written hits for other artists is just such a bargaining chip. You have nothing to lose by letting your songs be recorded, and much to gain.

Many people we know today as artists got their toes in the door by letting others record the songs they had written for themselves. Among these are Richard Marx, Taylor Dayne, Siedah Garrett and Michael Bolton, who made his own hit with his song "How Am I Supposed to Live Without You?" ten years after it was a hit for Laura Branigan.

Even with a hit-song track record, a record deal may not be in your future. We know hit songwriters who have wanted to be artists for years. We're talking about major hit songwriters and many, many years. They might even get a recording contract from time to time, but not much comes of it. If they had held back their songs all those years, they'd be nowhere now. Instead, they're very successful as songwriters who have learned to live with the frustration of not having part of their dream come true. Better some than none.

Unless you are so far into a potential record deal that you are actually negotiating the deal based on the master demos on a particular set of songs, we think it's best to keep all your options open. Billy Steinberg agrees: "If a really great singer like Linda Ronstadt or Whitney Houston wants to record that song or might if they had a chance to hear it, I think it's a major decision to decide not to even play it for them because you're going to save it for yourself. That's why writer artists have to take a careful look at where their real potential lies and not delude themselves."

It's a delusion to think that your career as an artist depends on having one particular song exclusively to yourself. As a songwriter, you learn with each song you write, so the next one will be better, and the one after that even better, and so on. Breaking into songwriting is hard, but it's a featherbed compared to trying to make it as a recording artist.

The reason it is so difficult comes down to the bottom line, money. A record company is going to have to believe in you to the tune of $200,000 to produce your first album and $100,000 to promote it. That's a fair amount of faith. Many artists don't sell enough records to pay back that investment on their first albums. Bruce Springsteen didn't until his third. Jimmy Bowen, president of Universal Records/MCA Nashville estimates that his label invests $500,000 in a new artist before they see a profit, and only 50 percent of his artists make those costs back.

Clive Davis, president and founder of Arista Records, advises aspiring artists: "If you're college material and you want to be an artist, wait until you get your full education, because the chances of making it are not good. You should be prepared for alternative careers. But if you love music to the extent that you can't dream of anything other than that, you should pursue that career until you feel that you've taken it down the road and have gotten the best professional judgments."

It seems to us that writing songs for hit recording artists is the next best alternative to being one, and it has the advantages of not destroying your privacy or disturbing your family life. Instead of saying, "No, sir, that's my baby" when someone wants to record a song you wanted to record yourself, we recommend you try the time-honored phrase, "Take my wife, please!" with a new twist: "Take my baby, please!"

76

· · · · · · · · ·

HOLD IT, HOLD IT, NEVER LET IT GO

Know how to deal with songs that get stuck "on hold" with producers

In the beginning, even before there was the hold, there were two years during which the tape sat in a pile. Out of the blue, two years after the tape was sent, songwriter Allan Rich got a phone call. James Ingram said, "I've been so busy. I've had these tapes piled up in my house for years. I'm finally getting a chance to listen to them. This is the first tape in the last two years that made me cry. I want you to know that I'm cutting this tune. I want you to put it on hold for me." Then, there was the year "on hold" before the song came out and became the number one hit "I Don't Have the Heart." That was a hold that paid off.

When an artist or a producer asks a writer to put a song on hold, they are asking the writer not to show it to anyone else because they intend to record it. This is usually done on the phone or in person. It is a verbal agreement. There is no compensation to the songwriter for tying up a song and no guarantee that the song will actually be recorded. Meanwhile, if the writer holds to the hold, other recording opportunities for the song may come and go.

It is a common experience for songwriters to get burned by putting a song on hold. Many artists take holds very lightly, while the songwriters who are waiting for that elusive recognition are clinging to the hold for dear life. Another writer told us: "I had four of my best songs on hold for a year with an artist. I was having lunch with a bunch of music people and one of them said, 'Did you hear so-and-so's new album?' I almost freaked at the table. I had been keeping on top of the situation and, as far as I knew, my songs were going to be on that album. They weren't." In that case, the artist held the songs but did not record them. It often happens that the artist even goes so far as recording the song, but it gets bumped off the album after the fact. This is because many artists record more songs than they intend to release on the album, then pick the ten strongest from those.

If you are asked to put a song on hold, you have to judge for yourself how serious the artist or producer is about recording the song. If you feel se-cure that the artist and producer mean what they are saying and really will cut the song, try to get them to commit to taking action within a definite length of time. Follow up when that time has elapsed and decide again at that time if it's still worth keeping your song out of circulation.

If you have reason to feel that they are less than 100 percent reliable, you can commit to an equivalent percentage of reliability in holding the song. Show it to others, and if you get a definite bite, confront the first artist. Ask him if he is really going to record the song. Tell him you need to know because you have someone else who wants to cut it.

This can get very touchy. You can anger and alienate the first artist this way. It's always best to be as up-front as possible. When they first ask for a hold, you can tell them that you have already sent it to other people. Ask them to let you know when they make a firm decision. Tell them that you will advise them of the status of the song at that time. This route can also lead to missed recording opportunities if the artist or producer doesn't like your attitude.

This is one you'll have to play by ear.

77

·········

MAKE ME A STAR

*Don't think that someone is going to
"make you" a success*

Songwriters experience a lot of rejection, especially in the beginning. During this long time of knocking on doors and having them slammed in our faces, songwriters dream of a Prince Charming publisher or fairy godmother producer or *anybody* who will make the magic happen.

We remember the first time we thought it was happening. We showed some songs to a publisher in a multinational corporation. We had other connections with him and regarded him as a friend. He listened to two songs with no great reaction.

On the third song, he literally jumped up out of his chair and shouted, "This is a great song, I love it!" Pat remembers thinking, This is it. This is my dream come true. This publisher is actually jumping up and down over one of our songs.

We left his office flying high and waited for fame and fortune to knock down our door. Two weeks later, when we had heard nothing further from the publisher, we called him and asked about the song. He had forgotten about it. So much for fairy tales.

This feeling that someone is going to "make us" leads us to stumble over our tongues and walk on eggshells around people we think can do the trick. These actions give the very people we want to impress the message that we are insecure and uncomfortable. (Especially with those eggshells all over our tongues.) This discomfort is contagious, and it makes people not want to deal with us. We make our worst fears a reality by believing that we are weak and they are strong.

It is sad but true that songwriters are not appreciated or recognized in many ways. The general public has the impression that the artists write all the songs they sing. Record labels contribute to this impression by not giving writers credit on cassette labels.

Organizations representing songwriters have to fight for our rights against encroachment by home taping, piracy, censorship, and users who don't want to pay for the use of our songs. Often this fight takes place in courts and legislatures that are neither impressed nor inclined to help unless Dolly Parton comes in to speak for us. This is in spite of the fact that the entertainment industry, especially the music industry, is one of the few U.S. industries that has a positive balance of trade. Countries in Europe offer higher royalties and more protection for their songwriters and copyright owners.

Considering the institutionalized disregard for the value of songwriters and the constant rejection that is number one on our job description, it's no wonder we wish someone would take care of us. The good news is, there is someone who can make you a star, someone who cares about you, knows your value, and will give you everything you need to achieve your dream. That someone is you.

Those who really know what's important in the music business have a saying, "It all starts with a song." Without a great song to sing, an artist is nowhere. Without an artist singing a great song, the record labels have nothing to sell and the radio stations have nothing to play. If you have written a great song, you are going to make the person who uses it very rich. They may be a vehicle for you to get where you want to go, but you are the source.

Now don't get all smug and uppity. That won't win you any friends. Just realize your worth and approach your song pitching situations with self-respect and a reasonable regard for the people you are dealing with. They are not gods; they are people like you who love songs. They want to love your song just as much as you want them to love it. Sometimes they do love a song of yours but still can't use it because it doesn't fit the project they're working on at the moment. This is a sugar-coated rejection, but still a rejection. For more on rejection, see the next chapter.

For now, remember that it's your belief in yourself as a songwriter that will "make" you. Your belief will make others believers. When you walk into a publisher's or producer's office, hold your head up high and don't be afraid. You have nothing to lose and everything to gain. Your songwriting gift may or may not be the gift that this person needs right now, but it is still a valuable gift that will find its proper outlet if you keep valuing it and offering it.

78

NEVER AGAIN

Don't give up after being rejected

A close cousin to the closet songwriter is the songwriter who shows songs to one or two, or even a hundred publishers, gets rejected and gives up. We know this feeling intimately. We could wallpaper several rooms with our accumulated rejection letters. It's all well and good to say, "Don't take it personally." Personally, there have been times when we've had such powerful emotional reactions that it feels like hitting a cinder block wall at seventy miles per hour on a motorcycle. Fun, it's not.

The temptation to chuck all this crazy songwriter stuff gets strong at times. What can we do with these feelings? Why, write a song about them, of course!

I'M NEVER GONNA' WRITE ANOTHER SONG AGAIN

I'm never gonna' write another song again
Everything I write down comes out wrong
I'm packing up my old guitar and pen
And putting them in the garbage where they
   belong

   CHORUS:
   I'm never gonna' write another song again
   It hurts too much to try to tell the truth
   And then somebody listens in a big glass
      tower
   He says he likes it
   But he ain't got no use for it
   I'm never gonna' write
   I'm giving up this fight
   I'm never gonna' write another song again
   I'm never gonna' write another song again

I'm never gonna hum another tune again
Never gonna' search my mind for words
I'm burnin' up my demo tapes and then
I'm gonna' try my luck at something less
   absurd

   CHORUS: *repeat*

I'm never gonna' stay awake at night again

Dreamin' I'll be on the radio
I'm trading in my Teac for a tent
And driving out to the forest to hear the wind
   blow

   CHORUS: *repeat and add:*

I'm never gonna' write
I'm giving up the fight
I'm never gonna' write another song again
This is the last one
I'm never gonna' write another song again

© 1977 Pea Pod Music

You can see by the copyright date that we're too foolish to take our own advice. How do we hang in there in spite of the incredibly bad odds and the constant rejection? You gotta be nuts. Nuts about songwriting. That's the bottom line. If you won't take no for an answer—no matter how many people say no to you—you make yourself inevitable. The game goes to the ones who are left standing after the rest have quit.

Johnny Cash tells a wonderful story about his early experiences with rejection. He was backstage complaining about how hard the road to success was, and Gene Autry heard him. Autry gave him a pat on the back and said, "Hell, son. If it was easy, everybody would be doing it."

If you know that it's going to be hard, you can brace yourself and not be so shocked by the harsh reality. We know it's hard for us, but it helps to know that it's hard for everyone.

Richard Marx went through six or seven years of rejection before he got the chance that let him find his place on the top of the charts with "Hold On to the Night" and "Satisfied." Julie Gold has been writing songs for twenty years. "From a Distance" is the only song she had recorded until that song won the Grammy for Song of the Year. Billy Steinberg, collaborator on "Like a Virgin," "True Colors" and "So Emotional," couldn't give away his songs for many years. "You Needed Me" was rejected over a hundred times before Anne Murray recorded it. There are the occasional overnight successes, but 99 percent of songwriters experience rejection 99 percent of the time.

We heard of a well-adjusted person who greeted each rejection with enthusiasm. She figured that she would have to go through a hundred rejections before she had one acceptance. Each time she was rejected she said, "Great! That means I'm one closer to that acceptance."

It helps to know that there are more variables in choosing a song than are known in your philosophy, Horatio. Financial politics, for instance, influence the choice of songs. A little bit of fine print in most new artists' contracts, called the controlled composition clause, says that the record company only has to pay three-fourths of the going mechanical royalty rate for any song the artist writes, co-writes, or has any control over. If outside songs are chosen that have to be paid at the full rate, the artist has to pay the difference out of his or her own pocket. This situation forces artists to keep their projects closed to outside songs.

One quick study of the songs on the *Billboard* charts will verify that most songs are written either by the artists or their producers. Maybe 2 or 3 percent of the Top 100 pop songs came from outside writers. The field is a bit more open in country music, where there is more respect for songwriters and songs in general.

For a song to be chosen for a recording project, it has to be the right song for the right artist at the right time heard by the right person in the right mood. That's a lot of rights to line up in a row. It's practically a miracle it happens at all. After that first person gets excited by the song, it has to be run through a gauntlet of ears, those of the producer, the artist, the A&R person at the record label, various assorted record executives, perhaps an attorney, and the artist's manager, hairdresser and astrologer. The point is, this is not one person's decision, and timing is everything.

Songwriters who are making it in today's market are tough, hard working, smart and well connected. They're competing with you and with each other for those same two or three slots on the charts that are open to outside songs. They make it their business to know who is about to record and is looking for songs now. They don't have nine-to-five jobs to cope with; they're full-time songwriters. They do their homework and

aim their songs with pinpoint accuracy at particular artists. And they live with rejection every day.

It's one thing when you do your pitching and get your response in the mail. You can weep in the privacy of your own room when you open the envelope you hoped would contain a lifetime contract with a million-dollar advance that turns out to have a fifth-generation photocopy of a form rejection letter. It's another thing to deal with rejection face-to-face. If you have the opportunity to show your songs to a publisher or producer in her office (a very rare opportunity), it will not do to show any anger or pain when the listener turns your song down. You may feel like screaming, but restrain yourself.

It's hard for the listener, too. They may feel guilty about saying no, and it's up to you to put them at ease so they will want to see you again. Relationship is the name of the game. If you can find a common ground to share as one person to another, such as sports, children, or a joke, do it. Don't waste your listener's time. Be friendly, but be businesslike. Get to the point and pick up any pointers the listener is willing to pass along. Be sure to say "Thank you" when you go. Then go home and scream into your pillow.

It's important to express that disappointment appropriately. If you hit your listener with it, you may never see that person again. But if you don't let loose with it somehow, it will build up inside you as resentment and rage until you are immobilized.

Songwriter/vocalist Morgan Ames put it bluntly: "Getting a thick skin and staying sensitive at the same time is a talent of its own. If you can't maintain your vulnerability while getting killed for lunch and breakfast, you really should not be in this business. I don't encourage people to be in this business, anyone who isn't driven to do it. If you do not have a built-in ability to not die when they kill you, you will be one of the bitter, defeated people of this business. My theory is that when they kill you, they don't mean anything by it. When they kill you and walk away, they look back and if you're picking yourself up, they take note of that as they move up."

Songwriter Sue Schiffrin was "killed" by a person she respected very much and the experience gave her something to live for: "When I started writing, there was this wonderful man named Irwin Schuster, who was at Screen Gems Music. He was a great song man. This guy had ears; he could hear a song. In three seconds, he knew if it was a hit or not. He picked up all these great Barry Mann and Carole King songs.

"I went into his office and I had been writing for about six months or a year and I played him my songs. He said to me, 'Sue, do yourself a favor. Get married and have kids.' I was devastated. I said to him, 'You know what, Irwin, you're going to eat those words one of these days.' And that was the thing that inspired me to do the impossible. Every time I wrote a song, I thought, 'I wonder what Irwin's going to think of this song.'

"It was true, I was not a great natural immediate songwriter. I had to learn it and I didn't learn it by going to school. I learned it by doing it. I don't care what anybody tells you, if you really want it badly enough, if you care, if your heart's really in it, you'll do it and get better.

"Years later, I had lunch with him and he said, 'I take it all back.' "

We heard of another story where the same change of heart took place in less than a half hour. A songwriter in Nashville brought a song to an A&R person at a record company, who was not impressed. He said, "I don't hear it," which didn't mean he was hearing impaired; he just didn't like the song.

Many of the publishers and record companies are near each other in Nashville. The songwriter had an appointment with a publisher across the street immediately following this rejection. He played the same song. The publisher loved it. He said, "This would be great for Tammy Sue Doe. Let's go show it to her record label."

So they walked across the street, back into the same A&R person's office. The publisher played the song and the A&R person said, "Yeah, that would be great for Tammy Sue." You figure it.

The secret of hanging in there as a songwriter is to keep saying yes to songwriting. Keep taking the next step. One step at a time. Write the song, make the demo, make connections, pitch songs, learn about the music business, and do that all over again a hundred times. Number 101 could be the one.

Even if it isn't, even if your number never comes up, aren't you doing this because you love it? No one can take that away from you. Songwriting is good for the soul, it's nonviolent, and it's not fattening. How many activities have all that going for them? Only you can prevent rejection burnout. *Never* say never again.

79

········

BURNING BRIDGES

Don't leave a trail of enemies behind

The other extreme reaction to the fierce competition and constant rejection of songwriting is represented by those who would rather fight than quit. We've heard of a songwriter who attacked a publisher with a chair because the publisher turned down his song. We've also heard of a big-name artist who starts out "wanting a piece of the song" in exchange for the favor of recording it and ends up claiming the entire song and all the writer's royalties. We know a manager who got an assignment for her songwriter client and then took it away from him because she decided she wanted to do it herself. All's fair on the songwriting battlefield? Might makes right? Wrong!

It's a small world, and the music business world is even smaller. Practically everybody knows practically everybody else. When the people who do music business gather to schmooze, they like to tell stories. The word got around about the violent songwriter, and all who heard refused to risk an appointment with him. Likewise, eventually no one wanted to deal with the artist, and his big name dwindled from household word to has-been. The manager lost her songwriting client and her credibility. The songwriter went on to get a big writing/production deal and lived much more happily after breaking with her.

If you think that you can afford to treat someone badly, think again. It's not just the bridge between you and that person that you are burning. You are scorching your reputation and damaging your credibility. The music business is like any other business: There are a great many wonderful, honest business people whom you can trust absolutely, and there is also a bunch of not-so-wonderful, not-so-honest people whom you can trust as far as you can throw. If you want to work with the good guys, you have to be a good guy yourself. They can afford to choose their contacts. If you look like trouble, they won't want to deal with you.

The music business is like life. Ideally, you don't do the right thing because you think you should or to impress others. You do it because it feels good to be totally honest in your dealings. That's the real payoff. The fact that people will be attracted to you and want to work with you because they know they can trust you is just a beneficial side effect.

So, we'll assume that you're resolved not to be the perpetrator of the low blow. What can you do when someone else does you wrong? If copyright ownership, a contract or significant income are involved, it may be time to see a lawyer about your legal options. Often, the money that's involved doesn't warrant an expensive legal proceeding. You need to examine the situation carefully. Didn't you have an uncomfortable feeling about how things were going? What made you think it was going to turn out all right despite your gut feeling about it? Could you have been indulging in some hopeful fantasy that clouded your instincts about this person? Why didn't you speak up earlier? If the bad ending was a total surprise, why didn't you see it coming?

These are questions we've had the occasion to ask ourselves when situations exploded in our faces. It's a healing and growing process to take responsibility for our own part in the bad things that happen to us. Each time we understand how we contributed to the situation, we get better at spotting the problems and avoiding them the next time. It is not healthy, however, to get into self-hate and blame or to obsess about the situation. Study it, learn from it and move on.

Part of moving on is resolving not to bad-mouth the person who did you wrong. It doesn't make you look good, no matter how you look at it. Are you bragging that you got involved with someone that took advantage of you? Does someone you can trust tell tales on someone else behind their back? No.

Find a safe, personal place to express your anger and resentment. Then you can be free to act in a businesslike way when it comes to dealing with people in the music business. Don't be fooled by the artistic nature of the product or the casual style of dress. Music business is big business. Look at every encounter as if it were a job interview. You wouldn't complain about how badly your last employer treated you. Not if you wanted the job.

If someone else burns the bridge between the two of you, forgive, for your sake, and remember. Remember to watch for the warning signals you missed. A friend passed on an image to us that has stayed for many years. Lessons in life are like bricks being hurled at your face. You stand there and the bricks hit you square in the face several times, catching you totally by surprise. Then, you notice the bricks are approaching just before they hit you. Twenty bricks or so later, with practice, you can get good enough to duck so the bricks miss you entirely. With a little practice, you can spot the not-so-honest people in the music business and gracefully avoid them.

Honesty is the best policy in every situation, including songwriting. The Golden Rule also applies in the music business. It feels good and it's good for your career to keep as many bridges intact as possible. A songwriting opportunity just may want to come across that bridge.

80

LET MIKEY DO IT

Don't expect to sit back and let the publisher or lawyer do all the work

It's a great day when you sign your first single song contract with a publisher. By all means, break out the champagne or the sparkling cider and celebrate. Look back on all the effort that got you where you are. The dozens of rewrites, the hours in the studio, the hundreds of rejections, the contract offered, the lawyer consulted, the contract renegotiated—and now, the signature. This is a moment to savor. All you have to do now is sit back, let the publisher pitch your song to Whitney Houston and collect your royalties after she makes it a number one hit.

Would that it were so. The reality is that, even though you have a publisher supposedly working to get your song cut, you have no guarantee that the publisher will do anything. All you have is your reversion clause, which says you'll get the song back after a set period if the publisher does not cause a commercially released recording.

Even songwriters who are signed as staff writers can't depend on their publishers to work their songs. A staff writer is signed to a long-term contract. During the term of the contract, the publisher owns all of the songs written by the staff writer, and the writer receives regular advances against royalties that her songs, she hopes, will earn.

You would think that a publisher would be motivated to ensure that the staff writer's songs are recorded and earn back those advances. Not so, says Sue Schiffrin: "They take a song, they don't even comment about whether they think the song is great or lousy or whether it's weak or whether it's strong. They pitch it to artists, but they put it on a cassette and send it in the mail. At the record company, they've got a thousand cassettes that came in that week. They all go in the garbage.

"You can't be just a songwriter anymore, you have to also be a publisher as well. Even though I have a publishing deal with the largest publishing company in the world, I still have to go out and get my own covers. Publishers have become col-

lection agencies; they're banks. When I trust my publisher to go out and get me a cover, it doesn't happen. But when I make phone calls to record companies and make relationships with people, I get more cuts."

So putting your signature on a publishing contract does not give you license to sit back and relax. It just gives you another calling card and a little bit of clout, because it says someone else believes in the song besides you. You're in partnership with the publisher. Depending on the individual you're dealing with, you may find that the publisher would appreciate your input and willingness to expend some energy to push the song. Perhaps the publisher would be open to a casting session, in which both of you talk about which artists each of you has in mind for the song.

You might also find that the publisher wants to have nothing to do with you. If that is the case, think twice before signing another song to that publisher. Music is a person-to-person business. Find a person who will deal with you as a person. You can get abuse anywhere. You can always pitch the song yourself and not have to share the royalties with someone who won't give you the time of day.

Another person who will not "do it" for you is your attorney. Your attorney's job is to explain the situation to you and to advise you of the pros and cons of the various alternatives. Your attorney can tell you what the contract means, but it's up to you to understand it. You need to ask questions until you do understand it, because you are going to have to decide what to do. Your attorney cannot make decisions for you.

You are setting yourself up for some nasty surprises if you think your publisher or your attorney is going to take care of you. Only you have your best interests as number-one priority. You may be high on your publisher's or attorney's list, but it's still a list to them. To you, it's your life. It is always going to be your responsibility to look out for yourself.

We don't mean that you should be hostile or aggressively demanding. But it is necessary to be assertive. Don't be afraid to ask questions. Get as many opinions and as much information as you can. Then, use what you learn to take care of yourself.

81

DO YOU KNOW THE WAY TO L.A.?

Know what you're doing before you move to a music center

Or Nashville? Or New York City? These are the Big Three when it comes to the business of music and writing songs. You can improve your writing skills and read the great selection of books on songwriting and the music business in your hometown. You can try to make connections for your songs through the mail and on the phone. But you will be in competition with the songwriters who are physically present in the offices of the people to whom you are only an envelope among thousands of other envelopes.

Some people will tell you that you definitely must move to one of these cities if you want to make it as a songwriter. They have a point. If you're ultraserious about being a songwriter, pack your bags. But don't make the leap until you take a look at what you'll be in for. At least, make a vacation/research trip to the music center that you think might suit you best. How do you decide which city will be your new home?

Let's take a look at L.A. first. If you don't live in Los Angeles, you might have a romantic picture of the glamour capital of the world where the streets are paved with stars. There are stars on the sidewalks of Hollywood, but they're hard to see through the dirt and smog. There are wonderful places to live on the beach and in canyons where you could almost forget that the city stretches for seventy miles in every direction but west, if you have lots and lots of money to rent them. Real estate prices in Los Angeles are sky-high. There is public transportation, but your music business appointments could be twenty miles apart, and it takes triple the time to get anywhere on a bus, so having a car and being willing to spend hours in it every day are practically mandatory.

The music business is very large in L.A., which means that getting some kind of job in the field is not impossible. Barry Manilow started in the mail room and so can you. L.A. and all the little cities that are surrounded by and surround L.A. also abound with employment opportunities of every description. The climate is mild, if you can stand the smog, and it never rains except for when it pours. And when you get your big recording, you can go to Disneyland to celebrate.

Another great thing about L.A. is that there are endless educational opportunities for songwriters. Almost every night, there is a workshop or a seminar or a forum or whatever where you can go to hear music business professionals talking about the music business. The National Academy of Songwriters has a full calendar of events every month. The Los Angeles Songwriters Showcase has a songwriters showcase every Tuesday. Other organizations, such as the Los Angeles Chapter of the Recording Academy, the California Copyright Conference, the Songwriter's Guild, the National

Association of Music Publishers, the New Age Music Network, ASCAP and BMI also produce informational events. Besides being highly educational, these events are opportunities to meet the people you need to meet face-to-face. L.A.'s the place for every kind of music, including country and particularly film music.

The Los Angeles Songwriters Showcase provides the perfect opportunity for you to test the L.A. waters with its annual Songwriters EXPO, usually held in the fall. If you are considering a move to L.A., try a research trip timed around the EXPO. You can overdose on songwriter information and scout out the territory. Allow for as much time as possible. L.A. is huge. People who live here carry a two-hundred-page map book in their cars and have to use it all the time.

Thinking of moving to Nashville? You are not alone. Musicians and songwriters flock to Nashville every day. Katherine Dines of the Nashville Songwriters Association International (NSAI) says: "Anybody who wants to move to Nashville should try to find some sort of job before they do that because the job market here is really tough. This is primarily because there are so many writers and musicians who have moved here, and they're all struggling. Wages are low and work is pretty menial—waitressing, bartending. There are very few positions in the music industry. If you plan to do a lot of gigs here, it will be really hard. All of the venues are busy because there are lots of musicians in Nashville. Even if you're at the top of the charts, you probably only get a paid gig once a month."

Nashville is a college town as well as a music business center, so people come and go all the time. Nashville natives who are trying to make their own living more affordable have opened up rooms or apartments in their homes to rent. Therefore, finding an affordable place to live is not the big problem in Nashville it is in Los Angeles.

The major record labels and most of the major publishers' offices are concentrated within walking distance of each other in an area called Music Row. However, a car is needed to travel to your home base, since Nashville's public transportation will probably not serve your needs.

Nashville has been called Country Music City, USA, but country is not the only kind of music being made there today. The song is the thing in Nashville, and it has the reputation of being the ultimate songwriter's town. NSAI holds weekly workshops and special professional writers' events several times a year. The Songwriter's Guild has a Nashville office that offers workshops, seminars, and monthly Ask-A-Pro and pitching sessions. Call ahead to these organizations to plan your research trip at a time when something special is happening for songwriters. Other organizations to visit that have offices in Nashville are the Recording Academy, the Country Music Association, the Gospel Music Association, ASCAP and BMI.

Looking to take a bite out of the Big Apple? Bring extra teeth! New York is a tough town. As native New Yorkers, we can tell you that there's an awful lot of cement in New York. The people move fast and talk even faster. We remember distinctly wondering why people talked about the weather when we were living there. We traveled in subways and walked through tunnels underground to work and never saw the sky. So what's the big deal about the weather? The forecast for New York: cold, slushy winters, and hot, muggy summers.

Finding a place to live is difficult and very expensive. The public transportation is great, if you are brave. Personal safety is an issue in New York. You don't need a car, and you probably wouldn't want one because there's no place to park it. Of course, New York is one of the major cities of the world, and jobs of all kinds are available for the quick and the persistent.

Numerous record and publishing companies have offices in New York, as do ASCAP, BMI, the Recording Academy, and the Songwriters Guild. All of these organizations sponsor educational events of interest to songwriters. New York is home for all kinds of music, especially musical theatre and jazz. But your country songs won't find a home here in the concrete canyons.

The three big music centers are not your only options. Quite a few cities generate their own special forms of music. Austin, Dallas and Houston in Texas, Atlanta, Bakersfield (California), Chicago, Detroit, Memphis, Miami, Minneapolis, Muscle Shoals (Alabama), Philadelphia, San Francisco and Seattle are among these. In addition, there are songwriter groups springing up everywhere, including Alaska and Hawaii. Do you know where your nearest songwriter group is tonight?

Our parental-type advice is to research your destination music center. Take a two-week trip to explore the area, preferably timed with a songwriter-related event. Research your housing costs and employment options. If you have to work a day job just to pay the rent, you may be too exhausted at night to pursue your music career. Ask people who know the city about which areas are high in crime, or call the police station that services the neighborhood you are considering. Also research the songwriting community to see if you could happily become a part of it.

If you decide that you want to move permanently, save up and have a three-month cushion of money after you've paid your first and last months' rent and the utility deposits. Then get yourself out there and meet as many people as you can. You came to the music center to make connections, so get out there and connect!

P.S. We arrived in L.A. with no money, four hundred dollars in debt, and no specific plan other than to be songwriters, and we're still alive to tell the tale. Back then, we were wild and crazy kids. Now we're just wild and crazy.

PART NINE

THE FINAL VINYL

Post-Record Release Problems

82
....

IN IT FOR THE MONEY

Don't think you'll get rich quick on one lucky break

After paying years of dues and suffering the slings and arrows of thousands of rejections, you finally get a song recorded. It may even be by a major artist. You're in seventh heaven. Your dream is coming true, and you are going to be a millionaire. The truth is out, you were in it for the money all along. You're going to take the cash and run to the farthest tropical island and spend the rest of your life on the beach.

As they say in the biz, "Don't quit your day job." Unless your song is a major hit, you're not looking at retirement-sized income. With one other collaborator and a publisher involved, you might get half of half of 6.6¢ per tape or CD sold, depending on the status of the artist's controlled composition clause. Income from sales of tapes and CDs is called mechanical royalties. In the case described above, your mechanical royalties would be $.0165 per copy, or $16,500 if a million were sold.

If your song is an album cut, that is probably all you will see from that song. If the song gets played on the radio, you will be entitled to performance royalties from ASCAP, BMI, or SESAC. If it gets played on the radio a lot, it could mean a lot of money. In fact, there are songs that earn their writers a million dollars from performance royalties collected around the world. If this book helps you in any way to get to that point, there is a way to show your gratitude. We're available for on-the-beach song consultations.

Your decision about which performance rights organization to join is one of the most crucial you will make as a songwriter. If you have a song that is going to be played on the radio on more than just a one-shot basis, you must join a performance rights society in order to get paid your performance royalties. Each organization has a different way of figuring how much to pay its members, and we have learned from married collaborators who joined separate organizations to compare the difference that the amounts can vary widely.

No other country in the world has competing performance rights organizations. For a long time,

we only had one, ASCAP, the American Society of Composers, Authors and Publishers. It is a non-profit membership society run by a board of members elected by members. Its job is to collect money, a.k.a. license fees, from the users of music, such as radio and TV stations, sports stadiums, concert halls, and stores that use music to make their customers happy and more willing to buy.

Back in 1958, the radio stations decided they didn't want to pay as much as ASCAP was asking for license fees. ASCAP withdrew their permission for the radio stations to use the songs in ASCAP's collection. All the radio stations could play were public domain songs; songs that were so old their copyright terms had run out. It became known as the "Jeanie With the Light Brown Hair" year. AS-CAP was declared a monopoly, and the radio stations formed their own performance rights organization: BMI—Broadcast Music, Inc.

The third organization is small but offers the special service of also collecting mechanical royalties. For that reason SESAC (which doesn't mean anything in English; it was derived from a French organization that it has nothing to do with any-more) is attractive to the small record labels' publishing arms, especially in country and gospel music.

Back to the big two and the big decision. We can't tell you which to join, but we can say that if you are about to get substantial airplay, you should thoroughly research both organizations and seek professional advice on which would be your best choice.

One reason not to quit your day job is that this money takes a long time to come through the record company's and performance rights organization's accounting systems. Expect to wait at least a year for the first check to arrive in your mailbox and three years for foreign royalties. Performance rights organizations pay quarterly, and record companies pay your publisher, who holds the money a while (collecting interest, of course) and then pays you at whatever frequency you agreed to in your contract.

Songwriting is not a get-rich-quick game. You probably have a better chance at winning the lottery. Yes, there are some top songwriters who do very well, even some millionaires. But they've been at it for twenty or thirty years, and they did it for love, not for money. The love of songwriting is the only thing that will make you hang in there long enough to make the money possible.

The Songwriter's Guild did some research among their members in 1980 and found that the average yearly income of all their published members was less than $5,500. Included in that average are some of those millionaires, so you can figure that there must be many more songwriters making little or no money to bring that figure down to $5,500.

Anybody want to chip in on a lottery ticket?

83
....

LOOK WHAT THEY'VE DONE TO MY SONG
Be willing to relinquish control over the finished product

You wrote the song, you own it, and no one can use it without your permission. Once you have given that first permission to record the song, others can record it without consulting you. But before that first recording, if you do not sign the song to a publisher, the song is totally yours to control. This sounds like a powerful position. You might get the impression that you had some say in how the song comes out. Forget it.

Unless you are the producer or related by blood or marriage, you will not be invited to the recording session. You will have no say in the outcome, no opportunity to contribute on the arrangement or the artist's performance. This situation prompted Melanie to write "Look What They've Done To My Song, Ma" in the sixties, and it's still true today.

You have to let go of the idea that you will have some say in how this song that you have so much power over will sound after someone else gets through with it. The best you can do to influence the situation is to make a great demo.

If your demo is hot, if it is rich with hooky riffs

between the vocal lines, if the groove is undeniable and the tracks are right on the money, the producer will probably copy your demo. We've heard of producers who, after trying and failing to get the same feel as the demo, have fallen back on using the actual tracks from the demo. This is easy to do in this day of digitally encoded music information.

The fact that you have no control over the outcome of the recording of your song may give you the impression that you should be careful to the point of overprotection when giving that first permission. We don't think so. If the record turns out bad, probably no one will hear it. You still have your demo to pitch, so you haven't lost a thing.

There are plenty of songs that have been recorded several times before the version that hit came out. "From a Distance" is a very good example. That song was recorded by thirteen different artists, including Judy Collins, the Byrds and Kathy Mattea, and in five languages before Bette Midler recorded the version that won Julie Gold the Song of the Year Grammy. This is not to imply that the pre-Midler recordings were not good; they just weren't the right artists at the right time.

As a songwriter trying to establish a track record, we recommend that you take any recordings that you are lucky enough to get on your song. You never know who will hear the song and make the recording of it that hits. The head of Almo Irving Music, the publishing arm of A&M Records, signed Julie Gold to a publishing deal after hearing "From a Distance" performed in a German cabaret.

The idea at first is to get your songs out there. When you have a sizable track record, you might be a little choosier about who gets to record your song. If the idea of letting go of the results of the recording session on your song is abhorrent to you, you might want to consider joining the growing ranks of songwriter/producers.

Getting a song recorded these days is like getting a camel through the eye of a needle. Many recording artists write their own material, and many others are permanently joined with producer/songwriters who supply them with songs. On the theory that if you can't beat them, you

might as well join them, many songwriters are developing their demo production skills into expertise at producing the final project. With today's technology, the line between demo and finished product is blurring anyway.

The songwriter who presents a record label with a package ready to go—artist, songs, producer all in place—is giving them something they want, less work. If one of the demo singers you hire absolutely knocks you out and you enjoy working with each other, you might want to try joining forces to produce an artist master demo. That is two to four songs of almost master (commercial release) quality to use for label shopping; that is, pitching the artist to record labels for a recording contract.

Your songs are like your children. At some point, they have to stand on their own two feet and you have to let them go to live their own lives. Fortunately, you can go on making new songs forever without threatening the planet with a population explosion. Keeping the long view of yourself as an infinitely creative source will help you over the rough spots when one of your song children turns out badly.

84

IT'S A SECRET

Index a song that is getting airplay with your performance rights organization

Getting a song recorded is the songwriter's dream come true. It's especially dreamy when you make the connection yourself with the artist, which makes you the publisher. The record company will ask you to issue a mechanical license, so you will do some research and deliver the appropriate piece of paper to them. You're already a member of a performance rights organization, so you've got your bases covered.

Sorry, but you're out on second. Membership in a performance rights organization and five

bucks will get you a cup of coffee. Your performance rights organization is not a guardian angel who watches over you and notes your successes on a golden scroll. If you don't tell them about your recording, they will never know. They won't look for it in their survey, and you won't get paid. But since no one will ask you to do this the way a record company asks for a mechanical license, you may not know that "indexing" your song with your performance rights organization is a prerequisite to getting paid for any airplay.

Ask your performance rights organization how to index your song when airplay is imminent. They will send you the proper forms. The computer age is coming to this process. ASCAP is instituting a new computerized Title Registration System and providing songwriter members with the necessary software. Please note that the paperwork with the record company and the performance rights society need only be done by you if you do not have a publisher representing you on the song.

How about that mechanical license? Is there anybody you should inform about that? It is possible to have the record company pay you directly for sales of records. However, we recommend that you let the Harry Fox Agency in New York City collect mechanical royalties for you. Harry Fox, which is related to the National Music Publishers Association, collects mechanical royalties for many of the largest publishers in the world. They charge a small percentage of the royalties for the service and it is well worth it, as we will explain in chapter eighty-seven, "Pennies from Heaven." When a recording that you have made the connection for is about to be made, contact the Harry Fox Agency at 212-922-3260 and ask them how to proceed.

After all you've been through to get this recording, don't keep it a secret from the organizations that are the conduits for your income from the song. In the end, the glamorous music business comes down to filling out forms, shuffling papers and accounting for figures in a column. But the check won't be in the mail unless you let someone know they should be sending it.

85

....

JOIN, JOIN AGAIN

Join ASCAP or BMI twice if you're self-publishing

When we had our first success with a song that we pitched directly to an artist, we made a mistake that cost us a substantial sum of money. We take solace in the fact that we can pass on what we learned to you so you will not make the same mistake. Since we had made the connection with the artist, we were the publishers of the song. We were already members of a performing rights organization, so we notified them of the recording. We figured we had done all we needed to do.

Ignorance is not bliss, we discovered. We did receive songwriting royalties from ASCAP in due time, a year to eighteen months after the release. But a couple of years later the light dawned; we saw that we had not received royalties as the publishers of the song. We called ASCAP and explained that we had neglected to join as publishers and to notify them that we were the publishers on the song, a paperwork process that use to be called indexing and is now termed "title registration." Unfortunately, the recording was too old for them to make any payment on the performances. The result was that we had collected *half* of the performance royalties that were possible on that song.

If reading this makes you realize that you have made the same mistake, it is possible to retrieve some back performance royalties. ASCAP will go back nine months from the current quarter. BMI is not obligated by its contract with its songwriter members to go back at all. However, as a courtesy to the writer and depending on the situation, they may go back as far as nine months from the current quarter. Any royalties from further back in time are lost.

It is not necessary, or advisable, to join a performance rights organization as a publisher unless you expect a song of yours to be recorded, released, and played on a substantial number of radio stations or on television. ASCAP publisher member dues are fifty dollars per year, which is deducted from your first royalty check. ASCAP requires submission of a copy of the commercial release as a qualification for membership as a publisher. BMI charges a one-time one-hundred dollar administration fee to publisher members and does not require a copy to be submitted.

When the time is right, the first step in the process is to choose which organization you want to join. This is a major decision, and again, we recommend you research the organizations to see which will pay the best for the uses that your songs are most likely to have. Each organization has its own way of determining payments for various uses. Ask specific questions. For example, "My album is going to have airplay on college stations across the country. Does your survey cover those stations?" or "What are your rates of payment for television show theme songs?"

Generally speaking, radio performance royalties are paid on the basis of a statistical survey. You are not paid every time your song is played, because no one can keep track of all that information now. There are over nine thousand radio stations in the United States. If you figure that each station plays fifteen songs an hour, twenty-four hours a day, that's 3,240,000 airplays to keep track of every day. Systems being developed for use in the future can track airplay exactly. For now, they find out what's being played at x number of stations and then extrapolate mathematically from the sample to determine their payment for radio airplay for the whole country.

Television music is reported more accurately and is paid for according to different formulas that depend on a number of variables, such as whether the music is featured—that is, a singer is center stage singing it—or just playing in the background. The amount of payment also depends on the length of time the song is heard during the television show. Performance royalties are not paid by movie theaters in the United States, but they are in Europe.

The next step is to choose a company name. First you will have to come up with three or four names and submit them to your chosen performance rights organization. They will tell you which names are available. We recently had to go through eight names before we found one that wasn't already taken. Then, each time you make the connection that means airplay for your songs, notify your performance royalty organization—twice.

We don't want you to have to learn this lesson the hard way, like we did.

86

......

IT OUGHTA BE IN PICTURES

Learn about the drawbacks of writing songs for films

Lights! Camera! Action! There's something special about having a song in a film. Seeing your name roll by on the end credits is a thrill. Many new songwriters see movies that feature songs and dream of that glorious day when they will be part of that glitter and glamour. The fact that the songwriters' credits roll by at the very end is telling. Very often, people who make movies throw in the music as an afterthought. When it comes to songs in movies, songwriters are on the bottom of a very big totem pole. It can really get you down.

People who make movies and people who make music are two different animals. They have trouble talking to each other because they don't understand each other's grunts and growls. The movie people think that, because they are spending so many millions of dollars, they should call the shots on the music, even if they can't speak the language. They wait until the last minute and then give a music supervisor the impossible assignment of locating/recording the perfect songs for two or ten spots in the film. The music supervisor has to act quick. He can't wait to deal with songs that have more than one person to go through to secure permission.

If there is enough time for songwriters to view a rough cut of the film and take a crack at writing songs for specific spots in the movie, the movie is screened for all the competing songwriters at once. Then they go off and invest their time and money in writing a song for the same slot that twenty other writers are working on, all of them unpaid for their efforts.

If your song is chosen for the film, it is usually taken for granted that you will not participate in any of the publishing royalties. Unless the songs in question have already been published, only songwriters with major clout like Marilyn and Alan Bergman and Billy Steinberg and Tom Kelly can insist on participating in the publishing of their songs in movies. Even when written by major league songwriters, songs get lost in the Hollywood shuffle.

Billy Steinberg says, "Tom and I have had nothing but misfortune in the area of placing songs in films. For example, film companies always want part of the publishing and Tom and I have never given up any of our publishing except in a few situations on film.

"Recently, we wrote a song called 'Listen To Your Heart' specifically for the *Karate Kid III* movie. The film company was saying, 'We need a hit with this film and we're going to push this song.' Tom and I wrote a song that we were really proud of.

"There are certain politics about songs in films. If the film company is going to do a soundtrack record with a certain label and you want an artist from another label to do that song, it's often hard to make that deal or accomplish that. Usually, they want an artist from the roster of the company that has the soundtrack deal. That's what happened in this case. We wrote this song and they came to us and said we want the Little River Band to record it. My instincts said, 'That's the wrong group for this song.'

"We should have, in our vigilance, specified in the deal either that we were going to have veto rights over who would record the song or have insisted that we produce the record, but we did neither. Even though I didn't feel the Little River band was the right group, the Little River Band recorded it and it came out very poorly."

Income from songs in films basically comes from the synchronization license. An agreement is made between the film company and the owner of the copyright that the film company will pay a certain amount for the right to synchronize the song with the soundtrack of the movie. Major league songwriters can charge a hefty synch fee for a song in a movie. Minor league songwriters do it for considerably less. It is the rare soundtrack album that sells enough to be a significant source of income for the songwriter. There may be some performance income from foreign performance rights organizations if the film is released overseas. ASCAP and BMI do not pay for performances in movie theaters.

We had a song in a movie starring John Travolta. The film was called *The Experts*, and our song, "Hometown, U.S.A.," was played twice in the movie and played a significant part in setting the scene. We were excited when this project came to us and couldn't wait until the movie came to our local theater, so we could watch our names roll by on the big screen.

Unfortunately, this was the film just before Travolta made a big comeback in *Look Who's Talking*, and his popularity was at a low ebb. The film company did some kind of test marketing in ten theaters in Texas or something and decided that the film wasn't strong enough to spend the promotion dollars it would take to release nationally. So, the film went straight to video release. Fortunately, they did release it on cable as well; many of our friends and relatives saw our names roll by and wrote to us about it on their Christmas cards. We never knew so many people read those credits. We're usually the only ones hanging out in the theater watching for who wrote the songs.

If you want your songs to be in pictures, the people you want to impress and endear yourself to are the music supervisors. Their names roll by on the credits, too. Then, when you get the cue to write a song for a film, get ready to roll with the punches.

87

....

PENNIES FROM HEAVEN

Don't think your royalties will automatically come to you

You've made and corrected three zillion mistakes in the process of writing, rewriting, demoing, and pitching your songs. Having made every possible mistake, you have nothing left to do but the right thing. The song has been recorded by an artist of note. You are the publisher or copublisher. You've filed the proper forms with the Harry Fox Agency and your performance rights organization. You have negotiated the deal with professional help; the papers have been signed. You await with perfect serenity the arrival of the check in the mail.

You may be disappointed if you expect business to be taken care of just because it's supposed to be. Some people who are supposed to give you your money would much rather keep it for themselves, thank you very much. If you let them, they will. They will not volunteer to pay you. Instead of serenely collecting your check from your mailbox, you may have to work up a sweat going after money that is rightfully yours.

For instance, we were copublishers on a song that was quite successful. The other copublisher was an established company, and the person we were dealing with there was well known to us in business and socially. We decided that the song would best be administered by a large international publishing company that would charge a small percentage for the service and then split the remaining income fifty/fifty and pass it on to us separately. The person at that publishing company was also well known to us. We spoke to him on the phone and he said (and we quote), "You and the other publisher will have the same deal."

We sat back and relaxed, waiting for the check to come in the mail. Waiting and waiting and waiting. Good thing we didn't hold our breath. A year and a half rolls by and still there's no money in sight from this song. So we started calling around and found that, not only had the large administering publisher not given us the "same deal" as our copublisher, he had sent *our* royalties to that copublisher, who had been holding them for a year.

We then called the copublisher and said, "Hey, you've been sitting with our royalties in the bank for a year now; you owe us interest." He must have thought that was a mighty funny idea, from the way he laughed at us. We did finally get our royalties with a lesson attached: Don't expect the other guy to be looking out for your best interests.

Lesson number two in this department has to do with a practice in the record business called the 100 percent returns policy. The record business is unique in that stores can return 100 percent of the product if they don't sell it. A few years ago, you'd hear about records shipping platinum and returning gold. That means they would send out a million and 500,000 would come back. In today's tougher times, the record companies are more conservative about the amounts they ship. The result of this acceptance of returned goods policy is that the record companies won't pay until they see how many come back. They also like to stipulate that they won't pay for a certain percentage of records because they break in shipping, even though there are no such things as records anymore. Do you get the feeling that the record companies would really rather not pay the publishers the mechanical royalties on the songs, which are the only things that give their product value? Without the songs, they'd be in the blank tape business. But they often don't act as though they know that's the case.

Enter the Harry Fox Agency with lesson number three: You have grounds for your suspicions about record companies. Every so often, the Harry Fox Agency does audits on record companies. That means they go into the record company's files and check to see if the royalties paid match the records sold. Many times they find that the record companies owe publishers money. Recently, the Fox Agency found over a thousand dollars that a record label owed us for one moderately successful song. Can you imagine how much the record company owed the major worldwide publishers with

hundreds of successful titles on their label? For the auditing alone, if you are your own publisher it is worth the percentage that the Fox Agency charges to collect your mechanical royalties. It would not be worth your time and money to do the audit independently. Also, when Harry Fox does your mechanical licensing, they don't allow record companies to withhold funds for those nonexistent broken records.

Don't count on your money showing up at your mailbox just because it's supposed to. Our stories are only a few examples of how your money can get lost in the shuffle. When it comes to the money that is owed to you, keep an eagle eye on your income sources and follow through to make sure your check actually makes it to your mailbox. Then you can sing all the way to the bank.

88

MADE IN THE SHADE

Cope with your success

You started out as low as you could go and made every mistake in the book, but your love of songwriting helped you hang in there through it all, right up to the top note. You wrote it, you pitched it, they recorded it, it went up the charts, it hit number one, and you even managed to get paid for it. You have finally reached the pot of gold at the end of the songwriting rainbow. Now your problems are over.

But wait, what's that on the horizon? A whole new set of problems. What a life! Thinking that your problems will be over if only you could have a number one hit will give you even more problems in terms of frustration and disappointment when the road after success proves just as rocky as the road to it.

It's true, fellow travelers on the songwriting road. We solve one set of problems only to be faced with another, perhaps more interesting, set.

You may wonder what could possibly be a problem after you've written the number one song in the country. You imagine that if such good fortune should come to you, you would live the rest of your life with a smile on your face. We have several friends who have reached those altitudes on the charts, and we'll tell you what they told us.

Once you have been on top, you have only one place to go and that's down. You could stay on top, but no one does that, not even Michael Jackson. Your own success will be the hardest act for you to follow. You will wake up the next morning and be confronted with the same blank sheet of paper that challenged you before the world recognized your talent. You will ask yourself, Can I do it again? and part of you may say, No!

Your success may attract many opportunities. People will want you to write songs for projects, songwriters will want to collaborate with you, songwriters' organizations will call on you to share your experience, and before you know it, you will be overwhelmed by the demands on your time. One friend of ours told us that he feels crazier than he ever did before his success, because he now has more in his life than he can handle. For him, the idea of success has progressed from "If I only had a cut" to "If I only had a hit" to "If I only had constant demand for my songs" to "If I only had peace of mind."

As time goes by, if you are not lucky enough to keep having major songwriting successes, maybe you'll just be a working songwriter. You'll be out there competing with all the other working songwriters and the new, hungry songwriters who hit town every day. You will have the challenge of making peace with the fact that you might never write a number one song again. You might be called upon to sing a "medley of your hit" for a songwriters' concert and listen as other songwriters dazzle you with their incredible string of standards.

Should you have the luck to continue to be a successful songwriter, you still face the stiff competition and all of the music business practices that disregard and threaten songwriters. It will be in your best interests to get involved in fighting record piracy, home taping, controlled composition clauses, omission of writers' credits on albums, censorship, attempts by users not to pay royalties, new technology that allows for the use of music without payment to its creators—the list of concerns is constantly growing.

Most people who have attained success want to give something back, and you will probably want to get involved in a songwriting organization. You might serve on the board or help with events. It will be important to do this in a way that doesn't keep you from being a songwriter.

Your songs will still be rejected, recorded badly, put on hold for too long, recorded and not released, released but not promoted, put in films that don't make it to the theaters, bought and sold by publishers who could care less about them, and used in ways that you won't like.

You can't get much more successful as a songwriter than Paul McCartney. He tells the story of a conversation between himself and Michael Jackson. Michael says something like, "Paul, I have all this money and I'm thinking of investing in a business. What do you suggest?" Paul says, "Music publishing is a good business and it's something you can relate to." So, Michael goes out and buys ATV Music, which is the publishing company that owns all the early Beatles' hits. Pretty soon, Paul hears one of his songs in an athletic shoe commercial, and he wishes he hadn't been so free with his advice.

The ultimate success is to thoroughly enjoy the process of songwriting and disregard the results. Most assuredly, you have to make all the right moves to write the best of all possible songs and make the best of all possible pitches. But the only way to hold on to your peace of mind will be to stop trying to control the outcomes; give yourself credit for doing the best you can and move on to the next song.

You will still have to open up to your tenderest parts, and risk exposing them and making a fool of yourself every time you write. For that reason, Paul Simon calls songwriting a dangerous profession. Songwriting is not something that you do until you get it right. You never reach that point. Songwriting is a lifestyle of adventure and learning. So, take your courage, your pencil, your guitar or keyboard in hand and write on!

INDEX

More Books for Songwriters!

The Craft and Business of Songwriting—From generating a song idea to signing a record deal, you'll discover how to create and market artistically and commercially successful songs in today's tough market. *#10429/$21.99/322 pages/paperback*

Hot Tips for the Home Recording Studio—Discover the tricks to recording a tight, polished, professional demo! Musicians acquainted with recording technology will learn how to lay down basic tracks, add vocals, and mix to get exactly the sound they want. *#10415/$18.99/160 pages*

Creating Melodies—You'll be singing all the way to the bank when you discover the secrets of creating memorable melodies—from love ballads to commercial jingles! *#10400/$18.95/144 pages*

The Songwriter's Market Guide to Song & Demo Submission Formats—Get your foot in the door with knock-out query letters, slick demo presentation, and the best advice for dealing with every player in the industry. *#10401/$19.95/160 pages*

Making Money Teaching Music—Discover how to find lucrative teaching opportunities. This guide shows you how to market yourself as a professional, recruit students of all ages, manage time and work schedules and much more! *#10428/$18.99/240 pages/paperback*

Who Wrote That Song?—If you're a music buff, you'll love the 12,000 songs listed here! Find everything form mid-nineteenth century ballads to today's Top Forty hits, with emphasis on the last forty years. Each listing includes title, composer, lyricist, and publication year. Where appropriate, listings also reveal who made the song popular, others who recorded it, and who sang it on Broadway or in the movies. *#10403/$19.95/448 pages/paperback*

Making Money Making Music (No Matter Where You Live)—Cash-in on scores of ways to make a profitable living with your musical talent (no matter where you live). This guide covers performing as a solo or in a group, writing music for the radio, jingles and more! *#10174/$18.95/180 pages/paperback*

Networking in the Music Business—Who you know can either make (or break) your music career. Discover how to make and capitalize on the contacts you need to succeed. *#10365/$17.95/128 pages/paperback*

Beginning Songwriter's Answer Book—This newly revised and updated resource answers the questions most asked by beginning songwriter's and gives you the know-how to get started in the music business. *#10376/$16.95/128 pages/paperback*

The Songwriter's Idea Book—You'll find 40 proven songwriting strategies sure to spark your creativity in this innovative handbook. Plus, learn how to use your unique personality to develop a strong writing style. *#10320/$17.95/240 pages*

The Craft of Lyric Writing—You'll get a complete guide on writing words for and to music, choosing song formats, and how to write lyrics with universal appeal from bestselling author and songwriter, Sheila Davis. *#1148/$21.95/350 pages*

Songwriter's Market—Find the inside tips on how and where to place your songs in more than 2,500 up-to-date listings of song markets. Each listing includes submission requirements and tips from the buyer. Plus get helpful articles on the ins and outs of the music business. *#10386/$21.99/522 pages*

Successful Lyric Writing: A Step-by-Step Course & Workbook—Write the kinds of lyrics that dazzle music executives with this hands-on course in writing. Dozens of exercises and demonstrations let you put what you've learned into practice! *#10015/$19.95/292 pages/paperback*

Music Publishing: A Songwriter's Guide—Get a handle on your songwriting career! This practical guide gives you advice you need on types of royalties, subpublishing, songwriter options in publishing and more! *#10195/$18.95/144 pages/paperback*